Mourie's All Blacks

By the same author

Bob Stuart's All Blacks
The Bob Scott Story
Bob Scott on Rugby
The Battle for the Rugby Crown
Great Days in New Zealand Rugby
Kings of Rugby
Beaten by the Boks
Cock of the Rugby Roost
I, George Nepia
Willie Away
Red Dragons of Rugby
The Bok Busters
The Lion Tamers
All Black Magic
All Black Power
Battling the Boks
Fred Allen on Rugby
Lions Rampant
They Missed the Bus
All Blacks Come Back
Goodbye to Glory
Winter of Discontent

Mourie's All Blacks

The Team that found itself

Terry McLean

HODDER AND STOUGHTON LTD
AUCKLAND LONDON SYDNEY

First printed 1979
ISBN 0 340 24217 5

Printed and bound in New Zealand for Hodder and Stoughton Ltd., 44-46 View Road, Glenfield, Auckland, by Wright and Carman Ltd., Trentham.

List of Contents

THE 1978 ALL BLACKS

Fullbacks

Clive Currie (Canterbury)*
Brian McKechnie (Southland)
Richard Wilson (Canterbury)

Wing-threequarters

Bryan Williams (Auckland)
Brian Ford (Marlborough)
Stuart Wilson (Wellington)
Robert Kururangi (Counties)

Centre-threequarters

Bruce Robertson (Counties)
Bill Osborne (Wanganui)

Five-eighths

Mark Taylor (Bay of Plenty)
Lyn Jaffray (Otago)
Doug Bruce (Canterbury)
Eddie Dunn (North Auckland)

Halfbacks

Mark Donaldson (Manawatu)
David Loveridge (Taranaki)

Number 8s

Gary Seear (Otago)
Ashley McGregor (Southland)

Flankers

Graham Mourie (Taranaki), captain
Leicester Rutledge (Southland)
Wayne Graham (Otago)
Barry Ashworth (Auckland)

Locks

Frank Oliver (Southland)
Andy Haden (Auckland)
John Fleming (Wellington)
John Loveday (Manawatu)

Props

John Ashworth (Canterbury)
Brad Johnstone (Auckland)
Gary Knight (Manawatu)
Bill Bush (Canterbury)

Hookers

Andy Dalton (Counties)
John Black (Canterbury)

Honorary Manager

Russell Thomas (Canterbury)

Honorary Assistant-Manager-Coach

Jack Gleeson (Manawatu)

* Currie suffered a hairline fracture of the jaw in his second international, against Wales. He was immediately replaced by Richard Wilson.

RECORD OF THE TOUR

Versus

Cambridge University, Won 32-12
Cardiff, Won 17-7
West Wales, Won 23-7
London Counties, Won 37-12
Munster, Lost 0-12
IRELAND, Won 10-6
Ulster, Won 23-3
WALES, Won 13-12
South and South West Counties, Won 20-0
Midland Counties, Won 20-15
Combined Services, Won 34-6
ENGLAND, Won 16-6
Monmouthshire, Won 26-9
North of England, Won 9-6
North and Midlands of Scotland, Won 31-3
SCOTLAND, Won 18-9
Bridgend, Won 17-6
Barbarians, Won 18-16
Played 18, Won 17, Lost 1. Points for 364, Against 147.

I

CHAPTER ONE

Strange Eventful History

HISTORY MAY CHOOSE to call it a tour that will not die by a team that found itself. Without doubt, the expedition of the New Zealand rugby team — the Eighth or Ninth All Blacks, according to choice — to the British Isles for 18 matches played between mid-October and mid-December of 1978 produced a strange eventful history. Achilles, returning to the wars, exclaimed: "You shall know the difference, now that I am back again". So with the warriors of Rugby from Down Under. Their predecessors in a number of teams during the 1970s had sung a wavering tremolo over and below the stave of average competence. In matches at home and abroad, they had fought and lost to Springboks, Lions, Tricolors, Wallabies; at home, they had been soundly beaten by an English team which was unable to win a provincial match. Many of the 1978 team themselves had only recently won, without conviction and with a shattering defeat by 30 to 16 in the last test, a series with Australia's Wallabies. Taking one consideration with another, one had to say that the omens for the tour of the British Isles were not encouraging.

But now the All Blacks, like Achilles, were back to the wars; and, like Achilles, they impressed their difference upon their foemen. In one match after another, sometimes in the last seconds of the eleventh hour, they were victorious. They lost, in fact, only one match; and such was the heroic quality of their defence that they yielded their goalline only seven times, an extraordinary feat. In terms of the application of coaching at individual and team levels, British rugby had not hitherto been so well prepared to resist an All Black team. Overall, therefore, the tour record represented a formidable achievement.

The causes of the change in character of these All Blacks, compared with too many of their predecessors in the recent decade, were three: management, by Mr Russell Thomas, general manager of a grocery chain based upon Christchurch; coaching, by Mr Jack Gleeson, a Feilding man who dry-wittedly called himself a hotelier rather than a publican because publicans were named in the Bible as sinners;

captaincy, by Graham Mourie, a Taranaki dairy-farmer who had captained an All Black team not of full international standing to Uruguay and the Argentine in 1976 and who had had command of a full-scale team sent to Italy and France in 1977.

Each man in his own field was expert. So agreeably and efficiently were their talents blended that the 31 players of the tour were soon discovered to be strong in spirit, valiant in heart and staggeringly consistent in physical fitness and output. They were not flawless. "What is it," Gleeson bawled after one gruesome display, "that is causing you to make mistakes? Is it lack of concentration? Or is it fear?" (Terry O'Connor, of the *Daily Mail,* half-hearing the quoted remark, translated the second part of it into "Or is it too much beer?") But, match by match, they came out as fit and fresh in the last minutes as they had been in the first. Justly, their reward was unique. They became the first All Blacks to score the Grand Slam — defeat of each of the four Home Unions at international level. True enough, their manner of achieving victory in some of these big games, notably against Ireland, Wales and Scotland, was enough to take years off the lives of many among the hundreds of thousands of their countrymen who fascinatedly watched between 2 and 5 o'clock on various Sunday mornings the telecasts of matches beamed from the grounds directly to New Zealand. But there it was; the play went on; and with a try here, a penalty there, a dropkick somewhere else, the All Blacks lifted themselves from the ruck to a starring role in the history of New Zealand rugby.

In the words of Milton, all was "dark, dark, irrecoverably dark" in the high noon of the All Blacks' achievement, the last trick of the Grand Slam which was the defeat of Scotland. Black figures scurrying o'er the sward of Murrayfield looked ghostly in the murk. But there was nothing impalpable about the result. It was there, forever. The All Blacks had taken the trick. They were unique.

Thus, in contentment, they faced toward the last matches. One was against Bridgend, a club granted the match primarily because this was its centennial year but well deserving in its own right because its team so consistently tried to attack. The last fixture was against the Barbarians, a club which was world-famed because of its high-minded attempts always to project the best in the game.

Sad the awakening, rude the jolting. This was the week that was, and will be, the blight of the tour. This was the week that released in the media a stream of vituperation against the All Blacks. Cynical critics who had tired of the team's scrupulous regard for the laws and spirit of the game went for the jugular. The tour hummed with controversy. In the bar of the Press Club near Fleet Street, a gentleman identified as belonging to the *Daily Mirror* said decisively: "I see that those blackguards have left for home today. What a good riddance!" Peter Bush, a New Zealand Press photographer, turned from the neighbouring group, tensely clutching his glass in both hands lest he react too positively. "Sir," he said, "would you mind explaining exactly what you mean when you refer to 'those blackguards'?"

It will be proper, later, to discuss Bridgend and the Barbarians in detail. Meanwhile, it ought to be emphasised that history alone must judge whether the unfortunate aspects of the two matches should prejudice the whole of the All Blacks' tour. Except for a few isolated incidents in the matches against West Wales and Wales and a monumental act of stupidity, by All Blacks, in the latter game, the tour before Bridgend, 16 matches in all, had been unequalled, in modern rugby time, for clean play. Jack Gleeson rode his troops hard. Under no circumstances whatsoever were they allowed to initiate rough play, or retaliate against it.

Until Bridgend, the house that Jack built and which Mourie so diligently furnished was next best to faultless. In terms of modern sport, in which the pressures of nationalism demanding victory, if need be, at all costs, have become implacable, the All Blacks' consistent performance was phenomenal. In the long view, it may be that it was too good for the team's good. It had offered no fuel for sensationalism. All of the team pleasantly and consistently performed aggreeable social tasks over and beyond the call of duty.

Suddenly, sensation. The loosehead prop, John Ashworth, intending, as he will maintain until his dying day, to heel the ball by raking for it, connected instead with the head of the Bridgend fullback and captain, J. P. R. Williams. A deep gash opened down the right cheek of Williams' face. He arose from the sopping field a figure of blood and mud. Departing, he left behind him, for the time that it took his father, Dr Peter Williams, to clean and stitch the wound, 14 comrades and many thousands of Welsh spectators who blazed against the All Blacks. In a select area of the grandstand, a young New Zealand woman found herself screaming out against Welshmen around her who were themselves screaming, "Kill the bastards! Kill the animals!"

Ashworth's intention had been, by his own explanation, honourable. Having regard to the consistent quality of the tour and the severe standards set by Mr Gleeson, it seemed unthinkable that he had deliberately booted Williams. "I have never kicked a man in my life," Ashworth said. "I would not play rugby if I had to." Amid the tempest of the match, time did not permit explanation. The horrid booing and shouting continued. When play was done, Fleet Street, radio and television moved in. Battle-hymns, so to speak, were sung. The New Zealanders, it was urged, should cleanse their souls lest their foul misconduct cast them eternally into the burning fires of Hell. It sometimes seemed, over the next few days, that on the hour every hour some psalm-singer reached for his typewriter to spell out rugby's wrath against the tourists. Among the most extraordinary statements was an assertion by J. P. R. Williams, who is a qualified medical man, that he had lost two pints of blood. Mysteriously, no one thought to ask how a player in such parlous physical condition could possibly return to the play.

Everything, not least the misreporting and/or misquoting, was regrettable. Few in Fleet Street seized on the oddity that Bridgend players had rather spoiled the show by joining All Blacks who had walked out of the dinner as a protest against some critical remarks by Dr Peter Williams who, though president of Bridgend, was not listed among the speakers. Dr Peter said he was sorry he had encouraged his sons to play rugby. As a parent, he was entitled to the view; but it did seem strange that Bridgend players had reacted in a hostile manner against his remarks. If they had been really steamed up against the All Blacks, they would scarcely have walked out, would they?

Still, the clamour and criticising and sermonising went on. Finding that he might have missed the bus, a serious blunder, Chris Lander of the *Daily Mirror* rushed back from London to Bridgend to procure from J. P. R. the wounding, sensational statement that he never wanted to play against the All Blacks again.

Such stuff was not music to the ears of the All Blacks or their followers, especially those of senior years who had seen for themselves the abrasiveness in J. P. R.'s style of playing the game. Nor was it edifying to listen to the opposition mounted against the All Blacks at significant stages of their match with the Barbarians. Whistling against and jeering of the All Blacks were constant to the game, especially in the moments when the New Zealand goalkicker, Brian McKechnie, was trying for penalty shots at goal. (McKechnie obliged his critics by missing a hatful of attempts.) After no-side and the singing of "Now Is the Hour", the traditional farewell, the proportion of jeerers to cheerers of the All Blacks as they left the field appeared to be in the ratio of not more than 1 to 3. Which was not a charming thought, considering that the 47,000 spectators had had the luck to watch a match pulsating with drama and excitement. The first half of the game may have been played at a higher average speed than any All Black match in history.

Plainly, many in the audience, surely not all of them Bridgenders, wanted the All Blacks to be beaten. They were resentful of the great demonstration of the New Zealand spirit which occurred in the last minute of play when the All Blacks, a beaten team, soared to victory with a dream drop-goal kicked by their five-eighths, Eddie Dunn.

But did this excuse, let alone explain, what now went on? As Russell Thomas made his way along a passage-way of the great north stand of the Arms Park, he was set upon by three men. Two seized each end of his long All Black scarf and tugged violently, trying to throttle him. The third grabbed an arm and with a violent gesture bent Mr Thomas' thumb painfully back. All three assailants were shouting insults and imprecations.

Though he had played hooker in Christchurch senior rugby 30 years before, Mr Thomas is not a big man. At 52, he had become a little bent, bespectacled, white-headed — not a man for a fast one-rounder against even only one opponent. He was shocked by the assault. A colleague described him as looking "ashen and grey" as he reached the All Blacks' dressingroom. In the Pressroom, David Frost, of the *Guardian,* hearing a whispered plea that nothing should be said of the incident, instantly reacted by handing over a very large Scotch. Mr Thomas swigged down the drink. With customary urbanity, he spoke about the match, the tour, the great good that he thought Gleeson and Mourie and their men had done for the game. He answered questions. He left the group with goodwill all round.

John Reason in the *Daily Telegraph* and Frost in the *Guardian* briefly mentioned the assault. The populars passed it by altogether. Yet this, as a foul and wholly shocking deed, surely ranked as a sensation and therefore, by popular Press standards, as a story. Its omission was mystifying, if not peculiar. What might be called the reasonable reaction of a reasonable man not at all interested in sensation but very greatly interested in rugby was expressed by the Scot who is honorary secretary to the International Rugby Board. John Hart is of the salt of the earth. He played once for his country, alas and alack in that deplorable match of 1951 in which Hennie Muller's Springboks beat the Scots by 44 to nil. But John is now more consequential to the game than most retired internationals. He has toured to all of the International Board countries, he is a friend of, and much admired by, administrators, players and Pressmen throughout the world, and he is, for rugby, a man of total integrity.

"I am appalled," he said. His eyes blazed. "I am appalled that anyone would do this to Russell Thomas — to *Russ,* of all people. I am shattered. For the good of rugby as a whole, I can only hope that the New Zealand Rugby Union, though they have every right to, will not express their resentment at this filthy attack on one of their men by withdrawing from their engagement to play in Wales in the Welsh centennial year. That would be a terrible tragedy. But the assault is also tragic."

Was it only by oversight that many papers and many radio and television programmes failed to mention the assault? Methinks not. I think the attitude was that the All Blacks had served their purpose to the media. They had permitted a howl to be raised against what was termed, not without just cause, a foul. Thus it was no longer significant that the honorary manager of an amateur sporting team visiting their countries as guests — special guests, let it not be forgotten; the New Zealand union immediately offered to stand in when the South African Rugby Board, contemplating the political situation, decided it would not be wise to accept a tour of the British Isles by a Springbok team — had been violently, sickeningly assaulted.

Looking back, Russell Thomas mused: "I should have made a statement after Bridgend. It might have helped." Looking forward, he said: "Something must be done to reduce the tensions between Wales and New Zealand in rugby."

Looking over the tour, a senior New Zealand official of unparalleled experience at the administrative level of international rugby remarked: "The trouble over there is that they still think of us as poor, simple, ignorant Colonials."

Poor, yes — and getting poorer, thanks to the Common Market. Simple, very likely; we trust British politicians. Ignorant, more than probably. Colonials, for God's sake never.

Rugby players. Why yes, yes and yes again. Seventeen out of 18, on a tour stacked against New Zealand, intensely demanding on fitness and discipline and spirit, was a cause for pride; and if poverty, simplicity and ignorance were the component features of such a performance, why the more of them the better. Decidedly, as I hope to show in many respects, this was a tour that will not die by a team that found itself.

CHAPTER TWO

New Lamps For Old

IN A LEFTHANDED sort of way, it is a comfort for a critic to learn that his wit, whatever he had of it, has not withered with the years and that in the opinion of those who matter he is still as bad as ever he was. A generation before the tour of Mourie's men was mounted, the *New Zealand Herald* generously supported my candidature for the job of Press Association correspondent for the long tour, about five months in all, of Bob Stuart's All Blacks to the British Isles, France, British Columbia and California. Aspects of the tour, especially the defensive patterns of play adopted by the All Blacks and the unwillingness of the selectors to take chances on such talented attacking backs as Guy Bowers at first five-eighths and Jim Fitzgerald in midfield, encouraged critical appraisals; and a young Englishman who was secretary of the tour, Philip Bradforth, gleefully remarked that the average team reaction to my criticisms seemed to be the earnest, energetic, if not passionate desire of players to abstain from sitting at the same meal-tables as myself. After I had been posted back to my job as sports editor, whence I was later transferred to the editorial department to engage in various kinds of special work, the *Herald* gamely rejected the notion that a critic ought not to criticise. With the exception of the tour to France in 1977, they posted me to every major rugby expedition, within and without New Zealand, during the next 25 years. Silver jubilees having become the fashion with the celebration of Queen Elizabeth's first 25 years in the monarchy, I could be said to be celebrating a bit of a jubilee, too, in touring with Mourie's men 25 years after being the only pressman with Bob Stuart and his team. What would be the verdict of the young as compared with the older generation? It was an exciting thought. We were waiting, All Blacks and outriders, at London airport for the outward bound flight which would end the Mourie tour when I was approached by Andy Haden and two or three All Blacks. They sounded, and acted, pretty high. Andy thrust toward me a scarf made up of the ties of the Rugby Football Union centenary of 1970-71 and the Bridgend club. "This is for you, T.P.," he boomed. "We have voted you the champion shit-stirrer of our tour." "Unanimously?" I asked anxiously. It would have been disappointing to learn that some of the team had asked for their votes to be recorded against the motion.

"Of course," said Andy.

"I am glad of that," I said to Andy Dalton, a little later. "The new lamp's not much different from the old, eh?"

Andy grinned in his easy, casual way. "Your shoulders are pretty broad," he said.

Perhaps it was an appropriate time, then, to look down the years at the many incidents and teams which had been crowded into my jubilee span. Had things much changed in rugby in the 25 years, in techniques, team-play, the temperaments and enthusiasms? Was the rugby of Mourie's team and time more interesting, better played, than the rugby of those other teams I had accompanied to the British Isles — Stuart in '53, Wilson Whineray in '63, Brian Lochore in '67, Ian Kirkpatrick in '72, Andy Leslie in '74? Was rugby as relevant and important to the New Zealand community in 1978 as it had been in 1953, when we were farewelled by a motorcade through Wellington and welcomed, formally, at a Town Hall reception in Auckland the day after our return? Were the new lamps, talking of the whole subject of New Zealand rugby, as brightly shining as the old?

Fascinating questions, too extensive to be answered with deliberation in a work intended to represent the qualities of the Mourie tour. I suggest that one can begin with the broad statement that no All Blacks of the past had travelled as rocky a road toward stardom as the men Russell Thomas, Jack Gleeson and Graham Mourie so ably commanded. Some were not yet of teenage when the bitter controversy over sporting relationships between New Zealand and South Africa struck their country. Influenced by television's replays, repeated ad infinitum and in the agony of slow-motion, the peripheral portion of the public of the time became convinced that much of rugby was thuggery — indeed almost the only memorial left by a New Zealander appointed Governor-General of New Zealand, Sir Arthur Porritt, were words to this effect. Of profound significance, too, was a gathering discontent among senior players at the paucity of their allowances while they were touring, especially in representing their country abroad. Viewing the vast profits of such expeditions as the Lions to New Zealand in 1971 and the All Blacks to South Africa in 1976, players vehemently asked each other: "What's in it for us?" When told that they could expect no more than the glory, plus some ancillary, incalculable benefits — "I built my home in Christchurch at a time of severe shortages of housing materials," said a justly-famous All Black hooker, Dennis Young. "I never had to wait an hour for anything" — some·players reacted as if they had been stung by tsetse flies or bitten by cobras. In the decade before 1978, that is, the period of profoundest influence in the rugby development of the players who were to become Mourie's Men, New Zealand rugby also suffered slashings and bashings on and off the field. Many events were disquieting. Some were deplorable. The nadir was the tour of the 1972-73 team in the British Isles. Events, some not of their making, turned this into a team of ill repute. Damage done to the New Zealand rugby cause in the British Isles, especially in Wales, was substantial. Inevitably, some of this rubbed off in New Zealand. It became commonplace for parents, expecially impressionable young mothers, to say they would prefer their sons, if they must play football, to turn to soccer.

So much for the general background to the 1978 tour. A particular point potentially posed problems. When the New Zealand Rugby Union sent an All Black team of non-international status on a pioneering tour to Uruguay and the Argentine at the end of the winter of 1976, the "big three" of the tour were Ronald Don, a sharp, alert, peppery Aucklander as manager, and Gleeson and Mourie as coach and captain respectively. The team was unbeaten and performed so well that the three were reappointed when in the following year another All Black team of full international status was despatched, again in the role of pioneers, to Italy and France. The French won the first test, the All Blacks by superb tactics devised by Gleeson and implemented by Mourie brilliantly won the second. As a reflection of improved team-play so soon after the unconvincing performances in the series in New Zealand against Phil Bennett's British Lions, the tour was encouraging. Diplomatically speaking, it was less successful. Mr Don, admittedly hampered by a want of careful preparation by the New Zealand union, attained a querulous relationship with some officials of the French Rugby Federation, especially in the all-important aspect of interpreting. New Zealand pressmen with the All Blacks were spectators of one particularly intense shouting-match. Mr Gleeson was uninterested in and unaffected by this side of the tour. He returned to New Zealand convinced that Mr Don was an ideal manager because he was so much of a player's man. "Ron doesn't give a darn about anybody," Gleeson said. "He just wants things right for the team." Unusually for a man who himself would be striving for office — broken hearts of men who had been beaten in ballots because, beforehand, they had courageously voiced opinions which were known to differ from those held by the Establishment, litter the highways and byways of New Zealand rugby — Jack Gleeson in the months before the elections of the manager and coach of the 1978 team frequently urged the appointment of Mr Don. Councillors of the union were unimpressed. It was whispered that Russell Thomas was a surprisingly decisive winner in the ballot.

Would this, it was wondered, cause problems for the tour of the British Isles? Would Gleeson take umbrage at what he might consider a personal snub — all councillors were aware of his championship of Mr Don? Would his association with Mr Thomas be difficult, perhaps frigid? The point was important. New Zealand rugby has had its share of incompetent management of teams touring abroad. Britons in the know were amused by the New Zealander who was sucked in by siren voices in the Establishment — and out of it. A South African audience was not charmed by the All Black manager who observed that the last time he had been in their city was during the Boer War. A home-coming manager was rescued from Customs prosecutions only by extraordinary efforts. The captain of a tolerably recent All Black team pithily described his manager as "a bloody fool".

So here, potentially, was a prickly problem for 1978. It was soon resolved. Russell Thomas is a leading member of that minority which understands that homework is even more essential in maturity than it is to young scholars. He soon took steps to apprise Gleeson of his plans for the tour. Before the tour, he was often in correspondence, by letter or telephone. They had meetings. Jack responded in kind. If he regretted the loss of Ron Don, he never mentioned it. He was soon to find that Thomas was also a player's man, to the death if necessary. Moreover, it was soon apparent that while Thomas could be stubborn in defending a point of view and stern in exercising authority, his diplomacy was silken. He did not lose his temper. It was inconceivable that he could be coaxed into a shouting-match about anything.

It was a fact of the tour that the two did not develop a truly warm friendship for each other. The respect was profound, no question of that. But where Thomas, a gregarious character, liked to end up a hard day with a few drinks in his suite, arguing the toss about anything and everything with such special friends as Lyn Jaffray, Doug Bruce and John Loveday, Gleeson preferred seclusion with an occasional break-out at the bar with All Blacks, the Press or locals.

It seemed possible at the outset, that the players, as children of a divided age, might become disaffected and that the managers would find themselves uncongenial, one to the other and therefore, as agents of authority, to the team. It was the triumph of the tour that the All Blacks and their managers set irreproachable standards of conduct on and off the field. The team took its character from its leaders. My peers and superiors of the working press from time to time take the mickey out of me because I sometimes — not too often — remember in print that I have been with this tour and that. My older daughter Jill, while taking physiotherapy at Otago, practically set up palisades to defend her statement that her old man had not covered, as was the foul rumour of the university, the tour of the 1905 All Blacks. I like the joking. It's good fun. But I am not joking when I say that the principal cause of the outstanding tour of the 1978 All Blacks was the quality of the leadership. Thomas was, without any doubt in my mind, the most accomplished manager of any team I have toured with. His intelligence was acute, his industry prodigious. If he waved a big stick, I never heard of it. None of the players needed such a warning. His daily meetings at 9.15 acquainted the players with what was coming and what could and should be done. At them, the players had the right to speak on points that irked or to offer opinions that might help. The character of the side could be assessed from the willingness of players voluntarily to undertake tedious duties. The sum of their journeyings to clubs and schools was thousands of miles and hundreds of hours. The headmaster of the Caerphilly school said of Mourie and other All Blacks that they were the finest sportsmen he had ever met.

This was a side-expression of the humility, a genuine and profound humility, which graced Thomas. He learned it, growing up in the Great Depression in a home whose breadwinner was the caretaker of a local school. Thomas as a lad was there to watch Jack Sullivan, the man who later was chairman when he himself was first elected to the Rugby Council, score two tries for the All Blacks against the 1937 Springboks. On that day, young Thomas was wearing short pants of which the linings came from flour-bags. He was well acquainted with the griefs of near-poverty as he made his way upwards, on merit and with considerable industry, to the general managership of the South Island branch of Foodstuffs, the large national grocery organisation, and coincidentally progressed through various chairs of amateur sport to the Rugby Council and the chairmanship of the Victory Park Board which administers Lancaster Park in Christchurch. He was offered inspiration, too, when his mother cycled hundreds upon hundreds of miles to teach first aid to thousands during the years of the Second World War. Not a penny piece would Mrs Thomas take in reward or expense. That, she said, was her war-effort. Russell did not forget. Somewhere in the distant past some ancestor must have pinched from the House of Wales the famous motto, "I Serve". He was faithful to it.

Gleeson, temperamentally an ascetic who preferred to keep his own counsel, was as a coach neither so stern and decisive as Freddie Allen, nor so warm and amusing as Carwyn James, nor so penetrating a critic of the qualities of the game as J. J. Stewart. In general coaching qualities, however, he was at least the equal of any one of these three great coaches in modern rugby. In powers of discerning the qualities, especially the potential weaknesses, of an opposing team and in motivating men he was slightly superior to all except, perhaps, Mr

James. Though he preferred not to do his thinking aloud, Jack sometimes cautiously lifted the veil on his thoughts. Some of these reflected his immense sympathy for his predecessors, Stewart and Bob Duff (of the 1972-73 team), because they had been required to tour with players of strong minds who were not easily disciplined. Jack had made sure that at least one such player, a favourite with part of the public and the Press, was not in his team; and, in fact, no apple in the barrel was even speckled, let alone rotten. Bryan Williams, the senior tourist whose rugby voyagings began even before the All Blacks' tour to South Africa in 1970, emphatically declared that Mourie's Men were the most congenial team he had ever toured with. This weighty praise reflected the qualities of the team; not least of which (and this was Mr Gleeson's special contribution) was the serious attention to duty.

Gleeson prepared for the tour by circularising a physical training programme recommended by Rothmans former national athletics coach, Brian Wilson, of Napier, who had done much to help the Hawke's Bay representative team which strenuously and often sensationally stalled off challenges for the Ranfurly Shield in the late 1960s. The schedule was skilful. The All Blacks were hopping fit from the start. When Gleeson suspected that staleness might be affecting play and morale, Wilson supplied him with further exercises which again were invaluable. Thus, on the physical side, Mourie's men were carefully and skilfully helped along; and their capacity for unceasing hard work and the stamina which yielded them victories at the eleventh hour of their great matches was directly attributable to Gleeson's discernment. Best of all coaches, he got on with the training as a job to be done vigorously, intelligently and, above all, briefly. Boredom was a state of mind with which the 1978 All Blacks remained unacquainted. They acquired and held fast to zest on the training-field. It is axiomatic that, in athletic activity, the body will only perform to the level to which it is accustomed. The zip and zing and sting of Gleeson's training were out of this world.

Gleeson stood apart from all coaches of my experience in an exercise which became critical to the tour. As early as Cardiff, the second match, he got tackle-bags. They were retained for the tour. The bags stood about six feet high. They were somewhat pear-shaped, rising from a base about 30 inches in diameter to the peak, which was about 12 inches across. The interior was packed with foam-rubber. This was firm but yielding. In the early stages, the bags were used for their prime purpose, as aids to tackling. Later, the exercise was extended. The bags were also used for training at rucking and mauling.

It would be impossible, in my opinion, to overestimate the importance of the bags to the success of the tour. Gleeson demurred at this statement. He shrugged his shoulders in a characteristic gesture. He had always used such bags in training, he said. Nothing was new under the sun. Mourie also sought not to place undue importance upon the bags. They were, he said, "a bit of a laugh". "The guys" treated them as such. Maybe, yes, maybe it was true that they encouraged competitiveness. Otherwise, there was "nothing to them". They were "good for a joke, that's all".

Untrue, untrue, untrue. The bags turned the 1978 All Blacks into the most powerful tackling team of my experience. In training, one man was required to hold the bag upright while the others ran in, one by one, with a hiss and a roar, taking off, two or three yards short of the target, so that they were flying through the air when they made contact. Because they knew there was no danger of injury, either to bones or soft-tissues, the All Blacks training-day by training-day built a greater confidence in themselves as tacklers and correspondingly acquired a stronger, more accurate tecnnique. They could laugh, too, as when Billy Bush, at Limerick, in the presence of Irish schoolchildren, solemnly came in at the bag with his right arm extended in a perfect demonstration of the stiff-arm tackle. Laughter was not what they were after when the whistle blew for kick-off in each match. Their objective now was the enemy ball-carrier. It was a sight to astound, and jubilate about, as Billy Osborne roared into the midships of an opposing centre, striking him with a power and authority scarcely less severe than that which made the famous Welsh centre of the 1950 British Lions team, Jackie Matthews, the most devastating tackler ever fielded by any team visiting New Zealand. In the Cardiff match, Brad Johnstone made four tackles, at least three critically important to particularly dangerous moves, which were exemplary by the severest technical standards — and props are not normally noted for their tackling. So through the tour, Mourie, Leicester Rutledge, Mark Donaldson, Osborne, Williams and many more struck down foemen with shuddering, devastating efficiency. None was unfair. All were invaluable. Science has not yet devised a means to test the psychological importance of efficient tackling, though it is an unusually strong and dedicated man in, say, the key position of first five-eighths who is prepared to take a third severe tackle in a game. As before remarked, Gleeson extended the exercise from the tackle to the maul and ruck, insisting that as men drove with the ball into opponents, they should strike at maximum velocity while turning their bodies to release the ball to teammates thundering in behind them. Here again, confidence was built. Men could concentrate on performing the proper actions with the ball without fearing injury to themselves or to teammates who, as in normal exercises of this sort, would be acting as Aunt Sallies. The momentum of the thrust became highly developed.

From an early stage, Lions' forwards who in New Zealand in 1977 had subjected All Black and provincial packs to humiliation because of the superiority of their techniques of scrummaging and mauling were amazed by the improvement and quality of the Mourie Men. Their compliments ought first to have been directed at Jack Gleeson. In material particulars, he was a master technician. The quality embellished his skills in discernment and motivation.

Critics soon carped at Mourie. They said he became an active obstructive force when, as his backline attacked, he ran from his flank position on the scrum on a line which kept him in front of his own ball-handlers and between them and the backs of the defending team. Critics always carp. It is their function. Life would be all but insupportable if they were not around to disagree with. In Mourie's case, the criticisms were soon muted. Later, they disappeared. Attention was instead directed at the man's incredible capacity for work done at an inhuman level of speed. Had Mourie's ankles been fitted with (a) a pedometer and (b) a speedometer, it is probable the one would have shown him to have run, during his 14 matches, scores of miles while the other would have established his speed as exceeding that allowed to paid-up members of the Flank Forwards Union. Doubting Thomases — who did not include Russell — who came to sneer at this latter-day wing-forward genius from Down Under stayed to marvel at Mourie's industry, mobility and diligence. Unlike the Duke of Plaza-Toro, "who led his regiment from behind while they were only fighting", Mourie was a king of the "Come on, boys".

That was the physical side; and it was staggering. On the mental, the tactical side, Mourie was not less alert. His rapport with Gleeson was complete. Thus Mourie was athletically active in mind from kick-off to no-side. He had the gift of sustained concentration exercised by a mind which appeared to operate on two levels. Which is to say that while one part of his mind directed his body to its incessant flow of activity, the other was constantly casting about, looking at the state, physical and mental, of the All Black team, assessing the effects of the wear and tear of the game upon the opponents as a whole and the weak sisters among them. For sentimental reasons, it is difficult to attempt the task of classifying the six captains of the postwar tours of the British Isles. All had noble qualities. But in the particular personal capacity to endure and in the general capacity to imbue his men with a ceaseless willingness, Mourie was probably unrivalled. An example fetches to mind: As a lineout was forming in the All Blacks' quarter against Midland Counties at Leicester, Mark Taylor sprang forward to wrest the long throw-in from a Counties' man. Accompanied by Osborne, he sprinted down the field. At a rapid regrouping of Counties' defences, the attack was in peril. Who should arrive, out of nowhere, but

Haden? With seven-league strides, he took a pass and at the right time made a pass himself. Taylor scored. It was a magnificent effort; but in what other team would the heaviest man of the side have run so far so fast for the dramatic intrusion which assured the All Blacks of victory?

Mourie spoke often during the tour, not least on television. Always, he communicated sincerity. The quality made profound impact. The man came to embody, to the British public, the virtues of the All Black team. Here was a plain-spoken, honest, modest, agreeable young man. He had a bit of a smile to him. He did not whinge about grounds or weather or referees. He was as gracious in victory as in the defeat by Munster. The latter was an experience the more lamentable because he seemed unable to devise counters to the relentless close-marking and decisive tackling of the Irishmen. But it was an experience of great value to the team because from it Mourie seemed to mature and henceforward march unfalteringly to his place as one of the great captains.

CHAPTER THREE

A Host Of Considerations

TAKING ONE CONSIDERATION with another, I feel bound to wonder whether the All Blacks' lot would have been a happier one if they had stuck to the tactics of the first part of their tour. Inevitably, they scratched about a bit in the opening match against Cambridge University. When the 1905 All Blacks won their first match, against Devon and Cornwall, who had been county champions in 1903-04, by 55 points to 4, it became an article of New Zealand's rugby faith that all teams in later tours must also win decisively. In fact, most have scraped along. Jet-lag of the modern age is inescapable. Young and old, strong and weak, alike are affected. At worst, the fatigue is severely debilitating. Thus, the failings of the second half at Cambridge were foreseeable; but it was encouraging indeed to discover the dynamic qualities in Mark Donaldson's running. In the next two games, against Cardiff and West Wales, the All Black 1978 edition, designer Jack Gleeson, exhibitor Graham Mourie, breezed to victory. When Bryan Williams intruded from left wing to right centre, beautifully drawing men and timing passes, Stuart Wilson in each of the two matches scored a try which was beyond criticism in construction and execution. The Welsh know their rugby and delight in the best of it. Each try left them entranced.

These were two difficult matches. New Zealand rugby minds are pragmatic rather than fanciful. The aim is to grasp the nettle. The Arms Park of Cardiff all the same exerts a strange dread. For reasons historical — and sometimes hysterical — New Zealanders are never sure of winning in Wales. Mourie's Men, you could bet, knew how Kirkie's Killers came a cropper, second time out, against Llanelli. They probably knew, too, how Whineray's Whoppers were beaten early on by Newport, 3 to 0, the only loss of a fine tour. Such as could cast their minds back a generation well remembered how Stuart's Stalwarts were done to a turn by Cardiff, 13 to 8. Thus the '78 All Blacks had cause to fear Cardiff, a great club, so soon as their second match. Moreover, it was evident that Swansea and West Wales might be a disruptive combination. Lochore's Larrupers in 1967, it was remembered, were put to no end of trouble to beat a West Wales team which had been diligently coached in seven sessions by Carwyn James. Now it was being said, in 1978, that anything James had done 11 years before would certainly be improved by Clive Rowlands, that, in fact, this would be the fifth test of the tour.

In the event, Cardiff and West Wales were each well beaten. The energy, vigour and, most of all, the enterprise of the All Blacks were startling. Gleeson was having to be careful. A shrewd student, he had soon discerned that Bruce Robertson, potentially his greatest midfield back, was wanting in confidence. At club and provincial level in New Zealand, the attention paid Robertson had grown the keener and more destructive as his reputation as one of the great backs of current rugby had expanded. He had so often been spotted by crash-tackling, some of it early, some late, that he had become wary and developed a defensive, human streak. So Gleeson, humane and understanding, took him quietly. Even so, the backs, especially Osborne, Stuart Wilson and Williams in the threequarters and Donaldson among the halfbacks, were at this stage in towering form. Mourie's vital style of leadership was encouraging the forward drive, too. The scrummaging had not yet expressed the Gleeson technique of feet moved forward, rather under the body, so that the leg-stretch, as the ball was put into the tunnel, would become a powerful thrust — but it was coming along. Gleeson was soon made aware that British teams, by placing three unusually tall men, none less than 6 feet 4 inches, at 3, 5 and 7 of the lineout, would not be easily overpowered. Because of power and strength and a mind which was totally committed, Frank Oliver, though an inch or so below the desired height, could safely be entrusted with 3. Haden had all the necessary height for 5. It was going to be just a matter of gearing him up. Being not so rugged of body or mind as Oliver, he might have his slack times; but Gleeson was confident he could attend to these. There was genuine anxieties about Number 7. Gary Seear had the height. After two tours to South Africa and France, he was aware of the tough demands of big-time rugby. The question was whether his uncoordinated body movements, which consisted of a series of unfoldings of torso, thighs and legs, would affect his capacity and speed for the defensive covering a Number 8 must do.

Gleeson was soon aware that he had problems with the second-stringers. The two Johns at lock, Loveday and Fleming, each caused concern at Cambridge. They were well held and often beaten by their markers, each mere striplings. Mentally and bodily, the two inhabited the provincial plateau. The question was whether they had the all-important temperamental qualifications for the higher plateau, and how soon, if they had, they could climb to it. One look at the standard British lineout pattern was enough to convince Gleeson that Ashley McGregor, second-string Number 8 to Seear, would not serve. For want of three or four inches of height, he could not, in the best of company, be trusted for Number 7. The belief that Gleeson had not been overjoyed at McGregor's selection for the tour was incidental. Now that Ashley, a silent man who looked much too young to be the father of four children, was a member of the team, he must be accommodated as and when possible; and if, in the severest terms, he represented a hole, that deficiency must be covered. When it became apparent from early in the tour that McGregor could have been awarded a placard, "Not Wanted on Voyage", his home-town supporters in Southland and his many admirers elsewhere became irritated and they were not pleased that, in all, he played only three matches. But it was part of the Gleeson straightforwardness that, early on, he told McGregor of the problems the All Blacks would encounter whenever they played too short a man at the back of the lineout. McGregor was advised henceforth to become a flanker. He did not openly grumble, or turn sour. He trained on steadily through the tour. This was a tribute not only to the man but also to the quality of the spirit in the team.

Notwithstanding the discovery of early problems, the particular anxieties being Loveday and Fleming, the All Blacks set about these early matches with zest. Their displays excited comparisons. It could fairly be said that no All Black team in the British Isles from Stuart's time onward had played so freely, adventurously. Needled by the low qualities of much of the provincial rugby of his time, Freddie Allen demanded — he never asked; you did what *he* wanted — that the '67 All Blacks fulfil the first requirement of rugby by picking up the ball and running with it. J. J. Stewart, who always asked and never demanded, was of a like mind to Allen, though he reached similar conclusions by subtle, circuitous philosophising. But Allen's fine team was held back, just a little, by a want of speed and elusiveness close to the scrum. Stewart's also had a defensive complex in about the same places. In the early stages, Gleeson's men looked superior close in. Moreover, Jack had a great way of dealing with potential crises. His fair and fatherly talk with McGregor has been mentioned. He was more decisive with both Loveday and Fleming. Loveday, a chiropractor who had trained at Palmer College in the United States had contemplated retirement at the end of the 1977 season. As an expert on backs, human, not rugby, he found his own to be sadly deficient. Having been worked over by the Lions and other teams, he could not see himself weathering the boots and buffets of further rugby, especially on tour. In the first days in the British Isles, his discs and vertebrae appeared to be out of joint. By way of treatment, he put himself to bed for a day, resting while the rest trained. Lured by the sound of music and revelry, he arose after dinner. He was spotted by Gleeson. Loveday may even have been on the dance-floor. Gleeson crooked his finger. "John," he said. "All Blacks who can't train . . . They go home." Not again did Loveday miss a training run. His play grew stronger with the tour. If he did not leap at the lineout like a broaching rainbow, there might have been point to his remark that this was because the All Blacks' throwers-in from touch, being prudent and cautious men, preferred not to place the ball in his proximity. Fleming needed no such draconian treatment. At the talk before the match with West Wales, Gleeson said: "John, I want you to play like an All Black today." The graph of Fleming's performances rose steeply, at an angle of not less than 45 degrees, for the remainder of the tour.

So much promise in those early matches. What would be the end-result? A backline comparable with that of 1905 — Roberts, Stead, Hunter, Deans, Smith, McGregor, Wallace; supermen all; or 1924 — Mill, McGregor, Nicholls, Cooke, Svensen, Steel, Nepia — not bad, either?

Alas. The humpty-dumpty All Blacks sat on the wall of Thomond Park in Limerick and took a great tumble. Not all the Queen's horses nor all the Queen's men could quite put them together again.

Gleeson displayed hypertension in his reaction to this merited defeat. He railed against the kamikaze-type tactics used by Munster's marauders, who knocked over everything that moved in case it carried the ball. He was not at all happy about a referee who allowed Munster men, especially on the fringes of the scrummage and lineout, to pinch yards of ground before the ball had become free. (Tactics of the same sort have decorated and desecrated New Zealand rugby year by year and match by match for generations.) Having aired his views, which were gobbled up by the Press, Gleeson took positive action. To a significant degree, he modified the all-out attacking plan of the first period of the tour. Having satisfied himself that Eddie Dunn had been unreliable at Limerick and excessive in his tactical punting once or twice elsewhere, Gleeson promoted Doug Bruce to be his anchor-man at first five-eighths. This was a decisive gesture. Bruce kicked swiftly, accurately and long with each foot. He was calm and solid. Not for him the blinding thrust on the short side or the hint of a break through the open field. He was one to be ready, two to be steady and three to keep the game under control.

Duggie was a fine instrument for the application of the new strategy. Demonstrably, the strategy worked. Mourie's Men continued unbeaten, if in hair-raising style from time to time, throughout the tour. Not until the Barbarians' match, which Gleeson welcomed the more because of the club's decision to field a team which would have a go, did the All Blacks resort to the all-out attack of their first period. This was a game of the most marvellous movement, almost as exhausting to watch as it must have been to play, and if the All Blacks had lost, as they so nearly did, Gleeson might have been accused of irresponsibility. Yet the failings that day were of individuals, not of the plan. If Williams had scored more than once, as he ought to have, if there had been just a little more precision in some movements, the All Blacks by half-time could have been so far into the lead, so dominant psychologically, that the rest would have been a procession. In victory, the faults of the game could have been written off as minor events. Yet it is a telling possibility, worth infinite argument, that the All Blacks by sticking to their original plan, Munster or no Munster, could have worked up such confidence in the backline as to make the finest line-up an all-conquering unit. It must always be held as a major criticism of the re-shaped plan that Stuart Wilson, who was a back of, at best, exceptional quality, having scored four times in the three early matches scored again only once more on the tour.

If I were to look back critically on the six tours of my jubilee experience, I would be inclined to say that the persistent, chronic failing in all of the teams was a want of confidence in their ability finally to decide how they should play the game. This was extraordinary. During each of the tours, the New Zealand forward-play had been, as a generalisation, superior, often decisively so. Stuart's team had a wonderful tight-core featuring Kevin Skinner in the front-row and Richard White and Nelson Dalzell, especially the former, in the lineout. With Whineray, Dennis Young and Ken Gray in the front row, Colin and Stanley Meads in the second, and a truly magnificent backrow of Kelvin Tremain, John Graham and Waka Nathan, the 1963 team at forward was all but unbeatable; this was certainly one of New Zealand's greatest packs of all time. Gray, Colin Meads, Tremain and Nathan were still there as the core in 1967, Bruce McLeod was a remarkably fast and powerful hooker and no team ever had a stauncher leader and servant than Brian Lochore. But the standard was slightly diminished; as it was, too, in 1972, despite the qualities of Ian Kirkpatrick and Ken Stewart in the backrow and of Peter Whiting at the lineout. With Whiting, Hamish Macdonald, Stewart and Kirkpatrick under command, Andy Leslie in 1974 fielded a pack of such quality that in the Barbarians' match which was played at Twickenham the Lions' pack which a few weeks before had all but annihilated the Springboks in South Africa, a feat never achieved by any of the five All Black teams which have toured that republic, was resisted, held and to a palpable degree overpowered.

Despite the predominance of one All Black pack after another during the 25 years of my own good fortune in touring with these teams, not one team developed a confidence based on the devil-may-care flair and panache of, as in example, a great French side. Backline after backline suffered itself to be inhibited exactly as Mourie's team did in relation to Stuart Wilson. Had Wilson played in the backlines of the 1950, 1959 and 1971 Lions' teams which toured New Zealand, he would certainly have scored many tries, perhaps even scads of them.

The fault in 1978, if it may be called such (in the pragmatic world of international sport, you really are nit-picking when you complain about, or pick holes in, an all but unbeaten tour), lay not in Gleeson, nor his team, nor such coaches as Stewart, Allen and the topnotcher in 1963, Neil McPhail, nor their many fine players. The fault was in the consciousness of the New Zealand public. Much and all as this leading spokesman or that might talk of free-flowing rugby, glories of attack, taking of chances and letting the devil come hindmost, the great continuing desire in the public mind was for victory. In a sense, New Zealand rugby has never outgrown, even at this distant time, the achievements of the 1905 team, which was beaten only once in the British Isles and France while scoring 838 points against only 47, and of the 1924 side, which lost not at all and which in the same five countries scored 721 points to 112. It is very likely, that to Mourie, who by his own admission does not trouble himself with rugby literature, the names of Charlie Seeling of 1905 and Maurice Brownlie of 1924 are scarcely names and that the famous backs of those times are unknown by him. Yet Mourie, I assert, suffered, as did Gleeson and Russell Thomas and all of their players, from the compulsive wish of their New Zealand public that they should win. Play well, yes, brilliantly if possible; but, above all, win.

I do not suppose there is much to be done about it. One looks at a burly schoolmaster standing five metres infield from touch while he hectors his 10- and 11-year-old boys who are playing in a Barbarians' day on the Auckland Domain; one looks at the parents lining touch of club matches between teams of midgets; one looks at club fixtures of all sorts upwards to senior and thence to provincial matches, especially when these involve the Ranfurly Shield; one looks at the tests, dirtied though they might be with late-tackles and broken jaws. Consistent to all is the public desire that, come hell, come high water, this team, or that, should win.

New Zealand rugby has wonderful players, wonderful people. I recall the man, though not his name, who came from Waihi to plead to the New Zealand Rugby Council for financial assistance in moving their ground from the town's centre to the rather more distant showgrounds. He talked of how, with two or three others, he customarily mowed the field, marked it, set everything up and, after the game, prepared for the match on the following Saturday. "How much would you get from a good gate at one of your club games?" asked a councillor. "Eighty shillings," said the man. Four quid! Yet, week after week, year after year, this man and his comrades had been keeping rugby in Waihi alive. I recall, on another tack, Peter Jones, the famous All Black of Stuart's and other teams, telling at a dinner how, at his small primary school in Mangonui in the far north he was compelled to desist from playing marbles, which was his passion, to play rugby. Being biggish for his few years, he was told to play at Number 8, packing down between the two biggest pupils who were at lock. "They were not boys, they were girls," Peter explained in his mild, light tenor. "This was in the days before Helena Rubinstein. That is how I became a flank-forward." I recall Bill Craddock who, long before he became mayor of Westport and a life-member of the New Zealand Rugby Union, spent uncountable sums from his own pocket to ensure that rugby in Buller resisted the encroachment of league from the West Coast. These are small samples of the humility, the humour and the unselfishness which have been characteristic of rugby in New Zealand and a material factor in its retaining, in spite of controversies, bitternesses and detestable aspects, its place as the great New Zealand game.

But humility, humour and unselfishness, great qualities though they have been, have not eradicated from the New Zealand rugby mind the mystical belief in the importance of victory. In this sense, the game may be described as permanently adolescent. All who are involved in it want to win. This is a human desire. Experience would suggest that, in relation to New Zealand rugby as it is played and watched by New Zealanders, the desire is unconquerable and so deeply rooted as to be considered an atavistic impulse.

Am I a lone voice in suggesting that there is another dimension to the game, that the factor of enjoyment, especially if it is desired that the sport should remain amateur in all particulars, is of greater importance than victory, however much victory may appear to enhance the enjoyment? I cannot answer the question. I know of many who wish, as I do and have done, for the legendary qualities of 1905 and 1924 to be reinstated. Jimmy Hunter as a midfield back scored 39 tries in the British Isles in 1905 and in 1924 Hart, Cooke, Svenson and Steel, threequarters all, scored 75 tries among them. It is desolating, surely, to think that because of a change of approach to defensiveness, backed wholeheartedly by the national will for victory, Bert Cooke, an ethereal genius, might in 1978 have scored no more than three or four tries.

The fault of 1978 was not in Jack Gleeson, Mourie or the players. The fault was in the system, the civilisation, that bred them all. As is so solemnly said by someone or other before each general election in New Zealand: It's time for a change.

CHAPTER FOUR

The Machine in Component Parts

IT WAS IN *Rugby World,* published in London, that, of all people, an American who works for, of all unlikely rugby newspapers, the international edition published in Paris of the *Herald-Tribune,* wrote a piece about a great French midfield back of almost a generation ago, Andre Boniface. Bob Donahue, a personable, capable young man with a fine feel for rugby, discussed many aspects of Boniface's career. This in relation to New Zealand included participation in the 3-0 defeat of Stuart's All Blacks in Paris in 1954 and the tour Down Under of Francois Moncla's Tricolors in 1961. As to rugby of the New Zealand style, Andre conveyed to Donahue a reverential regard. This was, he said, the true game. Alone among the rugby nations, New Zealanders had a spiritual appreciation of the discipline of the game; and he had always regretted, Boniface said, that he had not clasped the hand of his wife, who was only twenty at the time, and conveyed her Down Under so that he could immerse himself in this wonderful sport.

It was an unusual, moving tribute. Reading the passage, the average New Zealander could not help saying to himself: "Can Boniface be right? Is our rugby as good as he says? Does he really know what he is talking about? Is he aware of the continuing story of violence which desecrates our game? If he experienced, first-hand, consistently, the defensive complexes which we ourselves complain are the curse of our game, would he not throw in his hand and return to the rugby of France, so free, so passionate, so abundant with originality?"

This would be a good, average reaction from the average New Zealander, who becomes suspicious when he thinks things about his country, the good things, are being laid on with a trowel by visitors who do not understand situations as well as he himself does. But Boniface's tribute, coming out of the blue, was striking and stimulating. Among his many gifts as a player was a special one for setting up attacking situations by either a bit of a weave and a sprint which put him outside his marker for a vital moment of time and a vital fragment of space or else a pass, made with speed and delivered with precision

— the sort of pass which distinguished two great British backs, Jeff Butterfield of England in the 1950s and John Dawes of Wales in the 1970s. Centre-threequarters of the Boniface standard have not been much seen in New Zealand rugby, especially in the key place of second five-eighths, in the last generation. Could it be that Andre was talking idealised generalities in placing New Zealand at the peak of the rugby-playing nations, not in terms of proportion of victories but in terms of the ideal qualities of the game?

The coincidence of the Mourie tour and the Boniface tribute was a most interesting conjunction. By no means all of the tour was ideally played. The All Blacks were intermittently plagued, from first to last, by errors of omission and commission. They did silly, or unfortunate, things against Cambridge University in their first match. Eighteen matches later, by which time all of the gross failings should have been laundered out of their game, they were still maladroit in various particulars. They scraped home against the Barbarians in this fixture when, by rights of possession and proportions of attacking, including the chance of goals from penalties, they ought to have approached the finishing-post at a leisurely canter. Mourie counted the game against Monmouthshire, a team of many internationals and, more importantly, a forward pack principally made up of the tigers of Pontypool, as the best performance of the tour. Certainly it was a fine display. Richard Wilson, the replacement at fullback for the youngster, Clive Currie, who had been invalided from the tour by a brutal assault, rather than a tackle, in the international against Wales, set the All Blacks off into overdrive by cracking all kinds of goals in the first half and by half-time the match had become a one-horse race. Even so, the All Blacks, despite their lead of 22 to 9 at the break, were able to manage only one more try in the following 40 minutes. It was a niggling thought that a New Zealand team of the Boniface ideal would have used the large advantage to destroy the enemy in the second half; and Andre surely would have found it difficult to equate the number of avoidable errors which afflicted the attack with his vision of New Zealand's as the ideal kind of rugby.

Yet it may well be contended that even in the midst of their erring, a failing which distracted one from considering at true worth the true qualities of New Zealand rugby, Mourie's men did manage to convey, with a decent consistency, the sort of quality which appealed so intensely to Boniface. Except in such stupidities as the "dive" against Wales and the raking of J. P. R. Williams at Bridgend, the team conveyed a fine regard for rugby. Beyond a level reached by any All Black team with which I had toured to the British Isles, they had style. As a curtain-raiser to the tour, the All Blacks and interested Outriders attended at Twickenham to watch, four days before the match against

Cambridge University, the Argentinian team which had been touring in the British Isles play against a team which was labelled as an England XV but which was, as near as dammit, the full England international side. At the end of a game in which the Argentinian flyhalf, Hugo Porta, established himself as an exceptional player and in which the English were mighty lucky to escape with a 13-13 draw, the head of the New Zealand Press Association's London bureau, Ron Palenski, and I sped from the press-box in the East Stand to the area behind the West Stand, which is the preserve of the Establishment. Wishing for a word from Mourie, we encountered him surrounded by young autograph-hunters. Other All Blacks appeared to be already seated in the bus, located nearby, which had brought them from the Park Lane Hotel to the ground. I was a little astonished. My appreciation was that the committee of the Rugby Football Union, a body of considerable hospitality, would have had all of the All Blacks in the committee-room, or the Old Internationals Room, or somewhere pleasant and friendly.

"Are you," I said to Mourie, "going upstairs to have a drink with the Alickadoos?"

"No chance," he replied. "This is the Argentinians' day, not ours."

I lifted my finger. One up to you, sport, I said to myself. Such delicacy is not commonplace with touring teams, theirs or ours.

A couple of days later, the British Sportsmen's Club, which was founded in 1925 to allay the indignation and bitterness members of the 1924 All Blacks felt about the ordering-off of their loose-forward, Cyril Brownlie, in the match with England a little time before, gave a luncheon at the Savoy Hotel for the '78 All Blacks. Anybody who is anybody in British sport belongs to the club. The only gatherings are Savoy lunches at which teams like the All Blacks, the Australian cricketers and suchlike are entertained. On show in October '78 was the largest attendance in the club's history, a singular tribute to the All Blacks in itself. The special dignitaries were the former Prime Minister, Mr Edward Heath, and a Judge of the High Court, Sir Carl Aarvold, whose rugby career blazed with brilliance for Cambridge, England and the British team which toured New Zealand in 1930. More recently, Sir Carl had reigned as president of the All-England Lawn Tennis and Croquet Club, more familiarly known as Wimbledon. No one laughs more merrily at Mr Heath's jokes than Mr Heath himself; but they are excellent jokes; and his affection for rugby is profound and genuine. Sir Carl is not, perhaps, everyone's cup of tea. When the British team many years later held a reunion at Twickenham, he advised that he could not attend. But, happening to be at the ground on the day, he was offended not to be among his old teammates while they, mirthful up to the eyeballs, were being photographed by BBC television. "Carl

Aarvold," said one of the team, the brilliant flyhalf Roger Spong, "can, so far as the rest of us are concerned, jump in the lake!" However, here he was, an eminent figure in British sport; and the pitting of Mr Heath and Sir Carl against Russell Thomas looked to be a desperately unequal contest.

In the event, Thomas waltzed in. In tennis terms, he won in straight sets. Mr Heath had the touch of the practised politician. Sir Carl personified judicial wit. The company of more than 500 reacted to their speeches with "Hear, hears" and applause. Thomas, who is no orator in the accepted sense, offered, above all, sincerity. He had worked hard on his speech. He spoke simply. The time had come, he said, when international sport must be rid of vile chauvinism. What good could accrue from the tour of amateurs who had travelled half the world if, in victory, they were to be spat upon? Should it not be the first duty of all who were involved in sport to emphasise the quality of sportsmanship of the true sort? Mr Thomas could be pleasing in his wit, too. He said the Railways Department in New Zealand were still trying to collect from Sir Carl five pence to replace the cup he had broken in one of those wretched refreshment rooms which used to be provided for travellers of those times. As for Mr Heath, everyone knew that this eminent yachtsman had lately been sailing through rough seas (at a Conservative Party conference, a few days before the lunch, Mr Heath had been given a hard time by some speakers). These lighter touches went down as pleasantly as the wines the company were drinking (at their own expense). But the central message, that sport would command affection and respect only if insistence was placed upon the factor of true sportsmanship, came through so clearly, so decisively, so sincerely, that as Mr Thomas sat down, the company rose to him. It was a moving tribute. This was style, in excelsis.

Many other episodes of the tour demonstrated this pleasing quality. An English referee, Roger Quittenton, a young university lecturer whose unquestioned ability might be affected, so some experts contended, by a degree of hypertension visible in his control of players and events, called against Bill Osborne a penalty which presented Wales with a penalty kick 10 metres in front of the New Zealand goalposts. "That man," said Mourie, moving behind Mr Quittenton and indicating Ray Gravell, the Welsh back Osborne had tackled, "did not have possession of the ball." "Too late now," Mr Quittenton answered. It was Mourie's only reference. Another man might have persisted in recriminations against an award which could have cost the All Blacks the game. "I can tell you," said another referee, Alan Hosie, of Glasgow, who had risen to international status from a long apprencticeship, "that the difference between Mourie's team and the All Blacks of 1972-73 is as decisive as the difference between night and day. I have never encountered finer sportsmanship." Here, then, was another exhibition of style. It was a reminder of much of the *real* rugby of New Zealand; of the kids who played on mud-ridden fields with no more than a cold, cold shower for cleaning up, but who played, who would not have dreamed of not playing: of Jack Lamason, a remarkably astute captain of Wellington College Old Boys in prewar days, during which he toured England with the 1937 New Zealand cricket team, responding to a refereeing award in front of the enemy goal and obviously intended to redress a previous wrong by kicking the ball to touch and exclaiming, "We don't take presents from anyone, thanks, Ref"; of dozens, hundreds, thousands, of devoted men and women of all ages who in various ways exhibited toward rugby the fidelity and integrity of ardent lovers.

Subject to the few human blemishes which elsewhere will be described, the style was constant to the Mourie tour. Perhaps Boniface was right. Perhaps New Zealanders did have for rugby a selfless, lasting love which was unique to the game.

It was not a nambypamby, coquettish sort of love. Just as much as Mourie with his intellectualism expressed the spirit of his team, so did Frank Oliver with his tough, downright approach. No forward of the six All Blacks tours to the British Isles in the postwar stretch had outshone Oliver in earthy, pragmatic approach. It seemed curious he had to wait until 1976 to win his first cap until you remembered the curious rumour that he had been compelled to resign from the Police Force for firing revolver shots through the ceiling of his house. The whispering said Oliver had slightly gone round the bend because of the strain of duties involving confrontations with tough-guy elements in the freezing industry in Southland. The revolver-shots, it was said, had compelled the police to hold a departmental inquiry, the findings of which left Oliver with no option but to give up his job. I put this tale to Frank. He laughed. He had enjoyed the Force, he said. The cops had been a good bunch of coves to work with. But the work had come to interfere with his family life. That, and that only, was the reason he had resigned. Useless now to ask who might have started up the rumour which, I am quite sure, did stunt Oliver's progress toward the top. The great thing, so far as the team of 1978 was concerned, was that he had got there.

Between them, Mourie and Oliver expressed most of the finest qualities of the tour. Mourie was not an easy man to get to know. Apart from Ron Palenski, who had formed a profound friendship with him while touring with Mourie in the Argentine in 1976 and in France the following year, I doubt that any Outrider of '78 could say that he had penetrated the captain's wall of natural reserve. Mourie was always polite and cordial, though in Edinburgh he did get a little tetchy when I asked him whether he had been approached to join the World Invitation team the Northern Transvaal Rugby Union was forming for a tour of South Africa in 1979. He answered Press conference questions candidly and fairly. It was exhilarating to encounter so rapid and penetrating a mind upon topics which ranged widely far beyond rugby. At dinner in Leicester, Palenski, Kathy his wife and I were chatting along over coffee when Mourie joined us. The topic turned to farming and New Zealand's place in relation to the Common Market. Mourie was expert on this difficult subject. Having stayed on in France after the tour there to play for Paris University and to indulge an interest in Continental life, he could talk compellingly about the threat to New Zealand life of Common Market activities. Nor was he less eloquent in talking of his own relationship to farming on the 200-acre block he runs a few miles inland from Opunake in Taranaki. You could sense from his conversation about the comings and goings of the seasons, the burgeoning of spring and the decaying of autumn, the mystical relationship with the dairy-herd, the weather-eye cocked at the clouds which might spoil the haymaking, that he was a true yeoman, with a passion for the land and all creatures which moved upon it. Perhaps there have been other captains, starting with Whineray, who also have possessed penetrating and wide-ranging minds, the kind of minds needed in government, industry and, not least, the boards, meat, wool, dairy and so on, which are fundamentally important to New Zealand living. But who among All Black captains plays Beethoven on a stereogram while taking breakfast or places Bach foremost among composers? These were some of the many facets of the Mourie mind; and because the man, like Russell Thomas, had natural modesty and humility, he immediately conveyed to all others a hint of special qualities. These were fused into a pattern of leadership which was diverse in character, enterprising in nature and unfathomably courageous. His All Blacks had cause to be close to desperation in such matches as Ireland, Wales, Scotland, the Barbarians, North of England. You never saw this in Mourie. He did not appear to scream and shout at his men, or exhort them to make a supreme effort. His method rather was to step up his own pace. The example stirred his team. They, too, stepped up the pace fractionally, holding to the new level in spite of the demands of an exhausting game on their stamina. The rapidity with which Bruce Robertson late in the Barbarians' game closed in for a heavy tackle of the Scot, Andy Irvine, a half-metre or less from the goalline, was an instance of the speed Mourie by personal example generated among his players as the last trump approached. It was from the scrum — five metres after the tackle that Eddie Dunn dropped his goal right-footed — he is naturally left-footed — for the game.

Mourie trained hard. Socially, he fulfilled duties cheerfully. In many cases, these were outside the team's normal range of activities. Seldom did he trouble the bars of hotels or nearby pubs. He was no prude in these things. He was enchanted by the visit to and lunch at the Bristol cellars of the great House of Harveys, sherry-suppliers supreme, and there and elsewhere displayed a sound general knowledge of wines and vineyards, good years and indifferent. Mourie and a few others bought a few cases of French, mostly claret, on favourable terms. His own choice, Latour '68, was, he said, a bit of a gamble. The vintners quibbled at its current quality but believed it might improve into a wine of fine quality. Mourie was willing to take the chance and affably to discuss this and many other topics.

Essentially, however, Mourie was a private person. He did not put up barriers. They were there. You learned of them and, naturally, respected them. His one strange, inexplicable attitude was a feeling amounting to a fear of the Press and what he termed its power. Servants of the Press who like myself have had a fair experience are always confused by this attitude. We doubt that we have any power whatever. Most of us would not wish to have the power, even if its existence could be proven. We can be cynical. When the New Zealand Rugby Union in 1977 staged a week-long congress of Pacific and Asian rugby countries at Lincoln College near Christchurch, the 168 delegates who otherwise discussed all manner of topics of the game were "spectators" at a discussion in which various wights of Press, radio and television were invited learnedly to talk about the functions of their particular craft in relation to the game. I was first to catch the eye of the selector and repeated, briefly, the advice of a famous player and character of the 1890s named Will McKenzie, or "Offside Mac", a wing-forward who played for Wellington and New Zealand and who was one of the most celebrated men of several generations. "Always make friends with the local reporter," said Will. "You never know when it may be a help." To a man, the delegates stared at me. Few, by the look of them, had the faintest idea what I was talking about. The show battled along, becoming not so much a statement from the journalists as a free-for-all in which the objects of the exercise were all but totally obscured. Each of us in turn was then asked to sum up his views. Undaunted, I urged the delegates to "always make friends with the local reporter. You never know when it may be a help." They were as amazed as before.

Yet this is the only power in the Press, or its satellites. If your case is presented fairly, accurately and, shall we say, sympathetically, it is likely to receive warmer interest and support than if it is presented by an antagonist. I reject wholeheartedly the notion that the Press — and I speak of this with some experience — has any power. I doubt totally that any player whose cause I have espoused because he has seemed to me to have the right qualifications has ever been placed in any team on that account. We of the Press can hope for no more — at least this has been my consistent ambition — than to become, in the immortal phrase invented by the famous cricketer, Dr W. G. Grace, "critics whose views are worth reading". I found it troubling that Mourie with his keen and agile mind could seriously believe that anyone of us, or all of us acting with the kind of mysterious concert which appears to govern the writings of Fleet Street, was or were to be feared because of our occupation.

I doubt that Frank Oliver was ever troubled about the place and power of the Press. Frank was strictly a get-on-with-it sort of guy. While he was enormously proud of being an All Black, he did not wear his heart on his sleeve. You discovered the pride from associating with him and/or watching him train and play. Sometimes he let himself down and, worse, his side. His punch of Paul Ringer could have cost New Zealand the international with Wales if the penalty had been goaled. Likewise, his early charge of the English lock, Billy Beaumont, who was waiting to claim a drop-out from the All Blacks' quarter-line, could have cost the Barbarian match. These senseless acts no doubt derived from the uncompromising rugby of Oliver's youth and maturity when the subjection of an opponent by physical means was considered by players — and coaches — to be justifiable. It was fair to say, too, that Oliver had suffered his share of punches, beltings and rakings which somehow turned into bootings. In tests in South Africa during 1976, the All Blacks at the lineout were victims of deliberately unfair play in which the game's laws were flouted so that a massive Transvaaler, Kevin de Klerk, could dominate possession. If the games had been under the care of a neutral referee — and it will always rankle with those All Blacks that the offer of such an arrangement by the South African Rugby Board was spurned by members of the New Zealand Rugby Council — this bitter, win-at-all-costs sort of rugby would almost certainly have been outlawed. Nelsonian touches in South African refereeing made the illegal practices a feature of play; and the All Blacks were compelled to take the law into their own hands. Oliver became a gun-man in the confrontations of the last test and a most effective agent in the operations. He established himself then as a player without fear. Better, he established a reputation as a lock of exceptional strength and stamina whose work rate was staggeringly high. After his days in the police force, he had variously been a commercial fisherman and a forestry worker. Through these pursuits he had acquired a bodily hardness which in human terms was next best to diamond-level. To grasp his biceps was to feel corded steel. His torso and legs were of the same quality. Except that he could have been perhaps an inch taller, or two if this had not affected his strength, he was the ideal lock. He knew the technicalities backwards, he refined these as Jack Gleeson during the tour persuaded the forwards to move their feet forward, rather under their bodies, so that with the snapping straight of the legs as the ball was put into the tunnel an extraordinarily powerful thrust was developed. Frank chased in the open as ardently as he strove in the set-piece plays.

It was the luck of the 1978 All Blacks to have leaders who were perfectly complementary. Oliver was the ideal lieutenant. He had a mind of his own. His speech was decisive. He used words well. He had an independent mind, too. When a man can earn, as Frank claimed he could, $30,000 from a month of the prodigiously demanding work of commercial fishing, he need not bow the knee to anyone. But he was the most loyal of men, to Mourie, to Russell Thomas, to Jack Gleeson, to his team and, finally and irrevocably, to rugby. Perhaps his strategy and tactics were not so highly developed as Mourie's. The All Blacks he led in the final test might not have taken so much of a hiding from the Wallabies of 1978 if he had concentrated upon the inefficiencies of the Donaldson-McKechnie-Taylor partnership behind the scrum. But this was by the by. Every player and captain is entitled to an off day. In all general respects, Oliver was a supreme contributor to the 1978 All Blacks. It was his custom to sit alone as the team's bus wound along from here to there. One could imagine that a good deal of his thinking was directed to the games past and the match to come. He had intense concentration for the job that mattered.

If the tour had a special tragedy, it was that the symbol of unqualified greatness, as player and rugby man, which was Bryan Williams became tarnished by the exigencies and demands of the expedition. It would be impossible to overestimate the importance of Williams to the tour as the players came together in Auckland. He had twice toured in the British Isles, twice in South Africa, he had played 99 games for his country, he had won 34 caps. Despite suffering, in France in 1977, a gross dislocation of one hip which might have ended his career, Williams managed to come back in 1978 and to weather yet another troublesome leg injury before the tour. If one thing was certain, at the start, it was that he would be an automatic first choice in every first-team selection. If one thing was uncertain, from about the Munster match onwards, it was that he would be placed in the first team. He was, in fact, dropped for the first international, against Ireland, got a game when Brian Ford, who had replaced him, had to leave the field with a gashed leg, and, taking his chance, restored himself with fine, aggressive play. Intermittently, however, the slow-motion sidesteps of the match against Munster reappeared. He had long since been honoured by the Cardiff club with a silver salver and by the Arms Park crowd with a moving salutation for his 100th game; yet the damnable uncertainties which in all his career had never troubled him now not only sprinkled his play but by their persistence, especially in the diabolical game he played against Scotland, suggested that his confidence had taken all but mortal blows.

When dropped against Ireland — he had been forewarned by Gleeson that this would occur; it was a sympathetic touch — Williams reacted predictably. As a man of immense pride in his rugby, he said he would fight his way back, he would show all. After later days of indecisive play, his fathomless brown eyes and impassive countenance conveyed by little touches and flickers his acute self-disappointment.

But what would have been the worst experience of his career happily was averted. Glad though he was that the Barbarians had not chosen a British Isles' team to knock the stuffing out of the All Blacks, Gleeson naturally still wanted to win the final game. After the Scottish match of the week before and some fine play, including one extraordinarily brilliant run, by Robert Kururangi against Bridgend in the last match but one of the tour, Gleeson thought for a long time about placing the young Maori in the Barbarians' match and leaving "Bee Gee" among the reserves. It was touch and go. Omission would have been a paralysing shock for Williams. He played. He missed scoring chances of the first half but in the second smashed through a tackle for a try which carried his aggregate for New Zealand to 401, a mark of glory.

If we who had seen much of Williams during his career — I still rank his play for the All Blacks in South Africa in 1970 as the finest I have seen by a New Zealand back while touring abroad — suffered vicariously almost as severely as he did himself, we could still take pleasure in his unqualified station as one of the great members of the 1978 tour. With a guitar in his hand, he strummed and sang tunefully through the tedious hours of travel. His dry, sardonic, legal wit pierced the gloom of excessively serious discussions. He was scrupulous in dress and behaviour, limitlessly unselfish in his attitude to other players and the team, the very model of a modern major-general of a great game. Russell Thomas counted him as one of the principal factors in the success of the tour. Russell in these matters was an acute judge.

Two other misfortunes, tragedies if you like, affected the tour. One was the defection of the ranking fullback, Bevan Wilson of Otago, because of a leg injury suffered subsequent to his embarrassments in the final test with the Wallabies when he was twice fairly beaten on tackles he should have made. The other was the injury which put Currie out of the tour after he had had his jaw cracked in a violent collision with Steve Fenwick in the Welsh international. Wilson, a tall, stalwart man with a most amazing crash of a kick, especially at drop-kicks with the right foot, had been discovered for the third test against the 1977

Lions. He was the right kind of country fullback, solid as a rock temperamentally, well taught by a father who had played fullback for Otago in the 1950s, a fine, long kick with both barrels, with unfaltering courage under the highest of Garryowens and a sound sense of positional play. If the selectors, Jack Gleeson, Eric Watson and Peter Burke, did not weep on learning that Wilson was not available for Britain, they ought to have. He looked exactly suited, physically and mentally, for a tour. He might have come back from it with his foot wedged in the door of greatness. Currie's choice raised all sorts of eyebrows including, very likely, his own. His principal recommendation, membership of the Junior All Blacks, was not startlingly important. Juniors come and Juniors go and only a few become seniors to dream about. At selection, Currie ranked only third among Caterbury's fullbacks. It seemed unlikely he would win promotion at provincial, let alone at national level. His selection therefore seemed to be a criticism, if not a condemnation, of the quality of New Zealand's fullbacks of the time; a strange change; the country has seldom wanted for fullbacks of the first class and, starting with Billy Wallace in 1905 and carrying through to George Nepia, Bob Scott, Don Clarke and Fergi McCormick, has fielded its share of exceptional men for the job.

The hairline fracture Currie suffered was as great a misfortune for the All Blacks as it was for himself. He was just a Junior, yes. He took an abominably long time to prepare his place-kicks at goal. He commanded no remarkable length with his punted kicks. He was lean and trim, with a useful turn of speed, and the fine hands of a talented cricketer. Otherwise, he looked to be a goodish fullback, the sort you see all over the place. But with each appearance, Currie became more exciting to watch. Touches to his play were of genuine class. Given the chance to fulfil his evident promise, he might become, so it began to seem, a player of genuine distinction.

When Currie departed, the All Blacks were left with Brian McKechnie and the young replacement, Richard Wilson. The latter, who had toured with the All Blacks to the Argentine and kicked a good many goals, promised pretty well, though not so well as Currie. His goalkicking in the tight, tough match against Monmouthshire was one of the events of the tour. When McKechnie, John Ashworth and Dick Myers who had played in the final test against the Wallabies were deleted from the 30-man touring team in favour of Currie, Rod Ketels of Counties and Wayne Graham of Otago, sensation was, to coin the old phrase, the order of the day. Ketels, unlucky man, was soon announced as unavailable. He was doomed by an injury. Ashworth came back into the fold. As the news spread of the crippling injury suffered by Bevan Wilson, speculation about his replacement took in the possibility of McKechnie, who had played fullback against France in

1977, and of Ketels' teammate from Counties, Robert Lendrum, whose one cap had been won against John Pullin's touring English team in 1973. The selectors dithered. They would wait, Gleeson announced, until the match between North and South Islands had been played at New Plymouth before their choice was named. The delay suggested that Lendrum, a player with a well-founded reputation for ability which was sometimes marred by erratic patches in which he seemed not much interested, might be on the point of promotion for the second time. However, when McKechnie's name was announced on the Saturday of the inter-island match, it was discovered that the choice had actually been made on the Thursday. Hence, Lendrum speculation had been profitless and a waste of time. This did not please Lendrum supporters, some of whom were placed pretty high in rugby.

Gleeson would have been a man of abnormally strong temperament if he had not suffered, during the tour, doubts as to the wisdom of choosing McKechnie. What a man! Now you had him, now you hadn't. He placed the winning goal against Wales amidst tumult. Seldom in rugby history has a refereeing award of a penalty been so trenchantly condemned. The famous Welsh flyhalf of the 1971 Lions' tour in New Zealand, Barry John, screamed bloody murder in the Press Box about cheating. Barry's is a fine voice which can be wound up at will into higher decibels. But in all of that noise, that anti-New Zealand, that anti-McKechnie demonstration, John might just as well have been a whispering baritone. McKechnie reacted to everything as if he were a deaf-mute. He struck the ball as if he were Jack Nicklaus crashing another 300-metre drive down the fairway. What a temperament! you said. What ability! Yes — and could young Brian mess around if he felt like it! A clearing-kick which he tried to make against West Wales would have to rank among the abominations of All Black history in the British Isles. He missed 'em against the Barbarians with, you could say, a deathless skill. Now and again, or in between times, McKechnie was sublime of hand and foot, doing, precisely, that which needed to be done. Then he would switch off, becoming careless, neglectful and, most maddening of all, indifferent. He ended the tour as the All Blacks' highest scorer. He also ended it in a category all of his own. New Zealand can seldom have fielded a player who was so unclassifiable or uncomprehensible.

CHAPTER FIVE

Conquering That Complex

IT SEEMS A PITY, looking back, that Mourie's Men did not adopt and implement, early in their tour, a resolution compelling all of them at all times to avoid all but the inevitable human errors of close-quarter conflict. Had they done so, their impact would have been even more profound. The tour could then have been as decisive to world rugby as that which was made by David Gallaher's All Blacks of 1905 when they swept along like the panzer forces of the German Army which rushed through the Low Countries and France to the Channel ports in 1940.

Even so, the Mourie tour deserves to be ranked as climactically important to the strategical development of the game. For the purposes of argument, it may be reckoned that rugby turned the wrong corner during the tour of South Africa by Fred Allen's unfortunate All Blacks of 1949. The all-conquering coach of the Springboks, Dr Danie Craven, invented defensive patterns which achieved the disruption of the All Blacks' attack in midfield. The crafty doctor also put into practice some cute stunts at the front of the scrum for the purpose of ensuring that his pack never lost a ball on its own loose-head and won more than a fair share on the tighthead. The International Board, which is more often a Court of Appeal than an originating force, has since tried to steer rugby back onto the old path. It outlawed Danie's devilish invention of the Number 8 forward standing far out in midfield so that he could hammer the midfield backs of the opposing team. It created the ten-yard gap at the lineout to eliminate chest-to-chest defensive formations adopted by backlines. It legalised the so-called Australian dispensation — which actually had been invented in New Zealand about the end of the First World War — which outlawed punts into touch on the full from other than one's own defensive quarter. The board has since amended and modified other laws. Regrettably, it has refused to accept that its changes to the lineout laws have turned this key part of play into a shambles.

From 1949 onwards, rugby rapidly, you might almost say

tumultuously, descended into defensiveness. The aim in the game was to stop, not to go. Set-piece attacks were stultified by winging forwards, or marauding backs, or both. The great attacking invention was the second-phase play. A burly, powerful back of the size and strength of, say, Mick Bremner for Canterbury in the late 1950s or Ian MacRae for Hawke's Bay and New Zealand in the 1960s, was designated as a pointman who would rush at full speed into the opposing defence. Close in behind came his faster forwards, followed by the rest. They were instructed to win the ball by fast heeling from rucks so that the attack might be renewed against a defence which was now either disorganised in alignment or in a panic about its capacity to withstand a second attack delivered into a broken field defence.

Other inventions preceded, or followed, this famous second-phase. Jargon was invented. Coaches talked about "scrum time" or "lineout time" or some other time. They also spent much time on instructing players about first-time defence, cover-defence and related subjects. In effect, coaches and players reverted to the trench-warfare complex which governed life on the Western Front during the appalling horrors of the First World War. The deadly weapon of the front, the machine-gun, which snuffed out attacks with withering efficiency, reappeared in world rugby as the tackling, the covering, the mass-order movement which deprived the game of its pleasures in skilled backline movements, or coordinated thrusts by backs and forwards, or the ultimate thrill of the swift wing-threequarter swooping outside the clutching arms of the opposing fullback and heading like a deer for the goal.

What was to be done? What should be done? Some teams, some players, rebelled against the restrictive influences. France produced backs like Maso, Gachassin and Lux who disdained confined rugby. Like the flowers that bloom in the spring, Fijian rugby abounded in backs and forwards who did what came naturally and did it uncommonly well; but after his team, captained by John Pullin, had squeaked home by a point against a Fijian XV in 1973, the English manager, Sandy Sanders, blightingly said Fijian rugby would not improve because its players were fundamentally undisciplined; and discipline, Sanders implied, was the first, if not the only, essential of rugby of the first class. In so many words, one could infer from Sandy's statement, you played your rugby by numbers, or else! It was a cheerless thought.

Fred Allen's All Blacks of 1967 who were unbeaten in 17 matches did try to fulfil the instruction of "Needle", their renowned coach, to give everyone a chance by playing 15-man attacking rugby. The team is remembered with respect and affection in the British Isles. Indeed, it deserved to be. But it was woefully weak in some places, not least in the front row. Moreover, MacRae was there; and as often as not, the

All Blacks could not conquer their training in the second-phase situation. Once the tour was done, rugby, especially in New Zealand, rapidly resumed the wearing of its defensive cloak. Like the 1967 team, the British Lions in New Zealand in 1971 made a breakthrough, or, if you like, a breakback to inventive attack. By 1974, however, the Lions captained by Willie John McBride of Ireland through South Africa had reverted to the primary defensive pattern based upon a magnificent forward pack, a great scrumhalf in Gareth Edwards of Wales, and a goalkicking genius in Phil Bennett at flyhalf.

World rugby, or at least the rugby of the International Board countries — England, Scotland, Ireland, Wales, Australia, South Africa, New Zealand and, just recently France — could therefore be compared with the mountain-climber who, tackling a steep slope of scoria, advances one pace and falls back two. If the defensive pattern were to be arrested or, with luck, conquered, it needed a decisive statement or act. In Auckland, an elderly lawyer, N.A. or Archie Campbell, bombarded authorities with his proposal that the backs of the offending side at the scrummage should be compelled to take stations, as at the lineout, ten metres to the rear of the last line of feet of their pack. Mr Campbell, a man of small physique, played much of his rugby before the First World War but, marching into his 80s, he was still skiing, every winter, on the slopes of Mount Ruapehu. He was phenomenally industrious in seeking support for his proposal. ("I recognise that handwriting," Danie Craven said when I flourished an envelope in front of him at a meeting of the International Board in Sydney in 1974. "That man has some excellent ideas.") But, notwithstanding formidable learning and incessant pleading of his case, which was based on the sound grounds of his own experience and a keen memory of the magnificent attacking rugby played in New Zealand by all sorts of teams into and through the 1920s and hereafter spasmodically until the blight of the tour of Freddie Allen's Forty-Niners, Mr Campbell found no takers.

The decisive statement, or act, then lay within the power of the 1978 All Blacks. Almost, they made it. John Reason, the severe but outstandingly well-informed critic of the London *Daily Telegraph,* dismissed Mourie's men with the remark that among all of its players only the wing-threequarter, Stuart Wilson, would have won a place in the 1967 All Blacks. This was not one of Mr Reason's more perceptive judgments. The lingering, saddening and yet infinitely intriguing feature of the team that found itself was that in the finding the side all but made the vital statement which could have convinced men of sense and good will in rugby that the only secure future for the game lay in the deliberate decision of its foremost players and coaches to chuck this confounded nonsense about defence out of the game and put in its place, in all glory, the ethic of attack which governed the game in its most fruitful years.

I still say that, despite the mistakes which were such a plaguy feature of their tour, Mourie's Men came so close to the ultimate statement as to compel all reasonable men to examine their achievements, carefully, fairly and moderately; and, having assessed the special qualities of the tour, to vow now to turn aside from defence to the path rugby was so willingly following until the tragedy of the tour of 1949 wrought such damage.

The claim is neither preposterous nor exaggerated. The 1978 team faced a much stiffer tour than the 1967, which played only 11 of its 17 matches in the British Isles — none was permitted in Ireland because of an outbreak of foot-and-mouth disease in Cheshire and a consequent restraint on travel to that country. The coaching movement which was to have such a profound impact upon British rugby thinking was in the first stage of experimentation by the Welshman, Ray Williams, who had only been appointed in 1966. At most centres where Mourie's team played, the preparation of the home side had been detailed and extensive and to a degree beyond anything which had previously governed British resistance to the team from a hostile (in the sporting sense) shore. At international level, this preparation far exceeded standard New Zealand practice. Before the Second World War, the New Zealand Rugby Union sometimes brought its All Black teams together for a week before a test-match against a visiting team. After the war, by which time the International Board had acted to limit the gathering of home players for an international to 48 hours before kick-off, New Zealand abandoned the old practice. It did not substitute, as have done the Home Unions, squad training for a chosen group of players. In their terms as selectors and coaches, John Stewart and Jack Gleeson sometimes hankered, on behalf of the All Blacks, for the kind of week-end work-outs which are now commonplace for members of the Welsh international squad. Each would have given at least one disused wisdom tooth to imitate the Scottish practice of 1978 in which about 50 players were brought together early in the season for specialised training from which the group was gradually whittled down. More than for any All Black team, going back to 1905, the British and Irish were prepared. To what end? purists might ask. None but Munster managed to beat the Mourie men. Agreed. But in the losing, the British and Irish so staunchly resisted that had they not been engaged against a foe of exceptional qualities some of them — Ireland, Wales and Scotland at the least — must have gainfully used their preparation and won.

All hail, therefore, the merit of the Mourie tour! From the record in the big matches, the first team was undoubtedly of fine quality. One wrings one's hands about the fullback position. If McKechnie felt like "going", fine. If he didn't — how valuable are the hands in covering the eyes against the more shocking sights of life. The problems of Williams' tour have been discussed. One feels certain the cause was the hideous injury "Bee Gee" suffered in France. There were limitations in the play of each of the second-stringers, Brian Ford and Robert Kururangi. Ford, who was also handicapped by injuries which cursed his career, had limitless courage and on the run he was absolutely determined and most difficult to stop. Kururangi, an artless young Maori boy at the start, made rapid and dramatic improvement. He was almost ready, before the end, for international status; which was good going because, early on, he had personified the team's penchant for airy-fairy mistakes. He might not seem quite fast enough to become an exceptional threequarter. But, guided by Gleeson and the rest of the team, he responded keenly and effectively. Best of all, he was cheerful. The smile on the face of the lad from Te Araroa was as bright as the sunlight which strikes the peak of Hikurangi, not too far distant, before it touches any other part of New Zealand.

Stuart Wilson became quixotically impetuous before the end of the tour. He indulged the folly of rushing from his place at right wing-threequarter upon the outside centre of the opposing team. More often than not, he made a decisive tackle or in some other way checked the attack; and, to be fair, some authorities hold that a player's first duty is to go for the man with the ball. Wilson otherwise was of the first class in all particulars. He ran superbly. His trick of feinting with his body, suggestive of a movement here when actually he intended to go there, was a natural gift of the highest quality. He had speed, balance, good hands. Best of all, he could run as wanted with the ball held in both hands in front of him, wiggling it about with subtle touches which could be read by an opponent to mean a kick, a pass, a dummy, or anything. This was a supreme gift, seldom seen in even the very finest of wings.

Mr Reason might be right. Wilson might be the only one player of '78 worthy of the team of '67. I dispute this point myself. The best backline of '78 was never quite discovered in a match of the strongest class, but the components of it were unquestionably of high quality. Both of the halfbacks, Mark Donaldson and David Loveridge, were superior to the best British and Irish players. Donaldson was Jack Gleeson's choice at the start and had he not suffered a most painful injury of the foot in the last moments of the Irish match he would very likely have remained the first choice. His assets far outweighed his principal deficiency. This was his tendency rather to wind up his pass, so clearing the ball to his five-eighths with a perceptible delay. To offset the fault, he was amazingly strong, quick, combative and, in his running, elusive. I remarked after the first match that I would be interested to see Donaldson played at second five-eighths for the sake of the power, speed and deceptiveness of his running. As was to be expected and as I myself anticipated, no one took the slightest notice of the idea. By the end of the tour, I had not chucked the thought away. New Zealand rugby of the first class has for too many years wanted such a player, with a powerful, decisive, break, in midfield. Loveridge, a faster passer than Donaldson, more decisively charmed the eye with each passing match. His great gift was a dummy-pass which was offered at such speed that the opponent blinked while persuading himself that it must be a dummy, he ought not to buy it. The blink was enough for David. By then, he was gone. He otherwise had all the attributes of speed, courage and aggressiveness. It never was remarked in the British Press, or by television and radio, that the man was so brutally booted by Bridgenders that he ought not to have played against the Barbarians. Donaldson being unavailable, Loveridge insisted that he play; and it was just a little sad that, because of the Bridgend injury, he could not wind up to full speed when he made a second-half break against the Baa-Baas. At speed, he would have scored. This would have been something for him to dream upon while tending the pigs on his Taranaki farm. But he had already made his mark with the try he scored against Monmouthshire when, on their goalline, he dived describing a great parabola in the air, to touch the ball down before his opponent, Brynmor Williams, could reach to it. That was a try of incredible alertness. And that was Loveridge, dark-eyed, sallow-faced, Fu Manchu sort of moustache, lean, leathery and darting to the ball like the lizard that flicks out its tongue to catch a fly.

The talent elsewhere in the backline was not of the dull, trench-warfare type. I suspected that Gleeson, as a protagonist of attacking play, began the tour with the feeling that Eddie Dunn could be his man for first five-eighths. Munster unsettled Jack all around and not least in his estimation of Eddie's ability. So he opted instead for reliable Doug Bruce, "Old Faithful" from the top of his head to the tip of his venomously powerful left foot. Events justified the decision. Bruce was a clever, adroit player, unusually gifted in most requirements but sensibly wanting in the two which would have removed him from the trench-warfare mould he fitted so precisely. He lacked speed of foot. He wanted in enterprise.

Dunn, who had speed and who flashed a cunning dummy as he made for the gaps, was turned by the tour into a hewer of wood and drawer of water. In other words, he either judged or was told that his proper function was to take his halfback's pass while stationary and to send it on immediately. This paralysed his natural gifts and diminished the potential of the backline. While it may be argued that one of the greatest of all flyhalves, the immortal Irishman Jackie Kyle, tended, if he felt like it — and he was a whimsical sort of man — to catch and clear while standing still, the old-time prescription requiring a player in the position to move at speed into his halfback's pass is still hard to beat. The movement advances his team's attack before the defenders can deploy their forces and at best can compel the attacking threequarters to move at maximum speed with the ball. It could be observed, too, that Kyle varied his play so subtly and skilfully that his opponents were never quite sure what he might do. Dunn on the other hand came back into the fold. It was a pity.

Gleeson, as has been related, took care to bring Bruce Robertson along quietly, allowing him to settle, as the horsey folk say, before making demands of him. Whether Robertson fully developed his known ability in attack may be argued. The best he displayed was of infinite value. But it may be that Gleeson was too loyal to a player who had reached greatness. In the early matches, Bill Osborne was a powerhouse in his true position at centre, or outside centre as the British might call it. His enterprise was coupled with fierce body-strength which he used to break from all but the most decisive tackles and which he further used as an adjunct to skilful sidestepping and dodging away from tackles. As Robertson's confidence waxed, Gleeson became persuaded that the combination of Osborne and Robertson in the midfield was the soundest and most dangerous he could muster. The talent in each of the two men was undoubtedly a little stronger than the talent in their competitors, Mark Taylor and Lyn Jaffray. Jaffray's was an unexpected choice for the tour. He had rather faded from calculations and one or two youngsters were thought of as more likely to be chosen. On tour, Jaffray played capably enough, though his efforts to dominate the attack in the second half against Munster counted against him. Where he was invaluable, especially to Russell Thomas, was in his role as, so to speak, a senior prefect in off-the-field activities. As chairman of the dress sub-committee, he demanded sartorial standards of Saville Row quality. Parading for important events, of which the foremost for every player was the call upon Queen Elizabeth and members of the Royal Family at Buckingham Palace, Lyn even insisted that the silver ferns on cuff-links should all point the same way. He did these things in a mature, cheerful, good-humoured style and so effectively that he carried the team with him. But such matters, important though they were — a scruffy team off the field tends to be scruffy on it, too — were not relevant to the trench-war argument. One resolution of this lay in the non-playing of Osborne at second five-eighths. His club in Wanganui, Kaierau, satisfied themselves on this point in Bill's brilliant early days. New Zealand Maoris, too, rued his placing there when they played

Tonga at New Plymouth. Osborne was young then, and inexperienced; but with the passing years, the opinion strengthened that he was best — and a very good best; unquestionably of the first class — at centre. So the question was whether the attack would have been strengthened with Robertson at second five-eighths or whether Taylor was the man. In the tour of Australia in 1974, Robertson and Ian Hurst flirted pretty effectively with the British centre-threequarter system, one man playing left centre, the other right, according to the placing of the set-piece of the time. Robertson reacted effectively to the experimenting. He had so much class that, practically speaking, he could play anywhere in the backline and play well. But with him as with Osborne, the belief was that he moved most naturally and with the best use of his great speed when he was placed at centre.

Taylor might therefore be considered unlucky. He played at second five-eighths against Ireland. Later, he battled along as a second-string man, ready, willing and able to do whatever might be wanted. Being naturally strong, he shared with Osborne an unusual ability to break a tackle. More than anyone who played at second five-eighths, he had the gift for breaking the opponents' defensive line. His courage was abundant, his pace sufficient, he reacted calmly to crisis. Against Monmouthshire, he suffered an extraordinary injury which made him breathless. Before half-time he left the field. In the dressingroom, he mumbled that he was well except in breathing. Russell Thomas urged him to return to play. In the first move after this, he made a slashing break which soon yielded a try and which also advertised his attacking ability. Was it a misfortune that he did not get more chances in the bigger matches? On the whole, yes. This is the devil of tours of limited duration. On a tour of, say, 24 matches, Gleeson could have experimented, no doubt he would have experimented, with various formations in the knowledge that he had the time and the space, so to speak, to find the best combination. But a selector-coach faced with the first international in the fifth match and with Wales to follow Ireland a week later could not dare to experiment too much. With Osborne placed at second five-eighths, Gleeson was assured of infallible defence — though Taylor's was scarcely less strong. With Robertson at centre, Gleeson was assured of experience, enterprise and brilliance. So the die was cast. Which was the more regrettable, in a personal sense, because Taylor's contribution to the tour was as a whole even more valuable than Jaffray's. He was the character of it, cheerful, witty, the easy-going guy who came to be idolised by schoolchildren all over the place, but especially in Wales. Taylor and Stuart Wilson were those invaluable members of a tour, warm, informal, amusing men who did not try to be funny, they just were. When the team for South Africa was being chosen in 1976, Jay Jay Stewart desired that the Wellington halfback Ian Stevens should be included not as a likely first-string player but as a very funny man who could make the sun shine through the blackest of clouds. Jack Gleeson and Eric Watson, Stewart's fellow-selectors, would not entertain the idea. The loss was the All Blacks' — and the tour's. They don't come much funnier than "Nectar" — and big-time tours can become exercises in tedium if no member of them can take the mickey out of everyone and everything.

It will be immediately acknowledged that great backs are hamstrung unless they are playing behind, and can rely upon the constant support of, outstanding forwards. This raises the question whether the 1978 pack was of the first class and worthy of comparison with the packs fielded in the British Isles by Stuart, Whineray and Lochore in particular. It may as well be said, to clear the decks, that the tour contained forwards who were not quite ready for the topmost drawer. Barry Ashworth, who had apparently been a first choice while the Australians were touring, struggled along as a flanker and only once, against North of Scotland late in the tour, decisively displayed the qualities of an international. It was soon evident that John Ashworth — the two were not related — lacked some of the vital qualities of a loosehead prop and that Wayne Graham, who played flank or Number 8, had had luck in becoming first among the many equals who played the same positions for many provincial teams. As it happened, John Ashworth and Graham were committed against Monmouthshire amid feelings of apprehension that they would or could measure to the task. Yet the two, and John Loveday, proceeded to play magnificently. Each played above his best known form, crashing into the Welshmen like highly energised bulldozers, and doing themselves and their team very proud indeed. McGregor's misfortunes have been mentioned. Yet he was one of the few who could look back on the Munster match and say that he had emerged from it with his reputation enhanced.

A notch above these men and just about ready for the top drawer were such men as the Cantabrians, Billy Bush and John Black, Gary Seear, who had spent much of the New Zealand season at lock, which is not a good place for the training of a Number 8, Loveday, who became one of the most decisive movers of the tour when running with the ball, and John Fleming, who on the whole improved more than any of the untried forwards and who by the time the All Blacks confronted the Barbarians had developed into a true international. Black was an excellent second-string to Andy Dalton. His talents might not have been so broadly spread but he struck fast on the heel, he looked after the front of the lineout most capably, his left-handed throw-in from touch was accurate and he was a tough, solid runner with the ball. Bush's days at the top appeared to have ended more or less from the time he conceded the penalty which cost Andy Leslie's

All Blacks their vital third test in Cape Town. He roamed in the gloaming, lacking concentration in the tight-core stuff where his first duties lay, getting in the road in broken-field play. He may even have been shaken to hear of his selection. Yet Billy, a fine, manly, cheerful bloke, proud of his race, proud of his rugby, rapidly adjusted to the disciplines exerted by Gleeson and Mourie and, as always, became a favourite of his team. Gleeson then did a masterly turn by appointing Billy to lead the forwards in matches in which Mourie and Oliver did not play. The warrior-spirit was aroused in Billy. If it had been a help, he would have killed himself for his team. He led by example, whipping his men along. On the night of the Scottish match, he shaved that black beard which had made him look piratical. It was his celebration of the Grand Slam; and when the Scots got him to speak at the dinner (because Billy was also one of the 20-odd members of the team who could claim Scottish heritage), he spoke simply and sincerely of his pride at being, as an All Black, a member of the Mourie team. Maoris, when they are real Maoris, are wonderful people of rugby. Their natural talents compare with those of the French and Fijians. Billy was a real Maori, in excelsis.

When Bush was lost, stopped dead in his tracks by a torn hamstring on the wretched field of Rodney Parade in Newport, the All Blacks' front-row strength was reduced to Brad Johnstone, Gary Knight and John Ashworth. After Ashworth's affair at Bridgend, no other replacement was available for Johnstone and Knight, the first-string men. But John Reason and Carwyn James raised an awful hullabaloo when at Johnstone's retirement at half-time in the Barbarians' match Ashworth took the field. This was, the two men claimed, a provocative gesture by the All Blacks, arrogant and unfeeling in its overtones. What was to be done? Play Loveday, the only possible man who could be considered? In face of the fact that Loveday had had no experience of prop which, at loosehead, is the key place of the scrummage? This was carping, unfair criticism. Loveday might have made an excellent prop. Jack Gleeson had been looking at him speculatively from the beginning of the New Zealand season, though the Manawatu coach, Graham Hamer, thought the idea nonsensical. But against as expert a scrummager as the Englishman, Will Dickinson, Loveday might have been cut to pieces as decisively as had been his Manawatu teammate, Perry Harris, when committed, as a tour replacement — oddly enough, for Johnstone — against the Springbok ironman, Johan Strauss, in the third test of 1976. Loveday became a fine forward of the tour. For want of a couple of inches of height, he was a bit of an in-betweener, not quite of ideal height for lock and lineout. But he was a highly intelligent player who perceived pretty soon the need to step up his work-rate and who became a valiant contributor. Having trained as a chiropractor at Palmer College in the United States in the company of, among others, the Springbok fullback, Ian McCallum, who kicked goals galore to beat the 1970 All Blacks in the test series in South Africa, Loveday was a well-travelled, well-rounded personality who exuded genuine charm.

Despite the reverence shown toward All Black packs of postwar times, especially in the decade of the 1960s in which New Zealand placed first among the rugby nations and epic characters like Whineray, Colin Meads, Kelvin Tremain, Ken Gray, Waka Nathan, Dennis Young and John Graham figured in teams, it could be said, as a harsh judgment, that the New Zealand superiority might have been a measure of the inferiority of opposing forwards rather than a tribute to New Zealand techniques and qualifications. Things changed a little in 1970 when the All Blacks in South Africa encountered three great forwards, Frik du Preez at lock and Piet Greyling and Jan Ellis on the flanks. Things changed decisively in 1971 when the British Lions brought to New Zealand loose-forwards of the quality of Mervyn Davies, the beanpole Welsh Number 8, and Fergus Slattery, of Ireland, and two outstanding locks in Willie John McBride and the Scot, Gordon Brown. Most significantly, however, this pack contained an expert front-row built around England's unforgettable hooker, John Pullin. Ian McLauchlan of Scotland and Ray McLoughlin of Ireland were technical experts as props. They made the ranking New Zealanders, Richie Guy, who could run like Deerfoot, and "Jas" Muller, who weighed about 18 stone, look second-rate. Their influence is still being felt. Each had made a scientific study of the placement of feet, the gripping of hands, the binding together of players.

It was a fact, as was demonstrated not only in 1971 but again when the British Lions toured in 1977, that British techniques were infinitely superior to New Zealand — New Zealand techniques, it may be said, which had become hallowed by tradition. New Zealand players, notably Tane Norton, the hooker who captained the All Blacks in 1977, began to understand that New Zealand's was not necessarily the best fashion. The coach of the Canterbury team, Professor Jim Stewart, supported them, encouraged them, if necessary led them. Norton at a seminar in Napier urged that the new techniques were superior. His audience included the powerful hooker of the 1960s, Bruce McLeod, who looked disbelieving, then amused. The new-fangled thing which was the hot gospel of scrummaging could, he said, easily be overpowered. A well-aimed punch would soon unsettle the practitioners of the scrum. "But you can't throw a punch, even if you want to," said Norton. "The binding in the front row is too tight. You don't have room to do anything but scrummage." McLeod backed down. Norton instructed his own front-row to obey the new principles.

The contest was strenuous. As the packs, at a command, broke up, McLeod made a handsome admission. "You are right," he said. "Things aren't loose any more." At another seminar held in the presence of Jack Gleeson, who had become powerfully converted to the new techniques, Ken Gray began to give instructions based on his experience as a great front-row forward of his time. Gleeson interposed. "Ken," he said, "you can't teach that sort of thing now. Ideas have changed. This is what we want." Jack demonstrated how the loosehead placed his left leg forward and stretched his right leg far back, behind the hooker, leaving a wide channel through which the ball could be propelled. He demonstrated the British grip taken on the props by the locks, with the gripping hand reaching up to the waistband of the prop's shorts from between his legs instead of, as in the old style, around his thighs. "Ken stood around for a while," Gleeson reminisced. "Then he left. I don't think he was pleased. He didn't care to be told that what had been right in his time was not right now."

The 1978 All Blacks staggered British players, especially Lions who had played against some of them in the season before, with the power, control and decisiveness of their scrummaging.

"I would not have believed," said the captain of England, Billy Beaumont, "that any forwards could so greatly improve in so short a time. Mourie's is a very fine pack, by the best standards."

It is possible, certainly it is worth arguing the possibility, that Mourie's was in fact the best equipped pack, technically, of the six sent to the British Isles from the end of the Second World War. Johnstone had some limitations at loosehead. Smaller men, like Dickinson, who could get under him, just as McLauchlan had done in New Zealand in 1971 to the leviathan who was Muller, tended to make a bow of his back, at the cost of quality in the key position of the scrum. Brad made up for the deficiency by the honesty of his general play, his tackling, which was remarkably strong and consistent, and his alert following or reaction, which brought him tries against England and Barbarians. Elsewhere, the scrummage was consistently powerful. Eyebrows were raised when Dalton was beaten on his loosehead by Peter Wheeler, the Englishman, for Andy was a fast, consistent and accurate striker. He was also a tigerish man at ruck and maul and playing down the short side of the lineout, as against England, ranked as a heady, vital, great player. Knight came to profit slowly after suffering, as did John Ashworth to a lesser degree, from a beastly infection known as "scrum pox", an unlovely but descriptive term for the herpes simplex which spread over his face and placed him in hospital in Dublin. Haden was infected later. But as Knight was renewed in strength and spirit, he bacame an immovable prop, a decisive and powerful block at the lineout and an ardent contributor to the loose scrimmages. Though he weighed about the same as Muller of seven years before, he was much, much faster in reactions and movement and far superior in all-round ability. He had had an excellent record in amateur heavyweight wrestling, which is dull to watch but demanding to play, and had long since learned to keep his temper and get on with the job. To behold Knight at Bridgend, therefore, belting a man as hard as he could with powerful righthand blows, was to be informed that the methods of the club's team in its centenary year might very likely have been condemned by many, many of its predecessors.

Oliver, like Knight, was also like Tennyson's brook. This, as earlier generations of New Zealand schoolchildren were mournfully compelled to learn, went on forever. Which was Fearless Frank, day in, day out. Haden was not so consistent. In the modern jargon, he either had to be "psyched" up, or "psyche" himself up, to produce his finest quality. Allan Martin, the Welsh Lion in 1977, gave him a hiding in the West Wales match. Two games later, Haden was dominant against Ireland. On the evening before the match against Wales, one week after Dublin, I encountered at the Arms Park Denzil Williams, who had been a leading forward in Welsh and Lions' packs for about a decade from 1963. Williams was in the company of an Aucklander, Hallard White, who is seldom known in Rugby as anything but "Snow" and who, after touring with Bob Stuart's All Blacks in 1953, went on to play an enormous number of games for Auckland. White, I learned, had trekked from Auckland to Cardiff to see the All Blacks play Wales and two days later was flying home — he was keen or crazy, one of the two. We stopped to chat. Williams wanted my opinion on the match the next day. I said it was going to be difficult, especially if Martin again cleaned out Haden.

"That's nonsense," said Williams. "He won't." Well, with all due deference to a famous Welsh forward. . .

It was perhaps because he lacked the maturity of Oliver that Haden's form tended to wax and wane. He could be active, dominant, or passive, subdued. When active, he was pretty nearly in a class of his own against all comers. Perhaps the cause was that he was but a boy in men's company when placed in Kirkpatrick's All Blacks in 1972. For at least a third of the tour, he was a most engaging boy, eager to learn, a fine jumper, a journeyman who in getting on with the job was establishing himself as an outstanding prospect for the future. Whether the influence of hard men in the team or the hostile British public, especially in Wales, affected him could not be decided; but in the second half of the tour, Haden turned himself into a grim and tough player who did not always shape his aggressiveness within the bounds of discipline. He punched opponents. He set up scraps. He became, said Kirkpatrick decisively, "a bloody nuisance". In maturing, the youngster who had the gift of the gab, who was, in fact, lively and likeable, trekked to Tarbes in France for a couple of seasons of experience in the lively, likeable and sometimes lethal play in the national club championship, and having suffered the extreme disappointment of non-selection in the 1976 All Blacks to tour in South Africa he played for the Algida club in Italy. *Rugby News* of Auckland gave his occupation as "rugby player" when he was chosen for the 1978 tour, perhaps the most unusual designation in All Black history, but Haden's life had in fact for some years been committed to the game.

He was a leading figure in this new development in rugby but was in good company; Chris Laidlaw, halfback, and Robert Burgess, five-eighths, had each spent at least a year at the University of Lyons in France, Sandy McNicol, a replacement prop in the 1972-73 All Blacks, played for a couple of years for Tarbes, Ken Carrington and other Aucklanders headed for clubs in Italy, Alan Sutherland of the 1976 All Blacks returned first to Rhodesia and then Johannesburg; and so on; if you could play rugby well and wanted a change — diehards tended to use the word "some" before change — the world could be your oyster. Constant play sharpens the competitive edge. Presumably it was this which caused Haden to make his notorious flying dive as the two teams headed for the last round-up in the international at Cardiff Arms Park. But whether he was in top form or not quite with it, Haden was a leading figure in the Mourie team. Oddly, for all his experience, he still wore the cherubic look of the young lad who figured in Kirkie's Killers.

The last but not the least of the senior XV of the tour was the flanker, Leicester Rutledge, the quiet Southlander who was given a place against the Wallabies after Mourie had suffered a devastating kick on the back. It seemed risky for the selectors not to stick to the old system, best displayed recently by Ken Stewart as the flying flanker, Kirkpatrick as the support who made play from the checked ball and Andy Leslie as the chap who appeared to sweep everything up, because both Mourie and Rutledge had an instinct for chasing in the open and with Seear as the third member of the ranking loose-forward trio neither supporting nor sweeping was consistently of test-match class. It was to be wondered, too, whether Rutledge might have recovered from the shock of the death of his father, a few days before the second test against the Wallabies. In the event, Rutledge turned to be 24-carat gold, through and through. As a deeply committed player, he tackled fiercely, was utterly courageous in charging upon the loose ball, chased unceasingly. In the words of old, his nose was never very far from the ball. He had little to say. He faded, you could say, back into the wallpaper as soon as he thought he was not wanted. But when he emerged, which was usually when he put on uniform for training and, more particularly, playing, he immediately cast off his quietness and became a model of industry and a determined, dynamic forward.

The Big Eight, as one might describe the leading pack, of Johnstone, Dalton, Knight, Oliver, Haden, Rutledge, Seear and Mourie, could seem substandard when compared with, say, Whineray, Young, Gray, Colin and Stanley Meads, Tremain, Graham and Nathan of 1963, or with Gray, McLeod, Muller, Colin Meads, Sam Strahan, Tremain, Lochore and Nathan of 1967. But let it be put this way: British forward play of the 1960s was notable for individual, not for collective strength. The proposition that while all 15 players of a team should be considered equal but that seven of them, namely the backs, should rank as more equal than others, was applied by clubs and superior teams all over the British Isles. Two bright and shining Rays, one McLoughlin in Ireland, the other Williams in Wales, did much to change British thinking, the former as an expert technician in the front of the scrum, the other as an experienced coach who, appointed by a stroke of genius on the part of the Welsh Rugby Union to be their national director of coaching, set out to establish that without an effective Heavy Brigade even the finest Light Brigade of a backline could not function efficiently. It may be that All Black forward play of the 1970s was neither so strong nor so well disciplined as in the 1960s, though due attention ought fairly be paid to the work the coach of the 1972-73 All Blacks, Bob Duff, put in to scrummaging — Professor Stewart was one who successfully seized on the Duff ideas. But whether New Zealand forward play had materially weakened was inconsequential. The primary fact of the 1970s was that British forward play strengthened amazingly and at best was almost certainly superior to the best of New Zealand play of the 1960s. It was quite desolating to watch All Black and other New Zealand packs getting a hiding from the 1977 Lions.

It was also quite desolating, looking at rugby as a whole, that the backs of that Lions team were so inferior. This was a team bent upon heading as fast as possible back into the trench-warfare style of so much of international rugby of the postwar era. What a contrast was furnished by the 1978 All Blacks! Their forward play was demonstrably superior to the British. This represented an amazing development within the space of 12 months. Secondly, the backs at best were quick, enterprising, fluent and competitive. Almost, but not quite, the team as a whole changed the mode of top-class rugby from trench-warfare to the glorious and free and skilled adventuring of those days of old, the Golden Eras each country had enjoyed, before all of rugby felt compelled to chase after Fred Allen's Forty-Niners after they had taken the wrong turning. The miss by Mourie's men was not by a mile. It was by so small a margin as to persuade all thinking rugby men of the hereafter to retreat pell-mell to the corner which had been missed in 1949 and to resume the path to glory which was the right road to rugby as it first was, and always ought to be played.

CHAPTER SIX

Other Sides of the Coin

For one who was so scrupulous over so many things and so particular as to detail, Russell Thomas, as he himself later acknowledged, blundered over Bridgend. He made a sad remark. "I should have spoken out," he said. The day after the match, he prepared a two-page statement. As he had done with his speech to the Sportsmen's Club, he spent a good deal of time cutting and re-writing. The critics who were climbing in on him because he had not seen the television replay of the John Ashworth incident tended to be, as is the British habit in these affairs, unfair and unkind. These were the last days of the tour. Thomas had plenty on his plate, not the least the arrangement of a container to take home the heavy gear of the team. The All Blacks were located at Porthcawl, 25 miles and the best part of an hour from the BBC studios in Cardiff. Thomas could have lost a good part of a day if he had obeyed the critics and rushed to see the film. He was in a dilemma. He had talked with Ashworth, whom he had known for some years. He had been assured the incident was an accident. Ashworth told Thomas, as he told me separately, that if rugby required the deliberate kicking of unprotected men, rugby was not for him. Thomas's natural reaction was to respect the frank statement of his man.

So he dillied and dallied. After much consideration, he decided not to speak. His fear, so he said, was that journalists on the tour, or the sub-editors in their offices, would for reasons of space, or perhaps sensationalism, cut or vary the statement. Such a process, Thomas said, "could have altered the things I was wanting to say and might well have conveyed a wrong impression".

He decided against publication. It was an unfortunate decision. I have never seen the statement. I do not know whether Thomas sought in it to clear Ashworth from blame, or dissected Dr Peter Williams' unscheduled speech to the diners (The Rump perhaps they could have been called, after the walk-out) at Bridgend, or argued that J. P. R. Williams' statement that he lost two pints of blood was scientific balderdash. These points are now immaterial. What was, and is, material and ever more shall be, at least until Wales have hammered New Zealand at the Arms Park — victory is the great resolver of many Welsh rugby problems — is that the All Blacks at Bridgend imitated the Shakespearean character by losing their reputation after 16 pretty well blameless matches against tough and headstrong teams or players. It did not do to say that the appalling assault upon Russell Thomas after the Barbarians' match squared accounts. The New Zealand Rugby Union took a grave view of the assault. The chairman, Cecil Blazey, said he did not think the attack warranted a decision by his council to decline the invitation of the Welsh Rugby Union for the All Blacks to tour in Wales in 1980 to celebrate its centenary — "though we are still deeply concerned," Blazey said much later. But, at the least, the New Zealand union intended to require that the manager and/or players of All Black teams visiting Wales in the future should be assured of protection. This remark was in itself a severe criticism of the Welsh.

However, the attack upon Thomas, though related to Bridgend and a dreadful indictment of the lunatic fringe, could not be used to dissipate the anti-New Zealand feeling which was generated by the Ashworth incident and which was epitomised in J. P. R.'s emotional and tragic statement that he never again wanted to play against All Blacks. Mourie was right when he said the game was of the sort which was bound to produce incidents. We have often seen such in New Zealand in matches involving touring teams or the Ranfurly Shield and into which players are projected in a state of, if not hysteria, then most certainly hypertension. On New Zealand's behalf, it may be asked why the authorities placed the game in the care of a referee who had had no experience of international teams. On Wales' behalf, it may be asked why the manager of the All Blacks did not speak out. It is perhaps best to leave the matter there. Time, the great healer, worked wonders for the All Blacks of 1974 when they played a Welsh XV, a team which was in fact Wales in everything but name. Andy Leslie's men were greeted with delight and acclaimed with pleasure. When Ian Kirkpatrick scored the try which made the New Zealand victory quite certain — the final score was 12 to 3 — the tribute from the crowd was almost as thunderous as for Wilson Whineray's try after his immortal sidestep and dummy against the Barbarians in 1964. These stimulating reactions from the Welsh were an extraordinary contrast to the treatment of Kirkpatrick and his men, particularly in Cardiff, during the 1972-73 tour. The bitterness began in the early match against Cardiff when the home team, undoubtedly by design, systematically assaulted the All Black forwards. I had the impression that the Cardiff club's president, Hubert Johnson, a great friend from our first meetings during the Stuart tour, restrained himself with difficulty from knocking me down, or taking a slash at me, after I had complained at the conduct of both the team and the crowd. Further experiences of the All Blacks in visits to Wales were not merry. Kirkpatrick, though no Oscar Wilde in the manufacturing of witticisms, fathered the unforgettable crack that "You never beat the Welsh. You only score more points than they do". Kirkpatrick also said at the end that "if our team had played only in England, Scotland and Ireland, this would have been a great tour".

After the '72-73 tour, the future of Welsh-New Zealand rugby relationships looked bleak. There were also strains in the relationship with the other Home Unions and, as Jack Gleeson discovered early in the 1977 tour, the French remembered the tour with less than pleasure. The 1974 tour remedied some of the bitterness. Before Bridgend, and not forgetting two or three unfortunate incidents, the 1978 tour appeared to have repaired every breach. At their first visit to Wales, Mourie's Men delighted all with their playing skills and adventurous spirit. Ireland, next on the list, was a delight from end to end. In suffering defeat by Munster, the All Blacks enhanced their qualities as sportsmen by praising the victors and marching up the hotel stairs chanting "Heigh-ho, Heigh-ho, it's off to work we go" with variations suitable to their situation. Scotland was a wonderful experience with men of integrity whose notions of hospitality seemed to be boundless until a few gate-crashers tried to get into the international dance without tickets. England was cold at Bristol and miserable at Chester but the lights of London Town were as alluring as ever.

But visits to Wales awakened bitterness, until at Bridgend the atmosphere crackled as it had done six years before. Was it right, or fair, entirely to blame the Welsh? Undoubtedly no. The three major incidents of the tour on the debit side involved the last lineout of the Welsh international, Haden's punch of Alastair McHarg in the Scottish test, and Bridgend. The first and the last were self-inflicted wounds suffered by the All Blacks. Thomas upbraided himself for not declaring his point of view about Bridgend. He would have profited, too, if he had reacted decisively to Haden's incomprehensible and childishly dramatic effort which smudged the match with Wales. No one could quarrel with Thomas's policy, adopted from the start of the tour, of never complaining about refereeing decisions. But foremost in the minds or, if you like, duties of men given managerial appointments must be a concern for the good of the game. In announcing, as the hubbub about the dive started up, that he had no intention of discussing Roger Quittenton's decisions and in imposing a gag on Haden about the incident, Thomas stood to be accused of neglecting this responsibility. When approached by two of the New Zealand Pressmen covering the tour, Palenski and Kevin McMenamin, of the *Christchurch Press,* Jack Gleeson was more forthright. The two men, both capable and experienced reporters, published Gleeson's comment. This was, in effect, that Haden's act was unbecoming. It was good to learn that an official of the tour was prepared to offer such an old-fashioned, austere opinion about an act which, I am sure, would never have been contemplated, let alone tolerated, by most of the All Black forwards of history. But here again, confusion developed. When the clippings from New Zealand newspapers came back to the team, Gleeson attacked the two reporters for their interview. They had, he said, misunderstood or misreported him, or both. Jack's was an unfortunate gesture. Sententious though it may sound, the good of the game is paramount. If rugby matches are to be won by acts which look like cheating, it is better not to play rugby.

Russell Thomas acknowledged at the end of the tour that he was apprehensive about the state of the relationship, in rugby, of Wales and New Zealand. He intended, he said, to work for an improvement so that the rivalry of these two great playing-countries could become adult, amusing and congenial instead of bitter, adolescent and antagonistic. Many are the faults of the Welsh in rugby. At sight of the Red Dragons who represent them on the great fields of world rugby, a red glaze descends into their eyes. All that is good is Welsh. All that is bad is the other side's. One of the best-known of Welsh rugby writers, Malcolm Lewis, of the *Western Mail* published in Cardiff, put this sort of view in the programme of the Monmouthshire match. "Sad to record," he said "a trend has developed in recent years where the New Zealanders have twice beaten Wales by very questionable methods. I have no wish to join in the mounting chorus of 'We wuz robbed' which has been rising to a grand crescendo since Wales lost to the men in black a few weeks ago but I feel our visitors have become so accustomed to rubbing our noses in the dirt that now they don't care how they do it. Remember 1972. In a frantic finale, the All Blacks held a storm of Welsh attacks at bay by resorting to the professional foul. Obstruction and late tackles littered their play. They got away with it because the Welsh goalkicking never matched the immaculate boot of Joe Karam, whose five penalty goals, mostly from technical offences, settled the issue. We thought we had seen everything after that but, lo and behold, up came something completely new at the Cardiff Arms Park — the 'dive-out' at the lineout in which Andy Haden and Frank Oliver produced the best piece of comic acting since the silent days of Buster Keaton and the Keystone cops. At least, it would have been comic if it hadn't been so tragic for Wales. As the TV camera so graphically revealed, the greatest 'con-act' of the century succeeded and New Zealand scraped home by the odd point."

I was writing my account of the Monmouthshire match when an old acquaintance, Ron Jones, a former president of the Abertillery club and the chairman of the dinner for the Monmouthshire and All Black teams, came passing along. He claimed to be furious with Lewis. Such bilious writing was, he said, unjustified, it could harm the rugby friendships of the two countries. "I am going to have a go about it at the dinner," Jones said. "I intend to say that the Monmouthshire committee does not condone the statement." We Pressmen returned from Newport to Porthcawl before the dinner. Next morning, I eagerly asked Russell Thomas for an account of Ron Jones's speech. "What speech?" said Russell. Not a word had been said. This was a further instance of reluctance to exhibit a concern for the good of the game. Very often in my experience, too often in fact, this concern has only been expressed by professional critics, especially of the Press. The reactions of most rugby men has been to denounce these critics, depicting them as leeches sucking money from the game. The attitude is childish. If critics of the capacity and tenacity of John Reason, who is esteemed by Carwyn James on one side of the world and J. J. Stewart on the other as the most incisive and discerning writer in English on rugby, were to be more carefully and generously studied, their opinions could have important and beneficial influences. As it is, men who reject such critics too often are incapable of exhibiting comparable moral courage in making and defending statements intended for the improvement of the game. Critics, of course, can also be mistaken. Even so, their views are usually worth reading.

Let me be brief about this sermonising. It is likely that as many faults in the Welsh-New Zealand relationship lie with New Zealand as with the Welsh. Since the Keith Murdoch incident of 1972, it has been distressing to encounter the proportion of New Zealanders who have deified the man and cursed those Welsh who, they claim, incited his expulsion from the tour. Their view has been as one-sided as Malcolm Lewis's. If only the public could sense and share the feeling of players, how different all might be. When the All Blacks played Cardiff in 1963, the match was turning sour. Whineray called out in a scrum, "How about playing rugby?" a Welsh voice answered, "Why not?" and to this day Cardiff men talk of the game as an event of their playing lives. It was a wonderful moment after the 1974 match (which would have been an international if the Irish, who had arranged the All Blacks' tour to celebrate their centenary, had been prepared to allow the match to follow their own test against the New Zealanders) when those great players, Gareth Edwards and Gerald Davies, came up the stairs to the balcony which looks down on the banqueting room of the Angel Hotel in Cardiff. There they joined the All Blacks for a drink or two, or more, before the formal proceedings later got under way. This was the friendship of men who had been out in the middle; and Edwards in his book, published in 1978, spoke of the "wonderful" night he had spent with All Blacks after his first encounter with such great men as Tremain and Colin Meads in his first international for Wales in 1967. Let it be recalled, too, how Edwards, Davies and Barry John went to the modest home of the All Black five-eighths Robert Burgess a couple of nights after he had been concussed in the third test against the Lions in 1971. The men dined in the company of Robert and Linda and swore, you might say, friendship for life. This was the true companionship of Welsh and New Zealanders in rugby. As a fellowship, it is probably the closest in the game. The speaking of Afrikaans is an impediment to such a relationship between New Zealanders and South Africans and the working-man philosophy of New Zealand rugby is in a sense alien to the rugby of England, Scotland and Ireland. But it is this philosophy, based upon the workaday life of men in trades and crafts, which is, properly harnessed, the bond between the Welsh and New Zealanders. There could be little doubt that, after Bridgend and the assault upon Russell Thomas, that there was room for much improvement by both nations in team relationships with each other.

It was strange for Mourie's Men to find that the outstanding and most consistent aspect of British rugby was the refereeing rather than the quality of opposing teams. Strange because, on past tours of the postwar era, the British, whether they were Welsh, Irish, English or Scots, had usually offered some teams and a number of players of exceptional merit. But the great backs, so it seemed, had withered on the vine of intensive coaching. Only Mike Slemen, the Englishman, looked remotely in the class of Gerald Davies as a wing threequarter. Workaday centres were a dime a dozen but nowhere visible was one to compare with the Michael Gibson of the decade from his first appearance against Whineray's team in 1963. Ireland's outside-half, Tony Ward, stood out as a quick, nuggety, brave player and superb goalkicker who with a little more enterprise on the break might turn into a Gibson of the late '70s and early '80s. But the general standard was below that which had been encountered by other All Black touring teams. A fixed belief was that coaching, hailed in the late '60s and early '70s as the hope of British rugby, had been overdone, stifling initiative and encouraging defensive patterns. Perhaps the problem was that coaching was not as good as it ought to have been. Gleeson's teams, even after Munster, were not surpassed and seldom were approached in attacking initiatives. By his record, the great man of British rugby had become John Dawes, whose Welsh teams had performed the incredible feat of winning three consecutive Triple Crowns. But the

Welsh team Dawes placed against the All Blacks was markedly deficient in attacking skills. The forwards, supported by two gifted young halfbacks in Gareth Davies and Terry Holmes, dominated much of the play for at least two-thirds of the game and in the case of such old hands as Charlie Faulkner and Bobby Windsor in the front-row looked likely to wheeze rather than breeze to victory. For want of fulfilment of the forward initiative, Wales failed. It was incredible that the team could yield leads of 9-0 and 12-4. Some Welshmen, in fact most, said the cause was the loss from the previous season of Edwards, Davies, Phil Bennett and Terry Cobner. New Zealand as easily might have said that its loss of Grant Batty, Lawrie Knight and, moving up in the geriatric stakes, Sid Going and Ian Kirkpatrick was also severe. But the New Zealanders tend to look forward where the Welsh enwrap themselves in Celtic gloom and look back.

Coaching qualities and standards in the British Isles might explain the indifferent performance of teams against Mourie's Men. On the other hand, it might be argued that the rarest bird in rugby is the qualified, seasoned, gifted coach who can seize the imagination of men of varying ages and mould their talents into a well-balanced weapon of the game. The stream of coaching talent around the world, even in the strongest rugby areas like Wales, France, New Zealand and South Africa, was thin. New Zealand was fortunate that Jack Gleeson established himself as the Coach of the Year. The strong man in British and Irish rugby was Tommy Kiernan, though it was a justified criticism that his methods with Munster were of trench-warfare standard rather than the combination of the heavy and light brigades which Gleeson pursued. Rugby was the more likely to fulfil its possibilities with the advent and encouragement of the Gleesons, the Carwyn Jameses, the John Stewarts and their peers — of whom there were not a great number — than by placing teams in the care of men wanting in imagination and, above all, confidence. Man-management, the supreme test of ability, was superbly displayed by Gleeson. History might prove it to be the most significant feature of the tour.

CHAPTER SEVEN

World Watershed

THE YEAR OF the tour by the team that found itself was marked in rugby by turmoil, unrest, drama and excitement. Discontent which had been growing among players of world ranking at the meagreness of their allowances while touring for their countries — something between thirty and forty dollars a week was standard for out-of-pocket expenses — promised much for World Professional Rugby Ltd, a company formed with a capital of $5000 in Auckland by theatrical entrepreneurs named Russell Clark and Benny Levin. Players contended that when they contributed to massive gate-takings at matches played by touring international teams — in South Africa in 1976, the team of Andy Leslie's All Blacks yielded about $5.5-million — they should be more sympathetically treated, especially in relation to the treatment of wives and families who had to remain behind. Despite expressions of lofty disdain in members of the Establishment, the company did in fact persuade many leading players to sign on the dotted line. A number resided in the British Isles. More were All Blacks of current or recent standing. In fact, the *New Zealand Listener* published a list of several men who had signed contracts; and despite the fact that one of them, not an All Black but close to it, threatened proceedings for defamation, no overt action was taken.

It may be that the importance of the tour that found itself was the principal reason why the company appeared to go into recess. Meanwhile, other events of the year were also dramatic. France accepted an invitation to join the International Rugby Board and its senior partner, the Four Home Unions committee which governs rugby in the British Isles. Russia played France and was beaten in injury-time in the test match between the countries. Vicious thuggery punctuated an unhappy tour of Australia by Wales and the Red Dragon dragged its tail in the dirt when its team was beaten in each of the two internationals, lamentations about the quality of Australian refereeing sounding loudly on the sidelines. Australia toured to New Zealand, lost its first test when one of its forwards stupidly threw a punch which yielded the All Blacks' winning penalty, 13 to 12, and was overcome by foul conditions of rain, cold, a streaming wind and a heavy ground in the second match in Christchurch. Then at Auckland, in the final test, the Australians greatly pleased a large crowd of 48,000, the largest by 12,000 in the history of test matches between the two countries at Eden Park, by the quality of their play while hammering the All Blacks by 30 points to 16. This sensational achievement emphasised how substantially Australia had improved in techniques and team-qualities from the massive and skilfully-organised national coaching movement which had been set up a few years before. It also emphasised — or at least the tour as a whole did — how deeply rugby was imbedded in New Zealand's sporting soil. The New Zealand Rugby Union's profit from the tour of $218,000 was more than extraordinary, it was miraculous.

Meanwhile, turmoil and drama were involved in a campaign by the Northern Transvaal Rugby Union to mount a tour by an invitation team which would be called, so it was proposed, A World XV, and which would tour through South Africa. The council of the New Zealand Rugby Union was twice in session on this proposal, once in October to decide against allowing 16 players to tour with the team, and then again in December, when after spirited lobbying it decided to allow six All Blacks individually to accept the invitations. Councillors stolidly argued that no breach of the Gleneagles Agreement reached by Commonwealth Prime Ministers in 1977 to ban sporting associations with South Africa or South Africans was implicit in their ruling; but anti-apartheid organisations and activists were not appeased; and when, in high secrecy, three councillors accepted invitations to join the tour, normally enthusiastic rugger types tended to wonder whether the government of the New Zealand game by a disunited body could be effective and efficient.

Much else went on. On the world level, 1978 was significant. For too many years had the International Board, made up of the largely Anglo-Saxon countries, England, Scotland, Ireland, Wales, Australia, South Africa and New Zealand, exerted arrogant dominion over a game which was now thriving in not fewer than 50 countries, including, most significantly, the United States. It had pleased the board and the Four Home Unions to keep France a little removed and to make no audible comment when the French became the principal functionaries of a European Rugby Union with affiliates in Spain, Italy, Romania, West Germany, the Low Countries and, most recently, Soviet Russia. Tales of the "professional" aspect of French and European rugby were commonplace. (It might also be said that old Welsh internationals claimed to have evidence of some British players receiving as much as £3000 a year for various activities associated with the game.) It became a fact of life that foreign players could be handsomely set up in France, not least as restaurateurs, while it was also alleged that Italian clubs were prepared to give overseas internationals allowances, apartments, cars, servants, round-trip air-tickets for themselves and their wives, and, at the end, $10,000 in the currency of their nomination — all this for a season of about six months in all.

What came to be feared by senior members of the International Board was the possibility that the success of "pragmatic", as it might be called, rugby would soon erode the amateurism which they considered to be fundamental to the game. It was more strongly feared that if they continued to maintain Anglo-Saxon domination, the formation of a competitive body commanding the interest and large affairs of the European countries and all others who might be interested would be only a matter of time. One very senior International Board man told me that there was no question that Russia would initiate the formation of such a union or association unless the IRB, in that old-fashioned phrase which has been sanctified for society by Prince Philip, pulled its finger out.

In the world sense, the invitation to France (which was accepted), might be discovered to be a case of too little, too late. The Americans, having lately come to market, were by 1978 still in their swaddling clothes as a national organisation with international affiliations, though their Eagles, a representative team, had toured in the British Isles and a subsidiary invitation team had toured through South Africa in the early winter of '78. Elsewhere, the criticisms of the International Board were numerous. Countries like Japan, Thailand, Malaysia, Singapore and the South Pacific islands of Fiji, Tonga and Western Samoa, in all of which rugby was strong and progressive, had no voice at international level, not even in an associate capacity. They could not contribute to the making of new laws, or the modifying of old. Their function was to wait for crumbs from the rich man's table, or to beg for favours. The aboriginal population of Fiji numbers no more than about 220,000 men, women and children which is scattered over many islands spread about league after league of the bounding Pacific main. But the penetration of rugby into the population is perhaps higher, on a count of heads, than in any other country in the world, Wales included; and the Fijians of recent years had proclaimed their strength, based upon extraordinary natural strength and speed, by chasing All Black and English national teams to within a point and by beating decisively Phil Bennett's wan and woeful Lions in their last match in 1977. Fiji were aggressive and bit of a pain in the neck to the New Zealand Rugby Union; but clearly, they were not going to sit around for too much longer as distant and forgotten affiliates of the International Board. Hence the very great dangers to the board if

Russia, or the United States, or some other country, set going machinery which might end up as another world body. The even greater fear was that such an organisation might regard pragmatic or neo-professional rugby as a logical development for the last years of the 20th century, thus eroding and perhaps destroying the amateur fabric of the game.

Fair reason, therefore, looking all about, for the year to be regarded as one of turmoil, unrest and, who knows, hints of revolution. Amid all this, the tour of the team that found itself, the expedition of Graham Mourie and his men, was like a shaft of sunlight striking through the blackest cloud or even, in the old phrase, like the first cuckoo of spring. "If this tour has taught our chaps anything," an English police officer, Richard Turral, wrote from Bedford, "it is, hopefully, that rugby is a running game, involving fifteen players who are amateurs, playing for fun." It was a statement coming from, so to speak, nowhere but certainly not from nobody, which warranted the closest study.

What were the qualities of the tour which made it unquestionably the great event of world rugby, 1978 (turmoil and unrest) edition? There were inhibiting factors to the success. Domestically, the Four Home Unions were very gravely at fault in failing to provide a touring secretary for Russell Thomas. The New Zealand council was scarcely less culpable in failing to insist on this appointment, which it regards as normal for all major touring teams to its country. Thomas was burdened by mail, by calls, by invitations, by God knows what. The arrangement made by the Four Home Unions and which appeared to be defended by its chairman, Mr Mickey Steele-Bodger, of local stenographers helping Mr Thomas as needed was second-rate and a reflection of the patronising attitude of the British to the Wild Colonial boys from Down Under. Mind you, this was not the first time the Brits had fallen down on this job. When the Four Home Unions committee appointed a retired bank-officer, Ted Howard, to the tour of 1972-73, they paid him £3 a week; which magnificent sum presumably was saved when Mr Howard was invalided from the tour, a bewildered and disillusioned man, some weeks before its end.

Although Russell Thomas and, so far as could be gathered, most of the players were satisfied with the Home Unions' travel arrangement of coaches for 19 of the 23 journeys around the British Isles, this, too, was unsatisfactory. British trains, even with the whimsical timetables which are arranged when industrial unions in that stricken community decide yet again to strike, or go slow, or work to rule, are exceptionally comfortable and are, in fact, ideal means of travelling for a team. Thomas was persuaded that the arrangement failed only when what he called the grid-system had not been employed in the construction of the All Blacks' itinerary; that is, when matches followed each other in centres which were not connected by the great motorway system of England, Scotland and Wales. However, he spoke without experience of travel by train with a team and thus was on shaky ground. Jack Gleeson was always a critic of the coaches, principally because he liked to work his week around the training-runs and was dissatisfied when these, as sometimes happened, prolonged the day for players. The worst instance of travel for the team was the day spent between Chester and Aberdeen by coach to Glasgow and thence by a short flight to Aberdeen. The Four Home Unions said, defensively, that they had been unable to arrange a charter-flight to Aberdeen. The answer to that one should have been short and bitter: Get one.

The aforementioned Mr Turral, who hitherto was unknown to me, struck at a point about rugby which was also a cause of widespread concern. He sounded a bit of a humorist when he wrote: "The All Blacks thoroughly deserved victory in the four internationals if only because, Scotland perhaps excepted, they were the only side trying to play football. As an Englishman, I shall always savour Brian McKechnie's last-minute penalty against Wales — how we laughed, down at the pub, and toasted New Zealand. After the laughing had stopped, I reflected that it was sad that I would rather see England beat Wales by a doubtful penalty than lose by the odd try in nine." He added: "I doubt that New Zealand supporters would feel the same shame today over D. B. Clarke's Dunedin feat. The game is now about winning, winning at all costs; and if the Lions were stuffed, so much the better."

Good old Anglo-Saxon touches there. No beating about the bush. But then Mr Turral went on to say: "When I joined the Police Force, two officers did duty at the local football match. They were old and decrepit, or so I thought then. The duty was a sinecure. Now, 140 of us have to attend. Supporters go for a result — some for a punch-up. Few go to watch the game or indeed applaud good play by the opposition. This is the way rugby is going in the British Isles. It is to our eternal shame that your country's team was often booed onto a pitch."

Mr Turral, a percipient man, made one other quotable comment: "My only regret is that the All Black backs were not entirely or comprehensively successful in scoring tries."

Now there's a pragmatic chap for you. Seeing things as they are, not through rose-coloured spectacles. The point of particular concern as to the All Blacks not scoring tries is shrewdly taken. The point of general concern as to the violence of play and among spectators is of world-wide importance in considering the world-wide structure of the game and, inferentially, the failure of the International Board to legislate against those areas of the game which engender the violent conduct which, in spite of all deploring, goes on and on. Principally, so I believe, the lineout is the place of most discontent. Laws which compel players to stand one metre distant from each other in the same line and not to move over a space of 500 millimetres, roughly 20 inches, between the two lines of forwards invite the keen attention of referees with a mind of mathematical bent and make easier streams of penalties against infringing forwards. Penalties stir feelings, not least in hard-working forwards, and feelings stir punches. Whistle, whistle and in comes a sour mood players are too heated to dissect but which compels even the gentlest-natured among them to indulge the snide stuff of jersey-holding, standing on a man's foot or putting an arm on his shoulder, or actually belting him, backhand or forehand. These are the originating causes of much violence; and violence unquestionably has lowered rugby's esteem in public eyes during the 1970s. Rucking is another source of trouble. Recent lawmaking by the International Board has convinced New Zealanders that legislators of sinister design and mind have deliberately set about the destruction of All Black strength by clause-making which limits the freedom of the ruck. This narrow view distorts a careful examination of the problem which is inherent in rucking — that is, the heeling of the ball from a loose scrum. It cannot be questioned that New Zealand rucking as prescribed and practised by the great Otago teams of Victor Cavanagh's days just after the Second World War was an art-form. Finely-disciplined men went for the ball, got it in style and at the all-important moment of their wish, and set their backs racing, as often as not into broken-field defences. But the difference between finely-disciplined men and men charging in anyhow on a ball on the ground can be as wide as the Pacific Ocean; and even in New Zealand, supposedly the one country capable of consistently practising well-controlled rucking, the sight has too often been seen, especially in recent years, of boots flying without reck for the safety of the man or men nearest to the ball. The Ashworth/J. P. R. Williams was a prime example.

This has been, and will continue to be, where desperate men and incompetent coaches are concerned, dangerous play; and dangerous play rather than violent or deliberately foul play has been the jinx of rugby in its modern development. Not many coaches or teams tolerate the deliberately foul player. He gets a name, his deeds are sometimes laughed about and rougher men among old-timers tend to swear that he alone plays rugby in the way it used to be played and ought always to be played. But the fellow is a maverick, a rotten apple, a rogue elephant, and the sooner he is disposed of the better for the particular team and, naturally, for the game. Mr Turral has talked of the attitude of winning at all costs and of spectator involvement and incitement. Perhaps because of the influence of soccer and more particularly the

Manchester United element which can make contact sport so difficult to justify spectator-problems are, I believe, a greater menace in the British Isles than New Zealand, at least for the time being. But the nationalist element which the All Blacks so much detested while they were in South Africa in 1976 has surfaced in New Zealand audiences; and it will take a long time to believe well of that Wellington audience at Athletic Park which in the first All Blacks-Wallabies test of 1978 strenuously whistled and jeered to put off his stroke the Australian, Ken Wright, as he tried to place a last-minute penalty goal which would have won the game.

Hence, taking the gloomy view, the view justified by so many of the events of 1978, with special reference to the brutality introduced by the Welsh into their tests against the Australians, rugby was in that year, and more probably in that era, involved in unrest, turmoil, indignation and discontent.

All hail, therefore, the deeds of the team that found itself. Mourie and his men, a finely-disciplined band, were described by the Welshman, Ken Harris, who is a life-member of the Welsh Rugby Union and the strongest administrator of the International Board, as the best-dressed, best-turned out, best set of rugger men seen in the British Isles since the Australians who were led by the immortal halfback, Ken Catchpole, 20 years before. It was the warmest of compliments from a man of much experience and profound ability. (I have always had a soft spot for Ken Harris' impish humour after he told me: "The English, the Scots and the Irish have never forgiven us Welsh for allowing our rugby to become the game of our working-men.")

There were regrets to the tour: the Ashworth and Haden incidents; the tactical and strategical changes introduced after Munster; the want of the old warmth, and some humour, in the relations between the touring Press and the players; the sad discovery that Russell Thomas was not in full possession of the facts in his assertion that Mourie had taken theology at university.

In any contest, however, the regrets were well beaten by the joys of the tour. I cite as only a small, though highly relevant, instance of the quality of the general attitude that in one four-day stay at a hotel the whole team consumed no more than five glasses of beer even though, in terms of the tours agreement, each man was entitled to a glass at both lunch and dinner. These All Blacks did not want beer. They wanted to get on with the job. Like their captain, who was a man of restless, though well-ordered temperament, they looked to the next hurdle immediately after they had cleared the last. They were concerned to play well, to look well, to apply the Golden Rule in their relations with their hosts. They were highly, and justly, praised by such as Mickey Steele-Bodger, representing the Four Home Unions, Herbert Waddell, of the Barbarians, D. L. James, the Welsh president of whom they saw so much, and their various liaison officers — Alex Heming, of England, George Morgan, of Wales, Fraser McAllister, of Scotland, and Desmond Scaife, of Ireland, whom they saw so often and liked so much. It is always interesting to hear what the higher-ups say. It is more enlightening to hear what is said by porters and maids and waiters and receptionists in hotels. The praise for these All Blacks from these unconsidered people was warm indeed. In the best New Zealand style, the All Blacks behaved simply. The manner is, if New Zealanders would only realise it, New Zealand's greatest quality.

Toward the end of the tour, I asked the New Zealand High Commissioner, Sir Douglas Carter, for an opinion of the team. Sir Douglas, a stalwart farmer and rugby man, and his charming wife were constant supporters of the team. I suspect that the In tray on Sir Douglas's desk was piled up a bit in the weeks between October 14 and December 18.

No matter. He was there when he could be. Coincidentally, he was fighting quite desperately to convey New Zealand's case for warmer and more sympathetic treatment in the vital trade of farm-produce to the British Government and through it to the European Economic Community. It was not too much to say that his commission was of life-and-death importance to New Zealand.

"Sir Douglas," I said. "What do you think of the All Blacks and what they mean to and for New Zealand?"

It came out pat. "They are," he said, "doing *my* job for me."

For what Mourie's Men meant to rugby, all the wide world over, 1978 was a good year in the game.

II

CHAPTER ONE

Shake-down Cruise

MUCH WAS PLEASANT sailing for Graham Mourie's All Blacks in the first four matches of their tour. They won them all, against Cambridge University, Cardiff, West Wales (which, they were warned, would be their fifth test) and London Counties. In the doing they scored two tries, both by Stuart Wilson, which set men long in the tooth thinking back to the great days when set-piece plays more often than not yielded the ball swiftly to the wings and set them racing like gazelles at the corner-flag. This was stuff British rugby had expected of its finest Lions, pre-1977, perhaps even pre-1974, and to find it produced by New Zealanders, so dreary in their tactical thinking, so concentrated upon forward play wielded in concert with a swarming cover-defence, was disturbing, shocking and, to the fairest minds among them, invigorating and stimulating. Both of the tries were scored in Wales, one at Cardiff, the other at Swansea, and if you had put one on top of the other, as in a carbon-copy, they would have seemed alike in every particular. At the set-piece moving right, Bryan Williams came in from the left wing, appearing outside the centre; and, taking his pass and drawing his man, sent the ball deftly on to Wilson. What a sight the young man made, fair hair gleaming, as he ran down the touchline, ball held in both hands so that you could not guess whether he was going to pass, kick or keep going! What quality, too, in the wiggle of the hips, the movement off the right foot infield, then back again off the left toward the touchline! The Welsh, whatever their faults, know their rugby; and at these manifestations of superior rugby, these pyramidal touches built upon the soundest of foundations, they exclaimed in joy. This was the stuff, they said, of which great teams and tours are made. Blessed be the name of the All Blacks. Grace, at last, had descended upon them.

But not all was easy and effortless in this portion of the tour which represented a shake-down cruise and a working-up — and together — of the component parts of a team which Jack Gleeson and Mourie intended should find itself. In the preliminaries, Cambridge University had been dismissed as inconsequential. Mere boys, all of them eggheads with IQs of at least 140, brain and no brawn, earnest, lacking the gaiety of the bloods of old, now, so it was said, inhabited the famous colleges. The afternoon at Grange Road would therefore be, for the tourists, a pleasant stroll. Perhaps, every so often, a ball would have to be caught at the lineout or heeled at the scrummage. Perhaps, too, a certain speed would be demanded in the passing to avoid the attentions of some young sprog whose father, doubtless a Blue in the great days, might have insisted from the boy's birth onward that the first duty of an English gentleman was to tackle, tackle, tackle.

In the event, the Nostradamuses who flourished in the Press and the bars, assuring the All Blacks of the good fortune they would experience in the opening match, neglected the fundamental fact that any English gentleman, whether his IQ be 140 or a mere 50, tends to inherit as a birthright a belief that, where he or his are concerned, his duty is to tackle, tackle, tackle. Also overlooked by the prognosticators, perhaps because the lad had suffered injuries which might have crippled anyone of lesser spirit, was the fact that the 'Varsity were captained by an Irishman, John Robbie, who for all his very tender years had already played scrumhalf for his country and captained the Irish Universities in a tour of New Zealand in mid-1978. With his blue eyes, blond hair and rosy cheeks, Robbie looked an utterly charming 16-year-old, which is a bit young for international rugby against a touring All Black team. As it happened, he was an utterly charming 22-year-old involved in post-graduate studies after graduating from Trinity in Dublin. As it happened, too, he had spent much time in the company of an Irish coach, Dr Roly Meates, a Dublin dentist who had coached the Irish international team in New Zealand in 1976 and the Irish 'Varsities two years later. Roly's name may not as yet have been placed in the scrolls of the truly great coaches of rugby. Perhaps he is a prophet and thus not excessively honoured in his own country. But he, too, is an utterly charming man of lively, alert mind whose thoughts as to rugby are wholesome, sound and refreshing.

John Robbie played the first half against the All Blacks like a senior prefect. You were a little astonished that when he put the ball into the scrum, as a halfback is required to do, it was not he, as hooker, who heeled the ball. You were also surprised, when he cleared the pass after a lineout, that it was not he who had jumped higher than anyone to make the catch. In a word, he was in everything and did everything. Such enthusiasm was captivating, exhilarating; but it was not entirely appropriate because the best of rugby, after all, is the harnessing of the talents of 15 men, not the exploitation of the superior abilities of one unusually gifted man. Thus the All Blacks at the break were 21 to nil and the prognosticators in the Press Box, or around the field, were simpering "I-told-you-so"s to each other.

At the half-time break, it was to be imagined that Roly Meates reached out from Dublin, touched Robbie say on a wisdom tooth with his high-speed drill and exclaimed, "Steady, laddie, steady." Transformation! All those young sprogs, bearded like the pard or not, pallid though they might be from burning too much of the midnight oil searching and researching their books, appeared to put on several inches in height, several stones in weight and several megawatts in energy. Coincidentally, Robbie stopped being the senior prefect and became a captain, wise, serious and enterprising. His halfback play sharpened as if it had been put to the hone. In retrospect, looking down the corridors of the tour, it did not seem improper, or irreverent, to say that no other captain surpassed him in the power of inspiring his troops. The All Blacks won the match, comfortably so you might suppose from the score of 32 to 13; but they lost the second half by 11 to 13. Appropriately for so glorious a centre of learning, they had had a bit — quite a bit — of an education.

It would scarcely be right to suggest that the All Blacks approached Cardiff, next stop, like a shy husband entering the bridal bed. But they were tremulous and not a little fearful, no doubt about that. Some day, soon with luck, some student of psychology may pen a thesis upon the rugby relationship between Wales and New Zealand. In these later days, it has become customary for the fortunate few who have carried the banner of All Blackdom on a profusion of tours to say that South Africa is the place, it beats all other countries hollow as a country for a team to tour. Forgetting all the nasty nuisances of politics, one can agree that South Africa is a glorious place. Its climate, especially in the fine times of old when you could go north of the Limpopo to Rhodesia and even travel, as we with the 1960 All Blacks did, to Ndola and Kitwe, way north in the tropical zone of Zambia, is unbeatable. All is exotic, from the great grey mass of Table Mountain in Cape Town to the mine-dumps of Johannesburg. For rugby visitors, especially players, from New Zealand, there is exceptional warmth and exquisite hospitality. But the rugby, alas, is too often reduced to a mastodonic contest, mountains of brawn devoid of subtle intelligence and with goalkicking elevated to the highest platform of influence. An All Black approaching South Africa may fear the physical contest. An All Black approaching Wales fears also the physical contest, though with less concern, but he is also aware of some other impalpable quality, a mystique, which induces a dread. He may even feel that Merlin is in the wings, waiting to cast spells upon him. If, however, Merlin is off duty or has suffered the British disease of striking for shorter hours and higher wages, the All Black is aware that, out on the field, he is in the presence of countless foes wishing him well in the name of rugby and evil in the name of Wales.

So the 1978 All Blacks, like their predecessors all the way back to 1924 when the Invincibles set out to avenge the defeat of the 1905 Incomparables, were conscious that at Cardiff they could be set upon by the representatives of perhaps the greatest rugby club in the world and by many thousands of Welshmen who with various hymns and songs would appeal to the gods to bring victory to their men. Practically speaking, the All Blacks had to buffet their way through great masses of hwyl, the mysterious and magical Welsh quality of total commitment in the names of Wales, before they reached the pitch; and if some of the more sensitive New Zealanders felt like retching or peeing an excessive number of times before they got there, who could blame them?

All preliminary excitement and dread and terror were wasted. Cardiff was just another team. No spark of vivid Welsh ignited any players or illuminated the side. This was a workaday outfit, to be approached with respect and passed by with wonderment that a club so constantly famous for highs could now be plodding along on a low. Well, said the soothsayers, crestfallen, anything Cardiff couldn't do, West Wales, based upon Swansea, could. Certainly the St Helens ground at Swansea demanded respect. It was here that the 1935-36 All Blacks became notorious as the first All Blacks touring in the British Isles to be beaten by a club team. In 1953-54, too, Bob Stuart's All Blacks were held to a 6-all draw by Swansea and in 1967 Brian Lochore's team, playing West Wales rather than the city's club team, were being run ragged at the instruction of a fascinatingly dominant field captain, Clive Rowlands, until two young New Zealanders produced efforts which transformed their comrades. Grahame Thorne from his own side of halfway ran like an electrified eel all the way to a most remarkable try and Gerald Kember, silly as a two-bob watch from a terrible crack on the head, brought off tackles and catches of such quality that you wanted to shout in joy at the sight of such bravery. Mourie's men, despite the comforting defeat of Cardiff, were still not reassured that they had the beating of Welsh teams as they marched upon St Helens. Many, as authorities remarked, had told them that this was to be their fifth test. With the passing of time, Clive Rowlands had become the coach rather than the captain of the team and from a long and fruitless association with various Welsh teams against All Blacks in Wales and New Zealand he had, it was said, scores to settle. What was not mentioned, at suggestions that what West Wales had not quite managed to do in 1967 they most certainly would in 1978, amounted to a chapter in the continuing saga of Welsh rugby's parochial politics. Back in 1967, West Wales were prepared by Llanelli's coach, Carwyn James. In seven severe sessions, he acquainted his players with their duties. The product was a disciplined side, physically fit, aggressive, imaginative and damned unlucky to lose. This effort added a cubit to the stature of James as a coach. By 1971, when he was appointed to coach John Dawes' Lions in New Zealand, James was thought to be a coach of the first rank. The tour, phenomenally successful, with the All Blacks beaten 2 to 1, with the last test drawn, established James as one of the more exceptional coaches of rugby history. His perception in discovering the frailties in opposing teams and players, his ability to make his Lions speak by admirable deeds, especially in support plays, made him a rare bird. Had he wished, he could have shared, with Dawes and the manager of the team, bluff Douglas Smith, a Scottish doctor, in the award of an OBE in the New Year Honours. But James, fiercely Welsh Nationalist, spurned the English gift. In later years, he coached Llanelli to beat the 1972-73 All Blacks and to be established as about the greatest club team of its time. In these years, too, he discovered jealousy; stark, bitter envy of his abilities. Yet the biters who would not sanction his appointment as selector and coach of Wales, preferring instead the coaching first of Clive Rowlands and later of Dawes, were now to be bitten with the display of West Wales against Mourie's men. Rowlands was the team's coach and Dawes, now of demigod status because of the consistent success of Wales in the Five Nations championship, came in as the mastermind for a final training run three days before the match. Herein was to be seen a fundamental difference between James and the two men whose appointments had denied him the supreme distinction of coaching his own country's team to greatness. Where he had run West Wales seven times, they ran it twice.

Was this arrogance? Or misjudgment? Or folly? Most likely, a mixture of all three. The upshot was a very severe defeat indeed. This match at St Helens was principally notable for the sour hostility of the crowd toward the English referee, Alan Welsby, a 44-year-old schoolmaster of commanding physique and a haughty disdain of his critics. When commiserated with during the evening, in the course of which he was abused by a West Wales' player, Geoff Wheel, so vigorously that the All Blacks' coach, Jack Gleeson, who was in the group, was staggered at the bitterness, Welsby said, with excellent humour: "If you don't get booed when you are refereeing a Welsh team in Wales, you are out of touch, you are losing your grip!" It really was saddening to listen to the vehement name-calling, the personal vilification, of an honorary official who was doing a difficult job for love of the game. As to West Wales and St Helens, they were both crummy. Sensing that the All Blacks might feel bitter about the match because they had played to the whistle and taken each decision, good or bad, without complaint, Russell Thomas gathered his troops after the game. "Not a word," he instructed. "Not a word are you to say against the crowd, or West Wales, or anything. Just let things be." At Thomas's instruction, the All Blacks, after the dinner, visited the Swansea Rugby Club's pavilion. Here, so they had been told, they would be honoured guests. They would be brothers-in-arms with the West Walians. It is to be said, in charity, that there are more distinctive clubrooms around the rugby world. It was also odd that the West Walians did not trouble to attend. The All Blacks did their duty for half an hour. Back at the Dragon Hotel, they were glad to have each other's company. It was not a day to be remembered by New Zealanders with affection or by West Welshmen with pride.

Hereupon, the All Blacks' caravan wended back to London, to the match against London Counties at Twickenham. Here, too, an attitude of mind expressed the group. It was awe. All of the team had seen Twickers before. On their first and only free Saturday of the tour, they had watched the touring Pumas from the Argentine give the English international side thinly disguised as an England XV the very devil of a time in a 13-all draw. No back of the tour — New Zealand, English, Irish, Scots or Welsh — made a deeper impression of excellence than the Argentinian flyhalf, Hugo Porta, who appeared to be a master of the five-eighths' trade and all tricks associated with it. Yet in spite of that experience, the All Blacks, especially the more impressionable, still approached the game with Counties with awe. Twickenham is a vast place of rugby. The east, north and west stands jut out from the surrounding land like pyramids of the desert sands and the south terrace sticks up a bit, too. Capacious bars are accommodated in the various structures. The amount of drinking done on a big match-day is phenomenal. The guzzling goes on until a little before kick-off: and if, now and again, a late-comer to his seat suffers a sharp kick on the ankle, you can be sure he deserves it. Counties had its great moment of glory when its team beat the 1951 Springboks, reputedly the greatest team South Africa ever sent abroad, and the springbok head still decorates a doorway of the great stadium. At other times, not least against All Black teams, Counties' teams had been stubborn opponents who gave up the ghost only at the last whistle.

Mourie's men wondered, therefore, whether they might be made to suffer harshly in their match with the representative team of the metropolis. True, they had been told the Counties' selection committee numbered no fewer than nine men and that, the older All Blacks supposed, argued that the team might be rather a patchwork quilt than a well-organised entity. Barking away on the sideline, too, even for those who might not want to hear, the lively All Black five-eighths of the 1960s, Earle Kirton, now a dentist, most successful, in London and formerly a coach of the famous Harlequins club and the Middlesex county team, could be heard denying that Counties possessed the soul of a true team. Twickers was still Twickers and to sprint and slog on its glorious sward was to be rated a privilege.

That, at any rate, was how the All Blacks felt. As to Counties, beaten by 12 to 37 and deserving to be licked by at least twice the score, nothing could be said in extenuation. If this rabble, this shameful group of nondescripts who in going through the motions appeared neither to care nor to suffer, represented the best that was in rugby in the metropolis, then God help London: and God help, too, the game itself. Reporting the game for the *New Zealand Herald*, I told its readers that the All Blacks had produced a second-rate effort against a fourth-rate team. One turned from the struggle with distaste. I wager teams of East Coast or Thames Valley, mustered from only a few clubs, would offer an All Black team, even one as competent as Mourie's side, a stiffer battle than was produced by London's finest spineless.

I mentioned at the start of this chapter that the first four matches of the tour contained much pleasant sailing. A deeper look beneath the surface in each contest reveals some interesting facts and fancies that would have an influence on the rest of the tour.

The Cambridge University coach was none other than Murray Meikle, a valuable forward in Otago and New Zealand Universities teams and for Otago packs of the 1960s. These were coached by that earnest disciple of Otago method, Eric Watson, who by 1978 had become one of the Big Three in the selection of the All Blacks. Apart from Robbie, by now an experienced player whose abilities commended themselves more to foreigners than they did to his native Irish — at the least, he could repair Ireland's chronic want of strong-minded, alert and efficient captains — Meikle *prima facie* did not have much to work on. The backs were young and of middling build and the forwards wanted the pair of dreadnoughts who are now considered to be essential to rugby of the first class. But by alchemy or other mysterious means, Meikle had managed to make quite a pack out of his boys. Nigel Heath and Justin Ford, the locks, looked pale and young against the craggy All Blacks, Fleming and Loveday, and Richard Brooman, Jerry Grant and Steve Killick in the front row were fresh-faced children against the hardy Canterburians, John Ashworth, Black and Bush. Yet Meikle — presumably it was his teaching — had awakened his boys to the likely efforts of the men so effectively that they caused the All Blacks problems at both the lineout and the scrummage. The All Blacks did not manage to pinch a heel against the head and though they won the lineouts by 20 to 12, their margin of eight to six in the second half reflected the growing confidence of the youngsters and the admirably high rate of work they managed. Much good was done the All Blacks by Master Meikle. Not to diminish the Cambridge effort, which was in fact a good deal better than traducers of University rugby were prepared to allow, the men upon whom many All Black eyes were bent, Loveday and Fleming, did not measure up. The latter became so involved that he clean forgot his instructions to move back from 5 to 6 when Cambridge were throwing in the ball. Like Loveday, he scarcely leapt as high as an elephant's eye. Decidedly, if their efforts were an earnest of things to come, the All Blacks of the mid-week XV might have to spend unhappy hours trying to stop other teams from beating them.

Nor were the lamentations confined to the forward effort. In the recent test-match series at home against the Wallabies, Mark Donaldson had been found to be inefficient in clearing passes from set-piece plays. Nothing was wrong with his pass. It had length, speed and height. The trouble was that rather more time than was desirable was consumed between Mark's grasp of the ball and his delivery of it. The gap alerted opposing forwards to what was going on — and O'Callaghan and Butler, both Welshmen, and Glanvill, who came from the West Country, had been well coached by Meikle into breaking fast, so to speak, from the blocks. In the second half, it was decidedly alarming, bearing in mind the possibility, if not the probability, that British critics were right in assessing Oxbridge rugby as being of the lowest standard in relation to British rugby of the first class, that Donaldson with his cumbersome wind-up and delivery was standing, in relation to the markedly improved Robbie, in exactly the same situation as he had stood against the brilliant Australian, John Hipwell, by whom he had been all but eclipsed in speed of pass. Nor was this the end of the problem in the backline. Bruce stood so far wide of Donaldson that he looked like a figure seen through the wrong end of a telescope — the distance was quite unfair to Donaldson — and the outer backs accordingly tended to be all jumbled together or spread all over the place. No wonder Jack Gleeson's brow was puckered and his lips drawn down at the end of the contest.

But there were good things in compensation. Those gallant University forwards, among whom the lithe youngster, Ford, from that excellent school, Millfield, which produced Gareth Edwards and many other stars, continually took the eye, were supplemented by some lively supporters in the backline of Robbie's consistent adventurings. Tyler's try, initiated by a cut by the flyhalf, Thorton, was startling, the line had liveliness, and right at the end Robbie set going a run of about 60 metres which was quite glorious. As for the All Blacks, Donaldson, wind-up forgotten and forgiven, was sensationally quick, strong and elusive and at least one critic, admittedly marching inexorably toward senility, had a vision that perhaps the young man with the right training could become a powerhouse in the midfield, in the key position of second five-eighths in which New Zealand rugby has so often been deficient. Mind you, Taylor's contribution in this position demolished, on the day, most criticisms. He conveyed physical hardiness and mental dominance. The break he made for his try of the first half was so well judged that the 40 metres ahead of him to the goalline was peopled only by shades of the great players of University's past. Ford and Kururangi were invigorating and McKechnie by hitting five out of five, including three penalties, in the first half, promised to become another of New Zealand rugby's great exports, a goalkicking fullback who could draw a bead from any angle. He converted Donaldson's lightning-fast try, a great break across the front of a swirling defence, from within a foot — 304.8 millimetres, to use the cursed modern system — of the touchline and the ball did not waver an inch — 2.54 centimetres — in its flight.

Two sidelights to the match were interesting. The crowd of 8500 was a record for Grange Road and many hundreds who wanted to be there were shut out. Evidently, British rugby was arousing greater public interest than ever before. Secondly, no one had troubled to tell Cambridge that the All Blacks would be burdened by half a dozen or so New Zealand Pressmen who would wish to tell the folks back home all about the team; or if someone had troubled to tell Cambridge, none of its officers had thought to tell the very charming groundsman who was stricken at the discovery that the Press Box could not accommodate the strangers but who was willing to do everything he could to help them. The crankiest old-timer of the New Zealand corps spoke wounding words to his British confreres on their status as second-rate citizens and the same genial gent in the evening growled at the chairman of the Four Home Unions tours committee, Mickey Steele-Bodger, comparing most unfavourably the favoured-nation treatment given British critics who had toured New Zealand with the 1977 Lions with that offhand treatment, taking Cambridge as an example, which apparently was to be shown the lads from Down Under. Mickey glowered and said things would be better. Happily, they were.

In a defiant gesture perhaps intended to convey that, Welsh mystique or not, they could take Cardiff or leave it, the All Black selectors changed their Cambridge team in no fewer than 14 places for the great event on the Arms Park, Mourie being the only survivor. Perhaps the selectors — Gleeson was, in fact, the only one; Russell Thomas and Mourie at best were advisers, or counsellors, and at worst rubber-stamps — had been listening to reports that Cardiff were not what they used to be. Perhaps they felt that the emotional experience of playing with Bryan Williams in his 100th game for his country, an event generously recognised by (a), Cardiff with the gift of a silver salver, (b), the All Blacks in having "Bee Gee" lead them onto the field and then, as a Samoan, lead them in their Maori haka and (c), the public, whose salutation was prolonged and memorably warm, would invigorate and stir the tremulous and steady down old hands who otherwise might have lost their heads. The real gamble was to leave out McKechnie after his fine goalkicking at Grange Road. Currie was the newest of new boys, not much known for his goalkicking and, back home, ranked as only the third of Canterbury's provincial fullbacks. More than half of the team, including most of the forwards, had played against the Wallabies in the third test at Auckland six or seven weeks before, not necessarily the warmest of recommendations. In fact, if Cardiff were as strong as of old, the selection could be suicidal.

Other times, other manners, as the French say. In an amusing contribution to the programme of the day, Les Spence, a backrow forward in the Cardiff team which lost to the 1935 All Blacks by 5 to 20, recalled the "special training schedule" instituted twice a week for three weeks before the game. In running kit, the Cardiff men left the Arms Park and ran through various streets and fields to the suburb of Llandaff, which is not only decorated by a magnificent cathedral but which also harbours the Butchers Arms. "Those who wanted a rest," Spence recalled, "called in at the Arms." It was a pleasant break before returning to the other Arms. "It was all good fun," Spence said, "and we really enjoyed ourselves."

Imagine such flightiness in modern times! Now, the preparations by each team were exacting. Practices, training-runs, motivating sessions, team-talks, the lot. Cardiff's great hopes were their new boys, Terry Holmes, an unusually tall scrumhalf (6ft 1in), and Gareth Davies, the outhalf. Each had been capped during Wales' tempestuous tour of Australia in the early months of 1978, and although they were young, Holmes 21 and Davies a year older, already there was talk that they were natural successors to Gareth Edwards and Barry John. Edwards himself generously said he believed both were on the point of becoming truly great halfbacks. Fair cause, then, for the All Blacks to tremble. They had other cause, too, because Cardiff's captain, Barry Nelmes, the loose-head prop, was an Englishman. Not since 1885, rather a long time, had the club ceded its captaincy to someone born on the wrong side of the Severn. The natural inference had to be that Nelmes, both as player and tactician, must be very, very remarkable indeed. As for the rest, and taking into account Cardiff's reputation, it seemed certain the team would be both difficult and dangerous.

The score of 17 to 7 flattered, in fact, the losers. They gave the All Blacks one hiding — at the lineout. The disparity, achieved principally by Nelmes at Number 2 and by the locks, Norster and a very interesting and fine player, Hans de Goede, a Dutchman who had played test rugby for Canada and who embodied, especially as to energy, many of the best qualities of a lock of the first class, was serious. It argued that the New Zealanders might be plagued in this vital position. As to the rest, no comparisons were valid. The game offered no finer feature than three or four tackles by Brad Johnstone. One was crucially important — the Cardiff player was on the point of breakaway but the tackle, made at the lower thighs and reaching down below the knees, was so severe that the man had no chance to play the ball. The others were an example of the growing spirit in the All Blacks and their development into the finest tackling team New Zealand has fielded for many years, perhaps ever. Mourie moved with relentless speed, Rutledge was only a yard or so behind, the remaining forwards joined with their leader in swarming attacks or cover-defence with counter-attack always in mind. Loveridge and Dunn, especially the latter, eclipsed the two young Welshmen, Osborne looked breathtakingly good in his natural position at centre and Currie, for all his youth, was steady, not least in goalkicking. The All Blacks' three tries evolved on the level of great, very great and greatest. In a mix-up between Murphy and Daniels in the Cardiff centres, Wilson cut off a pass and, like Taylor in the Cambridge match, broke into open country. This time, the distance to the goalline was a good 60 metres. No one neared Wilson as he flew for a try which, with Currie's conversion, put the All Blacks 9-3 ahead at the half-time break. The next try was even better because it occurred within two minutes of the start of the second half. Dunn, moving left, snaffled Loveridge's pass and within a stride or two chipped the ball with delicate precision over the head of Gareth Davies. Jaffray at full speed made the catch on the full, without a falter in his rhythm, and rushed onward toward the fullback, Paul Rees. Hereabouts it was text-book drill to pass the ball to Osborne, with open country ahead; and if the little Italian of the Cardiff left wing, Camilleri, did look to be gaining as much as a yard on Osborne in the headlong chase no Cardiff man stood a chance of stopping the try. It was superb.

As the piece de resistance, 13 minutes before no-side, "Bee Gee" the Centurion subtly sidled from his post on the left wing as Loveridge again set the backline running, going right. By the time Osborne had the ball in his hands, Williams was outside him, his dark eyes so fiercely fixed on Camilleri that the little man, like a moth darting at the flame, closed in on him. That left Wilson with the ball in hand, Rees standing sentinel ahead, the cover racing madly across, the goalline beckoning, 20 metres ahead. Nearing Rees, Wilson held the ball out to him in both hands, inviting him to pluck at it. It was a masterly touch to set a man back on his heels. Then Wilson squirmed rather than swerved and with an heroic dive thrust himself at the goalline just inside the corner-flag. It was, simply, a great try, a very great try.

The All Blacks, after these three efforts, turned mortal. The ball was thrown over the top of their lineout on their own goalline and the West Indian, Carl Smith, amid a jobble of bodies gratefully seized the ball to plunge for a try the conversion of which Davies missed from so close to the posts that he could have flicked the ball over with his little finger. Two experts talked about Dunn as if he had been sent from Heaven itself. "I shall remember him for a long time," said Carwyn James. "That little chip over the top, that grub-kick, that offer of a feint-pass, that foray on the blindside — it was all thinking stuff, very fine, the mark of a good player." "Eddie does not have to think about kicking. He does what comes naturally," said Barry John, "The King" himself. "He has hands, rhythm, a head. He is a beautiful player."

Except for Stuart Wilson's second try, built up by Williams' superbly-timed intrusion from the left wing, memories of the match with West Wales soon will fade. It will be good to let them go. Sport which engenders in spectators as bitter an attitude as was shown by those at St Helens is best avoided. When Referee Welsby who, having long since proved his competence, failed to see a step into touch which yielded a try for the All Blacks, most of the record midweek crowd of 40,000 screamed for his blood. It was the more frustrating when he reacted with lofty disdain. It was mysterious Welsby was not seen in later matches. Perhaps his reputation for being excessively scrupulous in administering the law had been conveyed to the All Blacks. Even so, he was the man for today's job. He had excellent command. Geoff Wheel, trying to set off a rumpus, was soon quietened; and Fleming, who belted him, was astonished when Wheel turned the other cheek. When he had blown no-side, too, Welsby, indifferent to the bitter barking of a Welshman at his heels, walked coolly to the mouth of the tunnel to assist the West Walians in clapping the All Blacks from the field. Men of lesser spirit might have been tempted to sprint for the dressing-room. Russell Thomas did not hesitate to criticise the crowd. Citing his own reactions to ill behaviour in crowds at Lancaster Park in Christchurch, he said he had never hesitated to speak out against unmannerly activities. "The trouble is," said he, "that ill behaviour in crowds communicates itself to teams on the field and lowers the tone of play."

Not so easily forgotten was the propensity to error in the All Blacks and the severe cut on the leg which caused the retirement of the international wing, J. J. Williams. Presumably the gash was caused by an aluminium sprig which had been serrated in some way and turned into a lethal instrument. Donaldson threw passes hither and thither and much too often was caught by his marker, Clive Shell. Haden was cleaned out at the lineout by Allan Martin. McKechnie committed ghastly blunders of which the worst was a presentation try to Roy Bergiers. Williams' intended kick upfield entered touch close to his own corner-flag and Williams and Wilson in an intended crisscross in midfield managed all of the outer aspects well enough but neglected the vital one of hanging on to the ball. This sort of stuff was distracting and accounted for the bare advantage of 7 points to nil at half-time, little enough for internationals against a team well below test-match standard. Nail-biting went on for the first ten minutes of the second half, too, for in the third minute, after Dai Richards had punted deep, McKechnie's miscue presented Bergiers with his try and a chance to caper in mad exultation at his deed. When McKechnie somewhat, but only somewhat, redeemed his blunder by placing a penalty, Roger Blyth, a good fullback, replied with a goal from 30 metres. At 10 to 7, the situation for the All Blacks was grim. Only a little later, referee Welsby heard many things to his disadvantage when he did not blow up a movement on the blindside by Donaldson and Seear which gave Wilson a try; from a distance, it looked as if most of the players of the two teams stopped in anticipation of the whistle for a step into touch. Hereafter, most doubts of the capabilities of the All Blacks disappeared. The classic final try by Wilson gave the match a magnificent last minute. Much else was satisfying. "We depend on you at No. 8, John," Jack Gleeson warned Fleming in the presence of his teammates. "You must respond." Fleming, unrecognisable as the boy of the Cambridge match, became an All Black. Mourie, bloodied about the eyes from a scrape of the brow, turned on another fascinating demonstration of endless energy, Osborne struck at the powerful Ray Gravell with scything tackles of tremendous power, and in default of high leaps at the lineout Haden plunged vigorously with the ball.

One could not fault Martin as a leaper in the lineout, or his captain, Derek Quinnell, who most capably looked after Seear. The West Wales' halfbacks, Shell, who once won a Welsh cap by standing in for the last two minutes of an international after Gareth Edwards had been hurt, and Richards were capable men at the job and the boyish lad of the 1977 Lions, Elgan Rees, once or twice took off at startling speed, though with no precise idea of where he intended to go or what he intended to do. But West Wales as a team were laughably removed from test-match standard, fifth or otherwise. They suffered, admittedly, from injuries which removed the Lions, J. J. Williams and Trevor Evans, which stopped Roger Blyth in his tracks and which put Evans' replacement, Richard Moriarty, off the field for ten minutes with concussion in his first play in the game. It was quite a sight to watch Moriarty stand up, after his injury, and then fall down. But perhaps the ultimate judgment was delivered by a famous Swansea man, Gordon Rowley, the honorary surgeon to the Welsh Rugby Union who over a number of years had patched up many injured men and inspired them, because he himself had played Olympic ice-hockey for Canada after suffering a terrible injury to an eye, to keep on keeping on. Said Gordon: "My opinion is that Welsh Rugby has gone over the hill. It will take four years to rebuild." It was not, perhaps, the kind of remark to shout from the housetops of Swansea, or Cardiff, or Llanelli, but Rowley was the kind of man who, if he thought it necessary, would have. In further matches in Wales, the All Blacks were to have hard times and their escape in the international was worthy of Houdini. But Rowley's so to speak interim judgment appeared to be fortified by later events.

Forgetting Earle Kirton with his caustic comments, one could not easily find the equivalent of a Rowley in all of the vast city of London. If the display of London Counties was a criterion, however, it looked as if London rugby had not so much gone over the hill as fallen down a precipice. At times in the second half, Counties' captain, Philip d'A. Keith-Roach, summoned some sort of spirit in his pack. Each of the locks, bearded Chris Ralston, 34 and looking every day of it, and Maurice Colclough, whose holiday in France four years before had soured when he ran out of money and then soared because, as a rugby player, he had been financed into a cafe, won some lineout ball and the wing-forwards Sandy Pratt, Robert Mordell and Adrian Alexander, ran around a bit. But when the great man of the backline, Peter Warfield, was found to bear little resemblance to the mighty man who had principally engineered the defeat of the 1972-73 All Blacks by North-Eastern Counties, it was time for Counties to abandon all hope. Their West Indian wing, Robert Demming, a long, lean man, was at 13 stone the lightest of the threequarters, who in fact were vast in size. The Scottish scrumhalf, Alan Lawson, who toured New Zealand as a second-stringer with the Scottish team of 1975, had more recently won fame, or notoriety, by refusing a place in the Scottish reserves, a stiff-necked gesture not calculated to improve his popularity. But playing behind packs like London's was bound to have effect upon even the most genial of halfbacks.

It seemed strange to hear, at the temple of rugby, no better than recorded musiç. It was worse to watch Kururangi drop a high ball. He soon made amends. Dunn hooked a kick to the box where Wyatt misfielded. Kururangi was swift to the ball and quick to the try; and the whole movement took much less time than Currie spent on his careful, and successful, kick at goal. Dunn was equally slow in trying for a dropkick at goal and London were glad to charge it down. With a 6 to 5 situation building, Dunn chose to kick and the All Blacks suffered when Taylor was hurt in the move. But the All Blacks were beginning to run, Loveridge being especially smart, and the second try, also by Kururangi, promised that the demolition gang was moving in. Taylor broke to the right to bring Kururangi into the attack and poor Bushell was blinded by the simple science of a simple sidestep infield off the right foot for a try Currie comfortably converted.

So far, so pretty good. The rest was much more dismal than it needed to be. On the attack, Dunn first and, later, Robertson, became obsessed with tactical punting. This was no way to build the confidence of the threequarters or of Currie as extra man in the attack. On defence, the forwards became obsessed with errors, culpable errors, most grievous to see in a touring team. Counties managed only 12 points, six in each half, but each was a gift. When Rutledge caught a flykick into the All Blacks' 25, a black hand descended on the ball in the ruck and Bushell snapped over an easy goal. After Kururangi had made another comprehensive foozle of a kick to his goalline, Warfield, going hard, was stopped dead by Rutledge; but at the scrummage, another penalty was awarded and Bushell obliged once more. In the fourth minute of the second half, another blunder at a ruck brought Bushell up and from 36 metres he placed a fine goal. Sadly, Bushell had to leave the field, obviously concussed, a few minutes later; but when the All Blacks, late, committed another folly, the replacement, Ian Williamson, a left-foot kick, goaled without trouble.

Perhaps it was hypercriticism to snarl at Dunn and Robertson. Yet the All Blacks were not making a sufficient number of attacks or utilising their superior average speed and the obvious requirement was to concentrate upon the running game. One reward of a match which tarnished whatever glory the rugby of London Counties had had was that Robertson's confidence, partly because of a try he scored with the coolest judgment after charging down Warfield's clearing kick from close to the Counties' goalline, was sensibly improved. For the past couple of seasons, he had been spotted by one opposing team after another and crash tackles had been his lot in match after match. Now, at last, carefully nurtured by Gleeson, he was beginning to enjoy the game. The discovery gave some joy to a bleakish afternoon.

CHAPTER TWO

The Kamikaze Kids

NEW ZEALAND HAD IT COMING. No doubt of that. The All Blacks of 1978 who suffered defeat by Munster by 12 points to nil were only a point or two removed from their forbears of 1953-54, who on the call of time won by 6 to 3; of 1963-64, who scored 6 points in the first half and then, playing downwind, had the devil's own job to win, 6-3; and of 1972-73, who close to no-side brought up their fullback, Trevor Morris, than whom no aspen leaf ever shook more briskly, to place the goal that drew the match, 3 to 3. These events proclaimed that the men of Munster, whether projected on to the field at Cork or on to the cute little, beaut little Thomond Park of Limerick, where Mourie's men took their tumble, were actuated by a patriotism fiercer than a burning oil-well. Not ever will Mourie's men get out of their minds the chants of "MUN-STER! MUN-STER!" which, beginning as timid choruses, progressed, as no-side neared, to stentorian shouts that might have carried halfway across the neighbouring Atlantic. Fermented and spirituous liquors were consumed in substantial quantities at the park after the match. All Limerick was given over to libation in the evening. It was thought, for a time, that it might be a good idea to reprint the programme of the match so that gentlemen of Ireland who had not been there could, by gazing at the names of the heroes, dimly grasp the feel of the match and the holy ground on which Munster had performed its mighty deed. Heroes! In only the fifth minute, Seamus Dennison, him the fellow that bore the jersey number 13 in the centres, was knocked down in a tackle. He came from the Garryowen club, which might explain his subsequent actions — to join that club, so it has been said, one must walk barefooted over broken glass, charge naked through searing fires, run the severest gauntlets and, as a final test of manhood, prepare with unfaltering gaze to make a catch of the highest ball ever kicked while aware that at least eight thundering members of your own team are about to knock you down, trample you all over and into the bargain hiss nasty words at you because you forgot to cry out, while going down for the one and only time, "Mark!"

Dennison was pretty badly hurt. Later, he was hurt again, more seriously. "I think, Seamus," said the attending doctor, "that you would do well to rest by the touchline for two minutes. You will feel much better when you go back." "Push off," said Seamus — they know that naughty word in Limerick, too. "Seamus," said the doctor, more earnestly. "That shoulder is quite damaged. It will be the better if you rest it for two minutes. No more. Just two minutes." "Push off," Dennison said, flatly, finally, forever. He was in pain, no question. But was he going to leave the field? Not bloody likely.

There were, perhaps, two portents to the defeat. After flying from Heathrow to Shannon on the Sunday after the match with the Counties, the All Blacks in the evening were festively dined at Bunratty Castle. This ancient pile had been restored for the tourist trade which had poured into Ireland for 20 years after the end of the Second World War and which only tailed off after the bombers of Belfast had threatened, with an execution here and an assassination or a fire-bombing there, to set all of Ireland alight. Bunratty's banqueting rules were cute. The chief guest, in this instance Russell Thomas, was installed as the Earl of Thomond and in office was invested with enormous powers. Earl Thomas exercised one of these by bidding that Barry Ashworth be cast into the dungeon. To Irish songs sung by beguilingly beautiful colleens and with much pomp and ceremony, the All Blacks drank mulled mead, tossed the bones of their meat over their shoulders and were more medieval than they might even be in Patea on a wild Saturday night. Yet the earl was not entirely serene. Ashworth's shrieks and groans and cries of "Mercy! Mercy!" from the dungeon were a little too lifelike to make an appetite as keen as it ought to have been. They anticipated by about 48 hours, the innermost reactions of the All Blacks as they faced a nil-9 deficit going into the second half of a match against a team massively well organised in defence and boundlessly energetic in chasing anything and everything.

The other portent was offered about midday of the Monday, a little more than 24 hours before kick-off, in a training-run of the Munster team. Training runs may come and training runs may go and the faster and farther most of them go, the better. They are tedious and boring gallops-about in which unenthusiastic men commit errors without cause and silently bear the criticisms of their coach. Munster's run was another matter. It lasted no more than 20 minutes. After the inevitable and essential preliminaries of warming-up, the players were directed by their coach, Tom Kiernan, into an unusual exercise. Tossing the ball out in front of the forwards, he would command one or more of them to go down upon it. The others were then to move on to man and ball to practise the heel to the scrumhalf, Donal Canniffe, and the setting-up of a fast passing move to the wing-threequarters, as often as not with the fullback, Larry Moloney, joining in. Now this had been done before, times without number by teams without number. Tellingly, however, the bite in the rucking and heeling was genuine. The man who had gone down on the ball was not treated as a friend. Tellingly, too, the passes from Canniffe were not only crisp but also were not dropped. Most tellingly of all, the wing-forwards of the team, especially a nuggety man from Cork Constitution, Christy Cantillon, moved so fast in support of the backs that the wings, Moss Finn and Jimmy Bowen, were aware of their comrades, fewer than five metres distant, as they galloped into their passes. The merits of the training were threefold: Vigour, as to the forward effort; accuracy, as to the handling of the backs; and, most of all, speed as to the support-play of the forwards.

Tommy Kiernan is a lean, grizzled, slim man with a pale face almost cadaverously thin. He played fullback for Ireland more than 50 times. He captained the British Lions who set South Africa by the ears in 1968 by exhibiting the wild, juvenile behaviour of a military Mess on the wampo. It is his natural disposition to look on the darker side of things. The attitude expresses the Irish genius for conning outsiders into believing what they, the Irish, want them to believe. Kiernan's is a sharp, lucid, subtle and penetrating mind. His memory-bank of rugby knowledge has the depth of the Mindanao deep. Having played against All Blacks led by Whineray, Lochore and Kirkpatrick, he knew much, if not all, about New Zealand rugby; and he had taken very good care indeed to be provided with video-tapes of the first four matches of Mourie's tour. At the end of the training-run a New Zealander who in the practice of his profession had watched about a million training-runs by about a thousand teams said, sincerely: "Tommy, you've a damned good team here." "Ah, bejaysus," said Tommy in his flat, sorrowful voice, "they are no more than a good bunch of lads. They don't stand a chance against the All Blacks. Which team in Ireland ever has?"

Pow! In the first minute, the first time he received the ball, Canniffe uncoiled his right leg, which appeared to take up two-thirds of his body of more than 6 feet in length, and booted a Garryowen high into the air. The ball rose as from a howitzer and descended vertically. As it came down, those Munster forwards, who now did not have to worry about heeling the ball from the arms of one of their men, arrived in concert, snorting like St George's dragon. They did not, then or later, merely charge. They hurtled. Wilson was shocked into a knock-on, Donaldson into a wild pass. In their own quarter, Munster won the ball and Canniffe smartly passed it to Ward. This dark, chunky, powerful man who in the previous international season had equalled the Irish scoring record by tallying 38 points from various means, mostly goal-

Episodes in the life of a hero: Brian McKechnie enters the Arms Park to replace Clive Currie against Wales. He studies the mark for the famous last penalty. *Overleaf:* The ball is still in the air and so is McKechnie's triumphant fist. Task completed, bonny Brian rests. As anyone might say of a Foveaux Strait man, the world is his oyster.

Above: And they call this the handling game . . . That awful pile-up of All Blacks and Irishmen is a constant of modern rugby. Is there a way out of the mess and maze?

Left: Reaching for glory . . . Bryan Williams, 99th time in the black jersey with the silver fern, dives for the goalline against West Wales, J. J. Williams to the left, Roger Blyth to the right. He needed an ell. He got only an inch.

Opposite: Leaping stags from down under . . . Gary Seear (left) and Bryan Williams, with Ray Gravell between them, set upon Gareth Davies, and the ball, in the Welsh match. Graham Price (right) waits to assist.

Left: The man for all seasons: Blood seeps from Mourie's eyebrow. The wound is inconsequential. Here, forever, vigilance marks the great captain.

Portraits of the famous . . . Below left: Jack Gleeson smiles and, with good cause, smiles and smiles. *Below right:* Eddie Dunn looks unwontedly serious, a strange attitude in one so naturally gifted. *Opposite, top left:* Flying Stuart Wilson, ball in both hands, zooms downfield towards greatness. *Top right:* Christchurch physiotherapist Brian McKenzie, a man of immeasurable value to Mourie's All Blacks, does a spot of stretching on Russell Thomas's frame. Or was he trying to stem the manager's talk? *Lower left:* Doug Bruce is poised like a statue as he crashes another kick into enemy territory. *Lower right:* Mark Taylor once lost his breath, but never his poise as the humorous character of the tour.

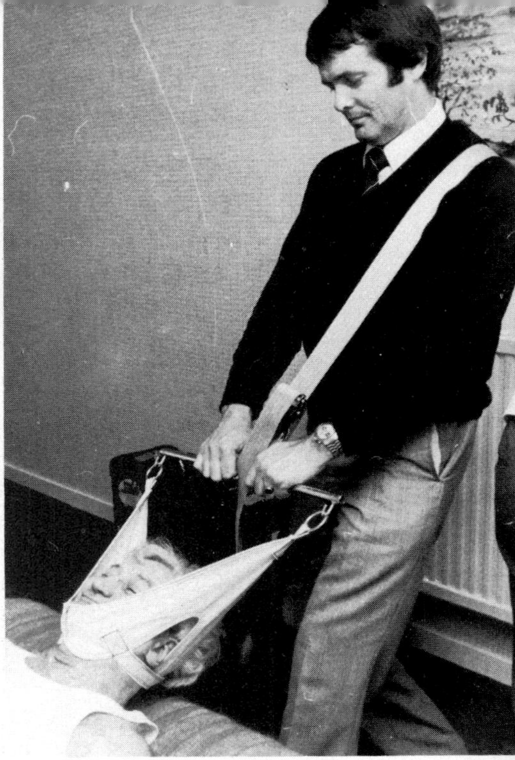

Bid for the grand slam: Three minutes from no-side, Andy Dalton scores the try that beat Ireland. Of the immediate spectators, Welsh referee Clive Norling looks to have cleared decks for action.

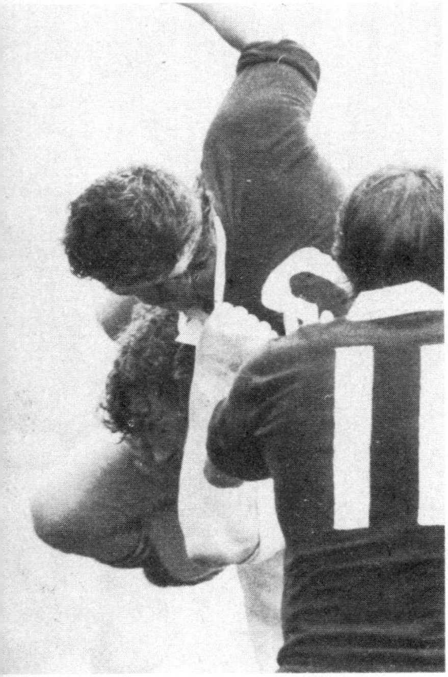

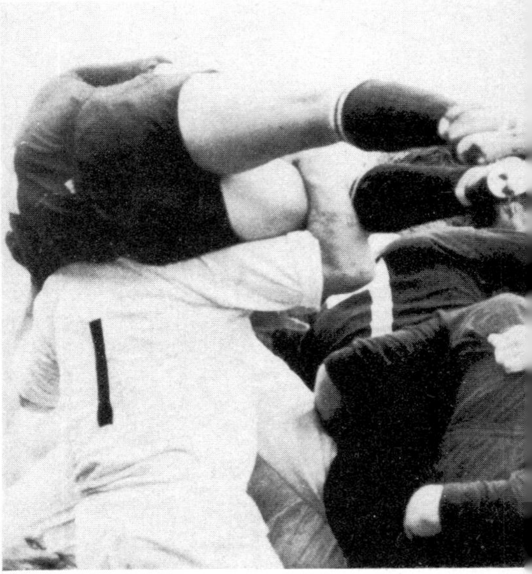

High, wide and handsome . . . Barry Nelmes, England's powerful prop, picks up Andy Dalton and in four decisive actions hurls him to the ground. *Opposite page: Friends for life* . . . Billy Bush finds a chum at the luxurious Lensbury ground of London training and the boy is even happier than Billy. *Why the All Blacks won so we*
. . . or, how to make tackling look easy.

Osborne is demonstrating yet again his
nderous body-charge. *Up in the air, sky-high,
-high* . . . At best, Andy Haden was almost
natchable. *You can't beat the Irish:* Billy Bush
Shay Deering, Ireland's captain, in conflict about
ball. Of the match, Deering said: "It was
ost enjoyable match." A gentleman, as well
scholar.

The black wall from Down Under: Donaldson, Bush, Dalton, Johnstone, Mourie, with Oliver and Haden peeking out from below, contemplate their task. Not the cheeriest of sights for opposing firemen.

Below: Attitudes on the job . . . Gary Knight, recovering from an attack of herpes, dauntlessl takes on the job. Ashley McGregor, played onl thrice, demonstrates the qualities of a fine tourist by trying every time.

3acks of brilliance: J. P. R. Williams, Vale's captain, discusses a point with ·oger Quittenton, the Englishman who not Wales's favourite referee. Michael iibson, soon to be 36 years old, looks ll class in his 64th appearance for eland. Bruce Robertson, beautifully alanced in evading the Barbarian Jim enwick, demonstrates yet again his uperlative skills.

he try of the century . . . Monmouthshire have safely heeled the ball over their own goal-line. The ball beside the right foot of Jeff Squire, their Number 8, and their scrumhalf, Brynmor Williams, has gone to tidy things up. Miraculously, David Loveridge, a spring-heeled Jack, has flown through the air to ore.

Left: On the way to the slam . . . Alan Tomes disputes possession with Frank Oliver at a lineout of the Scottish match. This was in daylight. Darkness later descended — but not upon New Zealand's hopes.

Below: Beaten by the bounce . . . Leicester Rutledge ought to have had this try against Scotland as reward for his splendid tour. Alas, in the tackles of Keith Robertson an Mike Biggar, Rutledge failed to force the ball down. *The Battle of Bridgend:* Every picture tells a story, so they say. This is it, o J. P. R. Williams, who said later that he never again wanted to play against the All Blacks.

Opposite page: Playing by numbers: In a perfect demonstration of techniques, Frank Oliver passes to David Loveridge as the Frenchman, Jean-Claude Skrela closes for the tackle for the Barbarians. *Mourie the Peacemaker:* As can be seen by the jerseys, these are early moments of the Battle of Bridgend, but already Geoff Davies (No. 2) is giving Gary Knight a push in the mush. Gary Seear seems concerned and Mourie moves in.

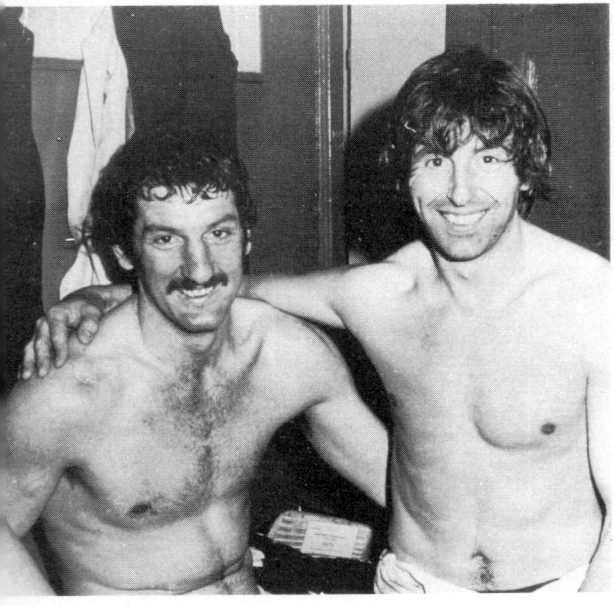

So near and yet so far: Loveridge sails for the Barbarians' line, with Stuart Wilson in support and Brynmor Williams coming across. If Loveridge had not been brutally booted at Bridgend, he would have got there. His bandaged thigh tells the story.

End of the Grand Slam: Mourie and Scotland's captain, Ian McGeechan, joyfully savour victory for one, defeat for the other. Would they thus have smiled if "Geech's" last dropkick had scored?

and dropkicks, immediately revealed why he could have, if he had wanted, made a career in professional soccer. His kick across field to Bowen on the left wing was, in effect, a square pass. The ball bounced kindly and Bowen, sprinting at his fastest, was clear of the first line of defenders as he grasped it. Far upfield, in the great vacant area which theoretically was the All Blacks' defensive zone, McKechnie awaited his man. In a nutshell, the contest was Ireland versus New Zealand.

No Horatius, this McKechnie. Not this time, anyway. Bowen faintly conveyed, with a feint, that he intended to veer left toward the touchline. McKechnie obligingly covered. Instantaneously, Bowen propped infield, still at speed, untouched by human hand. But now his speed was slightly faltering. Carrying the ball was a hindrance. So was the excitement — the match was only five minutes old. Bowen could hear the All Black cover moving at him, Jaffray with a dive almost clipping his heels, Wilson and others running helter-skelter in hurried defence. It was now that the fine moves of the training run paid a dividend. Not five metres from Bowen, Cantillon appeared, fresh, fit and fast. As securely as in the training-run, he held the pass. As he ran in to score beside the left upright, the entire audience of 10,000 and more Irish leaped madly in the air. They leaped madly, moments later, when Ward without the least concern placed the conversion. Yet again, in the 16th minute, with the game not yet into its second quarter, the Munsterians leaped in utter joy. Shaping to catch a very long penalty kick by Ward at goal, 45 metres if a centimetre, McKechnie mulled the ball, knocking it on. Scrum on the spot, Canniffe to put in, the goalposts 15 metres or so distant from Ward. Heel by Pat Whelan. Pass by Canniffe. Dropkick by Ward. Nine points to nil — and, to coin a famous old remark, the way the All Blacks were playing, they were damned lucky to have the nil.

Kiernan was among the critics who believed that the All Blacks could still have won the match but for shortcomings of a consistent and uniformly serious nature. Soon after Cantillon's try, Robertson retired hurt and was replaced by Osborne. In the development of plays, especially for a longish period from half-time when the All Blacks' forwards were decisively in command, it became apparent that Osborne and Wilson could be match-winners if they were given the ball. Regrettably, this was not done. Dunn stifled some attacks, especially on the blindside in the second half, by failing to bring Wilson into the running. Jaffray stifled more — more and more as the play developed frenetic touches in the second half — by aiming to break the line on his own account before letting the threequarters have the ball. Nor were the backs solely at fault. Haden, perhaps the best of all in the team, won ball comfortably against Brendan Foley and Moss Keane and Oliver was a powerful support. But the persistence of the pack in driving plays became the more wearisome at each instance of a succeeding move to put the ball to the backs being frustrated by the magnificent tackling of the Munster men. It could fairly be argued that Mourie was ingenuous in some of his tactical thinking. Certainly it was not a coincidence that the only time on the tour that his team suffered a beating was the one occasion when he was not coolly in command. He allowed excessive hobbling of Donaldson by failing to close the great holes in the front of the lineout through which Whelan, Gerry McLoughlin and Brendan Foley poured. Nor was he able to devise counters to the ball-winning of the tall Number 8, Donal Spring, against the relatively small men, Graham, McGregor and Mourie himself who were posted in the last three places of the line. No doubt, the blindside attacking was the right ploy against the well-poised and suicidally brave Munster defence on the open flank, but for want of adequate support when the ball was carried toward the touchline or turned back to the loose forwards insufficient profit was yielded. Most incompetent of all was McKechnie. Perhaps he escaped execution or the cruellest torture only because he was not to blame for the last, another Ward drop-goal 12 minutes from the end, from which point "MUN-STER! MUN-STER!" became a religious chant. A kick, very long, set Wilson to the chase. As the ball bounced into the All Blacks' in-goal, he moved rather too rapidly in trying to gather it for a punt back to touch or, better, a go at counter-attack. His feet slipped and involuntarily, as his feet went to ground, he touched the ball down. It was ABC stuff for Munster's forwards to heel the ball from the resulting scrum and for Canniffe to pass at such speed that Ward was able to make the kick in total comfort.

Total comfort for Munster, total subjection for the All Blacks. Except on a very, very few occasions, notably in internationals, All Blacks have always managed to score, even in defeat. This time, despite Tommy Kiernan's kindly appreciation, they were out of their class. As an immediate reaction, some of them blamed the Welsh referee, Corrie Thomas, for allowing Munster's men, particularly the wing-forwards and inside backs, excessive latitude in staging their offensive-defensive tackles from offside positions. The real gripe came from Gleeson next day. The All Blacks were waiting to board their bus to trip to Dublin. New Zealand newsmen were either waiting for telephone calls or preparing to catch the train. British newsmen, mostly from Fleet Street, were seeking copy for follow-up to the sensational defeat. Gleeson, not at all a jovial Jack, gave it to them. The Munster men, he charged, had been kamikaze types. Operating outside the law, they had tackled, unquestionably with extraordinary efficiency and bravery, but from illegal positions, sometimes, so Jack said, as far as ten yards — he must have meant metres — ahead of the ball.

Warming up and speaking sternly, Gleeson said the All Blacks had set out on their tour with the intention of playing 15-man rugby. It was vital to the good of the game as a whole that they should do this — rugby had suffered too much from obsessive and excessive defence. But if teams were to adopt the Munster pattern and do all they could to stultify the All Blacks' aims in attack, then the tour would suffer. So, too, would the game.

It was a stern, severe criticism which wanted in fairness on two grounds. It did not sufficiently praise the spirit of Munster or the presence, within the one team, of 15 men who each emerged from the match much larger than life-size. Secondly, it was ingenuous or, more accurately, naive. Gleeson thought it sinful Ward had not once passed the ball. It was worse, he said, that Munster had made aggressive defence the only arm of their attack. Now what on earth, it could be asked, was Kiernan to do with his team? Urge them to become as gormless as London Counties? The very thought was ridiculous. Kiernan held a fine hand with top trumps in Spring, Cantillon, Foley and Whelan in the forwards and Canniffe, Ward, Dennison, Bowen and Moloney in the backs — and even the very best man, who might be reckoned to be Cantillon, was only a wisp ahead of the very worst of the team. What was Kiernan to do — play as New Zealand wanted the match to be played, all open and free, with fine running from first to last? Or play to his strength; which, principally, was the absolute bravery of his men? Tommy Kiernan wasn't born yesterday. He knew what he wanted, and got it. He played to the strength of his team and upon the suspected weaknesses of the All Blacks. If you listen carefully, you may still hear, wafting o'er the Atlantic, the mad, glad cry of "MUN-STER! MUN-STER!" They call Limerick "The Golden Vale". Why not? The tears of the All Blacks may still be running in the broad River Shannon nearby.

No wonder Barry Ashworth cried, "Mercy! Mercy!" Bedad, the fellow must have been clairvoyant.

CHAPTER THREE

At The Watershed

FOR ALL THAT he suffered at and with every move of his team, especially when players blundered, for all, too, that by nature he preferred to make judgments by self-communion rather than by discussion with minds as sharp as his, Jack Gleeson reacted honestly and quickly to faults and failings. His reactions were the swifter when the sins were of commission rather than omission. Once he had had his say, a little more sourly than was justified, about the kamikaze kids, he quickly made an appreciation of the faults of Thomond Park. One was that the lineout defence, especially at the front, would have to be strengthened. Another, that it was essential to have at least one unusually tall man among the three at the back of the lineout. Thirdly, the ball must be controlled at halfback and first five-eighths so that even the liveliest of opposing forwards would be denied the chance to make tackles which would give them the chance to control the subsequent play. Other areas of concern were investigated. The choice of Currie, an untried hand for fullback against Ireland in the first international of the tour, was a bald statement that McKechnie had not measured up. No crystal ball had been needed, at the start of the tour, to ascertain that the selection of McGregor in the touring team had not been warmly supported by Gleeson; and though against Munster the lad had done his best — better than most, decidedly, in the last 20 minutes — his unsuitability on grounds of height alone was so manifest that Gleeson, by his own account, told Ashley he henceforth should play on the flank so that some taller man might be placed at Number 8.

Most significantly, Gleeson considered it essential to abandon, substantially, his intentions and ambitions to make the team a free-running, boldly attacking side, in each match. The approaching season for gifts and goodwill among men should not be anticipated by the All Blacks. Their attitude must be a decent cautiousness allied with a total concentration upon the plaguy stream of errors which had diminished the quality of their finer efforts.

In retrospect, it may be argued that Gleeson allowed himself to meet a new situation rather precipitately. Some of the passion of, for example, the matches against Cardiff and West Wales was reduced. Yet the record stands: Hairy escapes included, there were no further losses. The only reasonable conclusion was that, thanks to Gleeson with his gift for analysis and to Mourie with his gift for quenchless effort, this 1978 team had unusual character.

Meanwhile Gleeson had problems in preparing the All Blacks for their opening international against Ireland. He had been amazed and angered to learn, only a few weeks before the tour, that no fewer than 19 of the team's 23 journeys around the British Isles were to be made by bus; amazed because ample evidence was available of the harmful effects of long journeys on players cooped up in the discomfort of coaches, angered because no member of the New Zealand Rugby Council had troubled to invite his opinion on this mode of travel. (As a matter of fact, the councillors themselves were not even consulted; their role was to rubber-stamp an agreement made by one of their members, R. C. Stuart, while he was representing New Zealand at a meeting of the International Rugby Board in April of 1978.) The preparation for the match with Ireland was harmed in the view of Gleeson by the need to travel by coach from Limerick to Dublin, with a midway stopover for lunch and a training run; then, in the evening, to spend nearly two and a half hours getting to and returning from a reception for the team at the massive country home of the Dublin gynaecologist, Karl Mullen, who had sworn eternal loyalty to New Zealand and New Zealand rugby men from the merry months in mid-1950 when he captained the British Lions on a tour of the country. All told, the All Blacks were required to spend about eight hours in their bus during that day; and *that*, in Gleeson's view, was harmful, not helpful. It also seemed as if the All Blacks were being killed by the kindness of an excessive number of receptions. Limerick had offered them Bunratty Castle and the customary post-match dinner, Dublin offered Dr Mullen's reception (which was just moving into top gear as the All Blacks were being whistled out to their long journey back to the city) and, next evening, a gathering arranged by the New Zealand Ambassador to Ireland, Sir Douglas Carter. Also there were shopping bargains, at the cheapest rates for leatherware, and the excitements of mingling with the brilliant, the witty and the beautiful who are the Irish, whatever their social rank and station.

Not an easy job, therefore, to wind up the All Blacks for the first of their big ones. A special problem which, it could be surmised, cost Gleeson a good part of his beauty sleep, was to face the evidence, so obvious from the Munster match, that the great wing, Bryan Williams, had gone off the boil. As in the final test against the Wallabies, his play had been uncharacteristic. He was not driving irresistibly for the corner-flag. Worse, his venomously effective sidestep had slowed down to an old-fashioned waltz step. In all, he was not playing to international standard. It seemed a great sensation, back in New Zealand, when Williams was omitted from the team for the test. But to those who were there, it was plain that Gleeson was right — "Bee Gee", 100 matches and all, was not up to it.

The Irish, too, were not without their problems. Seldom has the selection of one player over another, this time Colin Patterson, the Ulster scrumhalf, in place of the ranking international, John Moloney, been attacked as fiercely as by the critic of the *Irish Times,* Edmund van Esbeck. "Mr God", as some of the less respectable Irish rugger wits described him, fired 15-inch guns at the selectors. Ned likes to write well-composed pieces and he has a care for good English. But this was an onslaught, a vilification; and but a dim grin appeared on Ned's face at the end of the match when some New Zealander remarked to him: "If Patterson is only Ireland's fourth-best scrumhalf, God help Ireland's opponents in the international championship". There were murmurings, too, against the choice of Michael Gibson, the legendary Lion and international of more than 60 caps, in the centres when his 36th birthday was only a month or so distant. In the previous season, Gibson, pre-eminent as a flyhalf in the 1960s, perhaps the greatest ever, in fact, and equally successful as a centre later on, had supplanted Ireland's captain, Tom Grace, on the right wing and in this strange position had with his genius still done his country proud. But a famous Irish back with 34 caps in the decade ending in 1934, Eugene Davy, presented what was perhaps an expert view. A back, he said, could be moved out from his positions, as Gibson had been, without losing form or quality. But he could never come back; in other words, Gibson the winger could not be restored as Gibson the centre. An interesting opinion, not strongly supported by play in a match in which, in fact, the Irish threequarters were too seldom used. But New Zealanders were among those hosts of Gibson admirers who cheered at the news, a few weeks later, that Mike had decided to retire from international rugby. They did not cheer because Gibson had gone. Rather they cheered because a great player who might otherwise have been beaten by the inexorable march of time had left with his banner fluttering high in the sky. In a tribute on BBC television, Gareth Edwards declaimed rather than suggested that Gibson had been rugby's greatest back. Extravagant praise? Perhaps. Who can hope to offer such a judgment? But it had been a privilege to see the man play.

A bit of Irishness aroused a preliminary interest. Tommy Kiernan's coaching had triumphed with Munster. Would another man of Cork succeed in the bigger job of coaching Ireland? The other chap was Noel

Murphy, a wing-forward with the 1959 and 1966 Lions in New Zealand, and the winner of countless Irish caps. What contrasts — Kiernan, lean, sallow, silent, Murphy, round-faced, bubbling, a constant talker. (Until you learned that Noel as a youth had signed the pledge, you might suspect, from his play at a party, that he was taking at least three jars to the one of every other man.) With a team, Tommy's commands were brief. Noel on the other hand both exhorted and extolled. The special interest for the knowledgeable was that the two were cousins, each harbouring a powerful wish to prove himself the better man.

Invincibility might not be the brand on Irish rugby but who could hope to beat them in any contest for serene civility and courteous sportsmanship? It was a dreadfully hard game. Only one touch of humour found voice. Duggan went to ground. "Willie's first rest," someone said. The Irish, back and forward, tackled heroically, ferociously. Their forwards, heavily outgunned in the lineout, mostly by the majestic Haden, yet thrust like a phalanx or spread to cover all holes. Starting the second half, 3-3, with the wind against them, the team exerted constant, enormous pressure. Anywhere within 40 yards of the posts, Ward menaced with his kicks at goal. The All Blacks resisted. Yet in the 20th minute of the second half, the match was still in crisis, perhaps favouring Ireland because of the soulful backing of the crowd of 50,000. At this point, within a short space, the untried man, the neophyte of the All Black team, made two efforts which were critical to the victory. First Currie tackled McLennan as he hared down the left wing. Next, he stood, silent and still as a statue, while a towering Garryowen by Ward fell from on high into his arms and the Irish pack in a mad charge rushed upon him. It was a supreme test not so much of rugby quality as of manhood. Currie did not falter. He claimed the fair catch as the horde engulfed him. One sensed that Clive Norling, a smiler as a referee, may have laughed in the joy of watching such courage as he awarded the mark.

This was a critical point, perhaps *the* critical point because if the Irish had capitalised on a Currie blunder nothing could have stopped them. But there were other critical points. The famous Welsh flyhalf, Cliff Morgan, who twice in the one season of 1953-54 helped to beat All Black teams and who two years later was a god among the British Lions who shared a series with the Springboks in South Africa, expatiated on one or two of them when he said: "With a little bit of quickness in their inside backs, the All Blacks could have scored twice in the first half and three times in the second. If the All Blacks are to keep on winning their big games, these are the weaknesses they must strengthen." It was sound criticism. Donaldson began nervously, steadied and, at the finish, brilliantly set going the winning move. Or nearly the finish. In the last moments of play, down by the New Zealand goalline, Duggan stood on his foot, tearing or straining tendons beyond hope of full recovery for the rest of the tour. Willie then administered a sharp kick on the backside. It was repayment for the boot Donaldson had put into his back when the Lions played Manawatu in 1977, a kick that cost Donaldson preferment until the All Blacks to tour France were chosen. Outside Donaldson, especially at Bruce and Taylor, the incidence of errors, or slow reaction to chances, was too high. Bruce, put into the clear in the Irish quarter, was gathered with ease. Running with a 3 to 2 situation building, he jabbed a grub-kick down the field. Taylor with fewer chances appeared to want a yard or so of the speed essential to midfield breaking at international level, in which the average rate of speed is so much higher than at lower levels. So the threequarters were not much used; and, defensively, it was scary to see Wilson rushing in upon McKibbin as the Irish backs were moving the ball to McLennan on the left wing. Perhaps the disjointedness of the All Black attack in the backline marked the start of the austerity required by Gleeson after the Munster defeat.

The play opened sensationally. Ireland were offside at the first lineout. From 53 metres, give or take a centimetre, Seear set the ball down to try at goal. What price glory? Alas, none. Nor was glory visible in Seear's next appearance in the limelight — he got in the way and Donaldson was caught trying to clear from an early scrummage. The contest was fierce, the All Blacks winning, on the whole, more of the ground. But they lost a heel on their own put-in, which was worrying because the Irish lock, Spring, at 14 stone 2 pounds was an odd pea in the pod of so many mastodons. But when a very long kick by Taylor compelled Moloney to scrabble the ball into touch about 15 metres in front of his own line, Bruce at a resultant scrummage neatly and assuredly dropped a goal for the first points. Joy was soon confined. Seear picked up too soon as the scrum was wheeling and from 40 metres Ward, dead centre, placed the goal. Currie might be good at catching but he was not good at kicking, chances of 40 and 25 metres being muffed. Soon into the second half, Bruce plucked from the air a fast, soaring pass by Donaldson and with calm precision dropped his second goal. Which was nullified a few minutes later when Ward, having lifted a high punt toward the New Zealand goalmouth, was hindered as he chased the ball. From 24 metres, after that stupid late-charge, he effortlessly placed the goal. Williams had come on vice Ford, who had suffered a serious cut on the knee and, very late, it was Williams who was called forward when New Zealand were given a penalty 44 metres distant. What a touch of romance it would have been if the man Gleeson had supplanted had kicked the winning goal!

He was no more fortunate than had been Ward with a kick of 40 metres a little time before which, remarkably, slewed in flight. So the game built up to the grand climax of a lineout 10 or 15 metres from the Irish line and from which it was intended that the All Black backs should attack to the right, with all forces chucked in for the winning score. A human error by Haden, who tapped the ball down before he could manage to grasp it, forestalled the planned move but, dramatically, won the game. As he saw the bouncing ball, Donaldson moved rapidly from right to left to pick it up and, at full speed, tore around the short end of the line, past Whelan. With extraordinary promptitude, Dalton and Johnstone saw the break and lined up inside, now on the gallop themselves, to offer support. At precisely the right moment, with Patterson coming across, Donaldson passed infield. Dalton made the catch even as Johnstone instinctively shaped to do so; and it was Dalton with a great heave who got himself over the goalline to score.

Irish eyes in the terraces were not smiling. In the nearby grandstand, complaint was raised that Donaldson had stepped into touch. (The Welsh touch-judge, Ken Rowlands, totally dismissed the suggestion.) Despite the disappointment, Shay Deering marshalled his men. They attacked hard, Kennedy going past Williams down the touchline and Gibson with artistic skill offering a dummy in a zealous attempt to thrust through the wall of tacklers at the left corner. They were still there, or thereabouts, at the last whistle.

Whereafter there had to be praise, with qualifications, for the All Blacks for jumping their first hurdle and praise unstinted for the Irish in their charming reaction to a defeat that must have been desperately disappointing to them all. "It was," said Deering, "a most enjoyable game." It was, too. All of the players, at no-side, and later, fell into each others' arms in the ultimate salute of champions who had expended every effort for their teams; but how many captains, beaten at the last trump, would stress as a first reaction the enjoyment of the game? Rugby does not breed more gentle gentlemen than Kevin Quilligan, president of the Irish Rugby Union; and from him, too, the salutation was memorable. "Victory," he said, "rested where it belonged at the end of an enthralling afternoon." It is the ultimate paradox that the Irish who are so bitter in their politics are so gentle — yet still fierce — in their sport. "Ah, what the hell," said one man. "We are the world's best losers. We have so much practice at it."

Magnificent were Haden and Mourie, a surging powerhouse of high voltage was Oliver, the lineout with Haden and Seear in control won 26 possessions to 9, an amazing superiority. Put to the test, all of the All Black forwards responded to a point past exhaustion. The courage of Currie, the speed and resolution of Osborne, Donaldson's sharp breakaways, the lightning moves of Wilson — these were all memorable aspects. But you would not easily match the Irish — Deering, Keane, Byrne, Spring and Slattery — for courage. Patterson in 80 minutes, first time out, established himself at international grade, Ward, no longer merely a cunning kicker, finely varied his play, Moloney's lantern jaw stuck out like an impregnable rock and in one moment here and another there Gibson's grace shone all round. Let Heaven be the more warmly praised if it can ordain that all rugger internationals can be as clean and sporting and exciting and manly as this.

CHAPTER FOUR

Time And Chance

IT WAS A quiet time for the All Blacks while they were in Belfast, preparing for, and then beating Ulster. As ever, Ulstermen were glad to welcome them. One never knew which was which, Catholic or Protestant. It was unimportant. What was important was that they were fine, decent, hospitable people. Their situation seemed to have improved. There was even talk that peace might be around the next corner, or the next but one.

Within a few days, mad bigots of each side were back on the job, killing and maiming with their bullets, blasting buildings with their bombs.

Except for the excitements inevitable to test-match week in Wales, it was quiet, too, at Porthcawl and in Cardiff. The principal activity was speculation, not on the market or in the exchange but as to the outcome of the international. Could the All Blacks take a further step toward their Grand Slam? Could Wales beat New Zealand for the first time since 1953? Arguments waxed, arguments waned. In the end, they were only arguments.

In the space of a few seconds, much was changed. At a late lineout of the match, strange events, unprecedented in all of New Zealand's international rugby history, occurred. Accusations, bitterness, hostility, a dangerous threat to sporting peace, developed. The All Blacks were accused of cheating. It was a hard word. It was a hard thought to stomach and live with.

It was, then, a week for becoming acquainted with the faults, even the murderous failings in other people and misguided enthusiasm in one's own. But had it not been said before, in Ecclesiastes, that "under the sun the race is not to the swift, nor the battle to the strong, nor bread to the wise, nor riches to the intelligent, nor favour to the men of skill; but time and chance happen to them all"?

Time and chance. What a phrase. It was complained as to the All Blacks while they trained to play Ulster that they should not have been cooped up in a hotel, the Dunadry Inn, about 15 miles from the heart of Belfast, with orders not to move without police escort. Rather, in the interests of their broader education it was said they should have been either quartered in the city or allowed to spend time in it, experiencing at first-hand the security checks at shopping centres and travelling to some areas, such as the Falls Road, where the murdered could be numbered, over the years, in scores. No doubt such adventurings would have made a profound impression on all of the New Zealanders. What outsider could fail to react to the quaint humour of the Irish who gestured toward parts of the Crumlin Road and the Falls Road areas while describing the places as "The Happy Dumping-Grounds"? At sight of the Dungannon club's ties, old hands naturally asked about the club which had entertained the 1974 All Blacks to lunch as a break in their journey from Belfast to Galway. What was the news, for example, of the club's president, David Steele, who had been so merry with his hospitality and so interesting in describing how and why Dungannon was no longer the seat of the Earls of Ranfurly, one of whom had presented New Zealand with its most famous trophy? "Did you not know?" was the answer. "Did you not know that David was taken from his car and murdered?" Moyra Gibson, the slim, brunette wife of the great player and as concentrated an enthusiast for rugby as you might find in the world, had to be drawn out before she would talk of the effect upon her, as a Belfast housewife, of the bombings. Yes, she said at last; at every blast — and she had heard plenty — she was in instant fear that Mike, at his legal office in the city, might be buried beneath the bricks. Ronnie Lamont, a slashing wing-forward of Campbell-Lamerton's British Lions in New Zealand in 1966 and, one would suggest, the finest type of schoolmaster, gestured through a classroom door at a little boy, perhaps 10, who, head on hand, doodled with a pencil. Matter-of-factly, Lamont said the boy's father, but a short time before, had been found guilty of the murder of 12 Catholics and a party to the deaths of another eight. "It is said about here, by both parties," said Ronnie, gesturing at his own area in Springfield Road and across a barren no-man's-land, 200 metres wide, of empty, battered, shattered houses and apartments, toward the Falls Road, "that the only good Irishman of the other party is a dead one." He did not declaim his patriotism by beating his breast; but, as a Northern Irishman, he wanted to see Northern Ireland freed of fear and violence and hatred; and he was prepared to keep on living there to do what he could to bring about these changes. "The only solution," he said, "is integrated education."

Time and chance. Would it have charmed New Zealand if, in the interests of liberalism for the All Blacks, they had been allowed to wander at the cost of the life of one of them from a sniper's bullet? The authorities dared not take the chance. Dunadry, therefore, it had to be.

Not entirely a house of pleasure. The bar prices, like the Belfast atmosphere, were murderous. Not entirely a place sympathetic to All Blacks, either. A wild rampage through the inn by a small group of the team of 1972-73 on the night of the defeat of Ulster had caused such damage that, before departure the next day, the team's manager, the late Ernie Todd, had to pay compensation of £500. It was during this wild party that security men, who in those hysterically anxious days were notably quick on the draw, fingered triggers while proposing to certain All Blacks that they abandon their intention to throw a piano from a first-floor window. The roisterings of that night were not without influence on the unique event of All Black touring, the expulsion of a player from the team.

The time was there but the chance was not taken when in the match with Ulster, won by the All Blacks by 23 to 3, Dunn and Jaffray as inside backs and Loveday and Fleming as lineout specialists were put out to the test to see whether they could be considered for the international team. The man of greatest consequence was Dunn. The average rate of speed of the All Blacks was high. Their stamina was sound. Man for man, they were rather faster and fitter than most opponents. At scrumhalf, they were well endowed. Their threequarters were fast if not quite, perhaps, express, though Wilson, wound up, moved into stride swiftly and held his rhythm well. The need seemed to be to improve the rate of movement next door to the scrum either in the passing of the ball or in a breaking run by a chosen player. It had been desolating to watch Bruce incapable of capitalising open ground in the Irish international, the more so because it was evident he himself knew he lacked sufficient speed. Could Dunn after that glorious piece of slick dummying and running for his try against London Counties be persuaded to utilise his superior natural speed and thus strengthen the All Black attack at a vital point?

In the event, taking Munster, Ulster and one or two other matches as a criterion, one had to accept that Eddie, as yet, wanted the confidence to exploit his potential. Had his brilliance as a youth of 18, newly entered into the North Shore Teachers College in Auckland, been decisively and consistently encouraged, it is possible that, by now, he would have been a seasoned international of exceptional quality. But Auckland's selector of the time, Mr Eric Boggs, preferred other men, as was, of course, his right and Dunn languished, unripened. Maoris as a race are shy. They find their own level by their own means. They cannot suddenly be rushed, or pushed, into explosive development of their skills. Unwanted in Auckland, Dunn tended to become isolated within himself, trusting too greatly, as his principal attacking weapon, on the ball held high in one hand and suggestively jerked in the motions of a pass. Now that he was wanted by New

Zealand, his confidence was awakened. He aroused the critical, and admiring, interest of such acute students of his position as Carwyn James, Barry John and Cliff Morgan, all three of exceptional skill in the same place. But his development was, at best, partial. Philosophising, one wonders whether Dunn might have repaid some special attention, an acute psychological understanding, by acquiring in the space of a few matches a confidence in his ability to react efficiently to the demands of his place in the team and especially to the development of the highest possible rate of speed in passing and handling.

So far as could be judged, Ulster was to be his final test of the tour for the internationals. Very sadly indeed, Eddie flunked. He fielded far too many of Loveridge's passes while anchored to the spot. In the second half, when the All Blacks, with the keen, cold wind behind them, could have been expected to quintuple their half-time score of 7 to 0, he kicked excessively. In all, the All Blacks managed only three tries; by Williams (grimly fighting to establish that he was still a first-choice player), Black and Kururangi. For the rest they had to rely upon goalkicks. Without diminishing Ulster's qualities of courage, not better expressed than by Patterson in sharply nipping around Loveridge's ankles and by the locks, Dermot Dalton and Willie Anderson, in outpointing Loveday and Fleming, the All Blacks ought to have scored more often. When Jaffray, at the times that he received the ball, also began to hoist it high with his boot, the rhythm and cohesion of the threequarters were undeveloped; and the strenuous foraging of the forwards, especially by Loveday, a human tank, Bush and the two Ashworths, while it was an outstanding feature of the play, still yielded insufficient dividends.

Ironically, Ulster suffered a similar grievous fault. Their flyhalf, Adrian Goodrich, was also obsessed with what is sometimes charitably described as tactical punting — in other words, getting rid of the damned thing and hoping for a mulled catch or a lucky bounce when the ball came down. So Gibson flourished on attack only once, with a lightning thrust terminated when an All Black came at him on the angle. For so wise a head he was most comprehensively beaten by a most delicate piece of skulduggery by Robertson at full gallop. Gibson's partner at centre, Alan Irwin, experienced little joy, too, and the right wing, Joey Miles, who six years before had stood toe to toe and traded blow for blow with Grant Batty in an exhilarating demonstration of wound-up threequarterism, was offered scarcely more than a walking-on part. Which was a misfortune because those Ulster forwards really were goers, even when Loveday, bent almost double, was charging into their groupings like a battering-ram. Dalton and Anderson were topnotchers at the lineout and in the backrow

Stewart McKinney, Harry Steele and a smallish but most industrious flanker, Alan McLean, all did their share of breathing heavily down the necks of Loveridge, Dunn and anyone else who was handy.

Did Gleeson's understanding of men, one of his strong points, fail in the rocket he later delivered at Dunn? It was an interesting thought. On the night before the match, he strongly emphasised in his talk to Belfast coaches that the capital sin was to kick away well-won ruck ball. "So what do we do next day?" he asked. "Kick away ruck ball!" In compensation, Jack was extraordinarily acute in appointing Bush to lead the forwards. Billy had been around a long time, on many tours, and temperamentally was more strongly armoured than Dunn. But Billy, too, could be self-doubting. To find himself promoted, appointed, so to speak, rangatira — ah, what powerful effect that stroke of genius yielded! No one slacked with Billy about. In fierce pride for his team, for New Zealand, he drove and commanded his men, leading, as often as not, by example. The consequence wasn't perfection; but if the backs had played as well as the forwards in the open running of the game, for a surety the half-time score would have been sextupled.

For all the cover of cloud, the sun was still up there, shining, when the teams of Wales and New Zealand emerged on to the Arms Park of Cardiff, the National Stadium of Wales, to play the tenth match between the countries. It was a question whether, under the sun, the race would be to the swift, or the battle to the strong, or whether time and chance would take command. The countries had met nine times before. Wales had won thrice, always at the Arms Park, in 1905, 1935 and 1953 and had scored 63 points. New Zealand had won twice at home, in 1969, and four times in Wales, three at the Arms Park and once, in 1924, at St Helens, and had scored 129 points. Would this be as grim a day as in 1972, when the decision of the English referee, Johnnie Johnson, not to award a late try to J. P. R. Williams because he had rabbited the ball over the goalline gave New Zealand the narrowest of wins, 19 to 16, and precipitated a violent blast of criticism against Johnson? It was to be hoped not. As J. P. R. was to say, later, after his unfortunate Bridgend wounding, rugby had lately taken a good many knocks and it could ill use a few more. Sharp little comic that he was, Cliff Morgan did his best to dissipate hostility in the atmosphere. For four hours of the test-match morning, he ran a BBC radio programme of reminiscence by a vast number of players and commentators who, with their gentle middle-aged humour amazed and amused with their stories of incidents and personalities. That madly-keen enthusiast, Richard Burton, the actor, told how he had become a supporter of the young Llanelli wizard, Lewis Jones who, because of injury to the great centre of the time, Bleddyn Williams, was first capped for Wales against England. In those days of 1950 before ear-transistors, Burton *had* to know from the cast of *Hamlet* at the Old Vic how his country and his idol were getting on. Well-versed Shakespeareans in the matinee audience may have been bemused, that afternoon, by the strange arm-wavings of Ophelia, Queen, Mercutio et al., as they made their entrances. The gestures conveyed that with the movement of the match Wales were in the lead, were establishing authority and were marching to triumph by 11 points to 5. So was Burton, or Hamlet, kept up with the news. At the last, Hamlet sinks down and exclaims: "The rest is silence". It was intriguing to ponder the possibility that this Hamlet, having expired, waited only for the last unwrinkling of the final curtain before rising to his feet with a bellow of triumph.

Other preliminaries were less edifying. Young New Zealanders who ran about the field waving banners reacted disagreeably when Russell Thomas later said, as a veteran of even worse goings-on at fields in South Africa during the tour of the 1976 All Blacks, that he intended to arrange with the authorities of all subsequent fields that these activities should be stopped. They were, said Thomas, undignified. Hear, hear. It was not in the least amusing for New Zealanders to gaze upon two young men — presumably their kinsmen — who marched up the field bearing a banner which proclaimed that "Keith Murdoch Walks the Water". Nor were the All Blacks glad to be joined by a Maori in civilian clothes when they offered their haka. Other preliminaries, Welsh, were more exhilarating. The singing was fine, clear, loud and tuneful. "My Hen Wlad Fan Dhu" — "Land of Our Fathers" — was glorious. Every Welshman there present — and there would have been 47,500 of them if the Welsh Rugby Union, through their most charming secretary, Bill Clement, had not been so extraordinarily generous in providing tickets for New Zealanders — felt uplifted.

By purpose, Wales took the kick-off. As arranged, Gareth Davies kicked deep. New Zealand, it was well known rather than surmised, would clear to touch just out of their own quarter. Wales would then assemble a short lineout, win the ball and require Terry Holmes, in the manner of a Gareth Edwards, to hoist a tremendous up-and-under to the goalline. Here the New Zealanders, in panic, would concede either a try or a penalty. By the time they emerged from shock, the All Blacks, the crafty Welsh well knew, would be a beaten team; and the Arms Park would ring again and again with cheers for the glorious Red Dragons.

Time and chance were not here involved. The riches were to the intelligent. At Gleeson's precise instructions, Wilson, who caught the kick-off, began a long run up the middle of the field. When the ball did get to touch, the play was at about halfway. And, Bobby Windsor later told Gleeson, the Welsh were confused. Their plan had come unstuck. What was to happen now?

What did happen for a minute or two was graceless. Wheel at the lineout punched at Oliver and after Bryan Williams had failed to convert the penalty from about 45 metres J. P. R. Williams was late-tackled and Billy Bush, eyes blazing, came out fighting. Mr Roger Quittenton as referee moved smartly to tell the captains they must subdue their men and only a little less quickly awarded Wales a 22-metre penalty which Davies goaled. The 30 players, it was evident, were in a state of fervour. As the saying goes, they were beside themselves in excitement and with the passion of the encounter. One expression of the qualities cost the All Blacks young Currie. Standing steadfast, as against Ireland, to claim a mark, he was ruthlessly smashed down by Fenwick. Slightly concussed, jaw fractured, he left the field and, most unhappily for the team and himself, the tour. As another expression of excitement, Mourie, defending desperately five metres from his own goalline, was penalised and from close to the touchline, 22 metres out, Davies expertly goaled. Four minutes later, McKechnie, the fateful man of Munster, took the field. It was a great moment for him. A greater moment, for New Zealand, because of him, awaited.

Amid the clamour, for by now every man, woman and child at the park was totally involved, the teams clashed, men hurtled at each other. It was not a question of courage. Men wearing red jerseys saw only men in black, men in black regarded men in red as being, for a space of time, mortal enemies. All were utterly committed. Allan Martin, a famous long-range goalkicker, failed with an effort from 54 metres. In a rousing counter-attack, Osborne, Bruce and Robertson slashed past many defenders until their last support, Wilson, was left with nowhere to go. McKechnie struck an unresponsive upright with a penalty kick from 32 metres and because B. G. Williams was adjudged to have late-tackled J. J. Williams — who it was alleged, acted his part better than Richard Burton could hope to have done — Fenwick was offered a penalty chance from more than 40 metres. He slashed at the ball rather than kicked it and, dutifully the goal soared over. After 22 minutes, Wales led by 9 points to nil. For New Zealanders, the end of the world was nigh.

It was not reasonable to suppose that New Zealand could win the game. Gordon Rowley might be right. Welsh rugby might be in disrepair and need four years of mending. The losses within the preceding year of Gareth Edwards, retired rather than be proclaimed a professional because of the best-seller book written for him by the former English cricket captain, Tony Lewis; Gerald Davies (John Dawes's candidate for best-back ever, a fraction ahead of Mike

Gibson); Phil Bennett and Terry Cobner were, it was said, tragic. No one troubled to mention that the All Blacks had lost, mostly by retirement, such first-string players as Grant Batty, Sid Going, Lawrie Knight, Duncan Robertson, Ian Kirkpatrick, Tane Norton and Kent Lambert — any three of whom could have strengthened the touring team significantly. But in the preceding Home international season, Wales had won the Triple Crown for the third successive year and scored a third outright win in four years in the Five Nations Championship. "This makes one wonder," said the celebrated critic, Vivian Jenkins, "what is left for them to achieve." "The results speak for themselves," said the Welsh coach, John Dawes. "The team deserves to be recognised as one of the greatest of all time." Since the bulk of the team were still available for selection and were in fact retained to play against the All Blacks, it seemed right to presume that the side was not a great deal removed from still being, in Dawes's estimation, one of the greatest. And, in fact, in building up a 9-0 lead in the first quarter and establishing in the third quarter undoubted superiority over the All Blacks in the forward encounter, Wales could well lay claim to being unbeatable on the day.

Even when, two minutes after the Fenwick goal, the All Blacks scored the only try of the match, Wales still looked unreachable and unbeatable when, two minutes later, Davies capitalised a gross refereeing blunder by placing a penalty from only ten metres in front of the All Black posts. 12 to 4 with 52 minutes of play remaining — no real Welsh team, let alone one of the greatest, could possibly lose.

Let us return to our muttons: Wilson's try in the right-hand corner was brilliant opportunism. Osborne, fielding from Bruce on about the Welsh quarter-line, weaved into position before punting toward the corner-flag. At Jack Gleeson's instruction, he had practised the move the day before. Wilson accelerated as he chased. He skilfully capitalised the advantage over Clive Rees who had to turn slightly before hunting for the ball. Wilson was a good yard or more ahead as he dived for the bouncing ball, eyes well open, everything concentrated on contact. He made it; and McKechnie, with one of his better kicks, was just a little unlucky not to place the conversion from wide out by the touchline.

The Roger Quittenton blunder would have been the more serious if it had cost the All Blacks the game. Round about halfway, the Welsh backs attacked and Fenwick, receiving, put in a very long kick which bounced about ten metres from the goalposts. Coincidentally, Osborne hindered, charged or tackled, whichever you like, Ray Gravell, Fenwick's partner. Quittenton reacted excitedly, whistling and pointing down the field. He quietened down as Mourie, moving behind him, said, "That man (Gravell) was not carrying the ball, ref." "Too late now," said Quittenton, in admission of his fault. (The All Blacks, it may be said, never publicly referred to, let alone criticised, the decision. Would other touring teams have been as restrained?)

At any rate, there it was: 12 to 4. The All Blacks could pack their bags and go back to Porthcawl, to New Zealand, anywhere. Because of artlessness, or dumbness, or something, they had thrown away the match.

The key to the mysterious misadventures of the Welsh in giving away a match they could not possibly lose occurred just on half-time when, after an attack on the blindside by Bruce, Seear and Williams, Holmes was penalised and McKechnie from about 22 metres placed the goal.

12 to 7 was a good deal more alluring than 12 to 4. The narrowing of the lead commanded in the All Blacks a more scrupulous attention to the job. Wherefore Oliver deserved to be larruped with a cat-o'-nine-tails when in the 14th minute of the second half he punched the new cap, Paul Ringer, after the whistle had blown. It was a fretful, childish, petulant act and the All Blacks could go down on their knees in gratitude when J. P. R. awarded the kick to Davies and not to Fenwick. The range was beyond Davies; and the All Blacks raged back behind a long dropout by Bruce and an even longer penalty into touch, 45 metres if a centimetre, by the same man, to a lineout of the 16th minute in which Johnstone won the ball and, coincidentally, the Welsh backs breached the 10-metre gap. From rather more than 30 metres, McKechnie knocked over the goal which reduced the Welsh lead to 12 to 10.

The Welsh still looked like doing it. Their forwards were magnificent. Young Ringer was doing a mighty job of foraging and tackling. Squire was his blood-brother, Martin was outleaping Haden, Quinnell as a battling old hand was keeping his men to their work. Had Davies converted the penalty against Oliver, the All Blacks would have lost. Had Holmes, helped by a whistle in the neighbouring crowd which momentarily checked many of the All Blacks and Welsh, made one more yard in a startling break toward the posts or been a little more careful in the pass which J. J. Williams comprehensively mulled, New Zealand most certainly would have been done all over again. Yet these gifts were withheld. So the play moved upfield and downfield, at pace and with power. Hymns and arias were sung out by the crowd and the New Zealand contingent at suitable moments chanted "Black! Black!" and feverishly crossed everything they possessed to ward off the evil moment of defeat.

Mere minutes from no-side, the forwards formed a lineout about 35 metres from the Welsh goalline. Bobby Windsor to throw in. He threw in. Very curiously, inexplicably, Quittenton ordered a re-throw by

Windsor. As the ball came in again, three events determined the match. Wheel was the party of the first part in error when he placed his left hand on Oliver's right shoulder and, using leverage, rose high for the ball. Haden was the party of the second part when, two places back, far from the ball, he abruptly turned and threw himself full length toward his own goalline. It was a dive to end all dives; and because Haden had neither been touched nor pushed, the only possible inference was that it was his intention to persuade Quittenton that he had been so grossly obstructed by a Welsh forward that New Zealand must be awarded a kick at goal. The party of the third part was Oliver. While endless playbacks in slow motion established that he was used as a lever by Wheel and that he, too, turned or was turned to face his own goalline, both hands about head-high or a little higher, before he flung down full-length, they could not conclusively establish that it was his intention to gull Quittenton into awarding New Zealand a penalty that might win the game. Oliver said: "We had to win the ball if we wanted to win the game. I tried to win the ball. I have never dived in my life. I would never dive." He is a fine footballer. More pertinently, he is a man of integrity. No more can be said.

But, so far as Quittenton was concerned, only the party of the first part counted. He was standing on the Welsh side of the lineout, facing infield. As Wheel began his climb, a finger accusingly pointed and a whistle piercingly sounded. In horror, Wales as a team and the Arms Park as a representative body of Welshmen grasped that a goalable penalty had been awarded against them. It was not in the kind of silence to which Hamlet departed that McKechnie came forward to act his part in the most important moment of his sporting life. Fifteen metres infield, 35 metres from goal. A lonely prospect, indeed. Not now the moment for determining whether the race was to the swift or the battle to the strong. Time and chance had coincided to happen to all in the game. The question was whether McKechnie had the skill to be favoured.

He hit his goalkick as Jack Nicklaus hits most 7-irons — high, far, dead-centre. The ball was climbing as it soared between the uprights. McKechnie turned about, clenching his fist above his head in triumph. Groans, whistles, cheers, jeers sounded and resounded through the last moments of the game.

"The Case of the Lineout Dive" was endlessly dissected on television, over the radio, in the Press. "They were cheating," said Clem Thomas of the *Observer*. "They were doing something entirely and directly against the ethics of the game." A kindlier but much more wounding word was used by Peter West of *The Times*. The All Blacks, he said, had used a ploy which was "unworthy".

Within the media, the reactions were bitter. The *Western Mail*, the

Welsh national daily, disappointed no one, friend or foe, by spending most of the week assailing the All Blacks. John Reason in the *Daily Telegraph* established beyond all reasonable doubt that Quittenton had been right to penalise Wheel. Russell Thomas put a zip on Haden's mouth, turned the padlock and threw away the key (it was not until the television playbacks had been dissected that the stones began to fly at Oliver). Jack Gleeson conceded to Kevin McMenamin of the *Christchurch Press* and Ron Palenski, head of the London office of the New Zealand Press Association, that he had not been pleased with Haden. He then was most mightily annoyed that they printed his comments.

The case could rest. Not all the king's horses nor all the king's men can get Roger to see it again — the other way. Yet, most curiously, as two great All Blacks, Kelvin Tremain and Dennis Young, from the day after the match led their 86-strong supporters' party hither and thither through Wales they in no place encountered hostility from the noble people who are the heart and soul of Welsh rugby. "Did we not have 75 percent of the ball and 75 percent of the game, I ask you," was the tenor of average statements, "and did we not fail to score? Who can be to blame for the Welsh defeat but the Welsh? Don't you worry about the newspapers, man. They don't speak for us, the real people of Wales. We could have won and didn't. Who is to blame? Us!" The Tremain party was entertained by, among others, the Treorchy Male Voice Choir, very famous, also, most oddly, 86 strong. "There were 86 of them and 86 of you," someone said to Tremain. "Did you not take up the challenge?" "We sang them 'Now Is the Hour'," said Tremain. "That was as much as we — and they — could take."

Nominate as heroes the halfbacks, Donaldson and Loveridge. Donaldson was first choice. He trained. He went to Gleeson. "I cannot do it," he said. "The foot will not stand the strain. You would be wrong to play me." Donaldson went to Loveridge, shook his hand and wished him well. Loveridge all of a sudden had to adjust his thinking from not-wanted to most urgently needed. The Welsh forwards came at him hard. He was constantly under pressure. He did not flinch. In the miraculous manner of Mourie's All Blacks, he kept right on to the end of the road, keeping right on to the end. Of such stuff as Mark and David were the 1978 All Blacks made. Who could ask for better?

CHAPTER FIVE

There'll Always Be An England

IF THERE'S ALWAYS to be an England in rugby, it might be helpful if steps were taken to eradicate Twickenhamitis from it. Sweeping through Bristol (worst hotel of the tour), Leicester (best hotel of the tour) and Aldershot (best dinner of the tour) before they reached London to play against England, the All Blacks encountered men and teams who were stiff of sinew, strong of fibre, proud and most unwilling to accept defeat. Whatever the record book may convey about the Bristol match against South and South West Counties, won 20 to nil, the Leicester match with Midland Counties, won 20 to 15, and the Aldershot match against Combined Services, won 34 to 6, the fact was that the All Blacks had to huff and puff to win all three. In each place, the opposition was vigorous.

Few of the Services' team regularly played in first-class club teams yet at half-time the All Blacks led by only 7 to 6. At Bristol, the All Blacks were startled by a young lineout man, Paul Ackford, who not only leaped to a remarkable height but who also palmed the ball down to his scrumhalf, Peter Kingston, as if he were delivering it on a plate. When Midlands' fullback, "Dusty" Hare — William Henry Hare, if you preferred formality — took a free kick from at least 40 metres, you came to be reminded of the individualistic qualities of great English players, starting with the most eminent of eccentrics, Peter Jackson, genius among wing-threequarters, who sold dummies and sidesteps as modern machinery shells peas. Hare turned his back on the All Blacks' goal. Was he, one wondered, cogitating? Terrified by his task? Overcoming some slight nervous disorder characteristic of his family in the presence of hounds? "Dusty" fiddled the ball. He dropped it down on his foot. As it rebounded into his hands, he swung about and dropped the most almighty goal you could ever wish to see. This was fascinating. So was the burrowing done by the Services' pack, led by an RAF man, Nigel Gillingham, on the Aldershot field, a superb example of well-planned spending of taxpayers' money on which the lights from tall standards blazed down through the game.

At the end of this brief swing-around through part of the heart of English rugby, the All Blacks returned to London. England, mighty England, was the goal. The England which had fielded some of the dirtiest but hardest forwards in history against the '24 Invincibles, which had walloped the '35 All Blacks by 13 to nil, which had yielded only one goal in losing in '53 by nil to 5, which at Eden Park in 1973 had swarmed all over the All Blacks after losing all three of its preceding matches against provincial teams. If history were a guide, Mourie's men would have trouble with this one. In the event, their victory by 16 points to 6 was a criticism of themselves. They were scandalously at fault in failing to win by at least 30 points. The chance might even have been there for them to win by a greater score than the 1951-52 Springboks mounted against Scotland in that mournful Murrayfield massacre of 44 points to nil.

Did English players invited to tread the holy ground now do so in fear where once their predecessors had thrust out the red rose on their white jerseys as if it were a rosette on their body-armour? Was Twickenhamitis a disease which spread from player to player like a virus? Or was it introduced by outside agencies? This debate was not fascinating. It was depressing.

Meanwhile, Bristol's Memorial Ground introduced the All Blacks for the first time to winter. Though the day to start with was dry, a cold, blustery wind blew across the field. The pitch was bare in places. Heavy rain fell later. Not, you might say, a comfortable place. But, like the Boy Scouts, the All Blacks had been prepared. Their rooms at the Unicorn appeared to have been planned by the architects who set up the Seven Dwarfs. It was checkerboard comfort. If you moved yourself, you had to move some other piece first. Seear and Haden among the longer-legged lads gazed speculatively at their beds, wondering what kind of ball they were to wrap themselves into. The Unicorn had been chosen, the All Blacks were told, because the Wallabies of a year or two before who had been placed in the Holiday Inn had not been welcomed with the warmth the West, a great rugger area, likes to show to its rugby visitors. But comfort means much to tourists and when the All Blacks, next stop, were placed in the magnificent Holiday Inn at Leicester, it seemed incomprehensible that this fundamental necessity had not been appreciated in the Bristol booking. Maybe it was at the Unicorn, or some place like it, that the composer of "Little Boxes" got his inspiration.

The West, as before remarked, has been great rugger country. Bristol spawned England's most capped player, John Pullin, the sturdy hooker whose teams of 1972 and 1973 brought off the extraordinary feats of beating South Africa at Johannesburg and New Zealand at Auckland respectively. In 11 seasons from 1966, John, as straight, as fine, as true a rugby man as you could ever hope to meet, won 42 caps. It was in Bristol that New Zealand rugby men first learned that oft-sung song. "Ting-a-ling, you're a bloody liar", which takes the mickey out of the boring, or pretentious. "Thank you, All Blacks," said the West Country captain, J. A. Gregory, to Bob Stuart's team of 1953, "for playing robust but not rough rugby." Like a shot his West Country lads bounced out their "ting-a-ling" and in the best of good humours told him he was a bloody liar. (It had been the kind of game, in fact, in which the teams, without indulging in stoush, had left marked impressions upon each other.) From the West, too, had come the wistful memory of one of their greatest players, Tom Voyce, a wing-forward of legendary qualities during the 1920s. He was talking to a group of New Zealand supporters about the match at Twickenham between England and New Zealand in 1924 — January 3, 1925, to be precise — from which the giant Hawke's Bay forward, Cyril Brownlie, had been banished for kicking a man on the ground. It had always lain on his conscience, Voyce said, that he had not walked, too. Fifty-five years later, he was still about, lean and spare and, among initiates, and for a long, long time past, a legend in his lifetime.

Now that they were approaching the halfway point of their tour, the All Blacks, it was to be supposed, would be consolidating their techniques, forsaking all errors, concentrating their strengths and burnishing their attacks. With the unfortunate defection for South and South West of the fullback, Alistair Hignell, a Cambridge Double Blue and England cap, the counties were reduced to two internationals in the backline, Alan Morley at wing and Peter Kingston at scrumhalf; and though Barry Nelmes, captain of Cardiff, and all of the backrow of John Watkins, John Scott and Michael Rafter, were English caps, the standard of the opposition did not promise to be high. Accordingly, the All Blacks, having passed off a touch of homesickness at suffering New Zealand weather and ground conditions, would, it was supposed or hoped or both, gallop madly to a stirring victory.

If you can count three tries, one of them a Father Christmas gift of a penalty try, as components of a stirring victory, bully for you and may your children have the luck to acquire a sounder education. It took the All Blacks 36 minutes to open up with a try by Williams, who from time to time also scored two penalty goals and a conversion to the penalty try. Very clever indeed was the long pass by Dunn to Robertson which cut out Jaffray as middle man and gave "Bee Gee" the chance to bolt for the corner-flag in his inimitable style. But the game was 50 minutes old before Dunn with a clever dribble scored the second try and it was into the last quarter as Seear, unfolding himself in various bits and parts in *his* inimitable, if not unique, style, while the All Blacks poured on pressure at a scrum five metres, was surprised to find himself established as the cause of the penalty try. Being a Scot from a faraway place, Mr Norman Sanson, it was to be surmised, did not understand that the unfoldings and refoldings of the lank Seear frame until all parts were assembled consumed amounts of time which might profitably be used by opponents to stop either his forward drive or the last of the unfoldings. Hence the gratification with which the All Blacks of the day observed Mr Sanson's rush along the goalline to the midway spot between the posts, whence he gestured like a traffic officer to announce the try, was tempered with a certain disbelief that the Ref. actually was sound in mind. However, there it was; the try was in the books; and 40 days before due time, Father Christmas was giving out gifts to the New Zealand party.

Perhaps Mourie could have done more for the All Blacks if he had distrusted Jaffray and trusted Taylor. The latter, brought into the match late so that McKechnie, as the only available fullback for the time being, might be kept for higher things, was placed at fullback; in which unusual place, he was quite the outstanding man of the day. The record-books which said that Taylor weighed 13st 4lb failed to indicate that within those 186 pounds he packed goodish speed, wide-eyed alertness, fearlessness and the natural strength of, at the least, a 15-stoner. The sum of these parts was aggressiveness. Going forward or back, into men or away from them, Taylor acted decisively. He might not have the prettiest sidestep, but unless you were firm of grasp you could not hold him. Being zestful and gay in heart, he reacted pleasurably to challenge. Counter-attack was an excitement he could not resist. He lightened up much of the All Blacks' play this day. Coincidentally, Jaffray was booting the ball hither and thither in a wind strong enough to limit accuracy and at a time when Robertson, Williams and Kururangi (later replaced by Wilson), were all eager to go. A switch by Mourie might have been resented; but it could have given the team that touch of inspiration which, in absentia, was failing to unite the general effort. For example, the forwards, though thoroughly beaten at the lineout, where the count against them was a whopping 23 to 13, made up in good part for the deficiency by some excellent chasing and particularly fine efforts in moving the ball onwards in maul situations.

Looking at, in particular, two of the finest players in the game, Ackford and Kingston, one was tempted to wonder how talented English players greeted their selectors. "Quo vadis, Domine?", perhaps? Admittedly, Ackford was competing against Fleming, who grazed no low-lying nimbus as he leapt for the ball, while Roger Corin, who at 3 was matching Loveday, could be assured that the latter's customary leap was usually a rhythmical movement of the foot from the heel to the ball and back again. Nevertheless, Ackford was so extraordinarily accurate in his timing and palming, certainly enough to place him among the three best leapers of the tour, that one was bound to wonder why he could not get a chance at international level. Admittedly, he was lean. But he could leap. He kept on leaping. Kingston once, in 1975, was capped against Australia. He was then passed by and forgotten. Extraordinary. This day, he caught everything and cleared it at speed, nine times out of ten to the right place. In the first requirement of halfback service, safe and accurate passing to his outside backs, he ranked among the foremost scrumhalves of the tour, if nor foremost. Well might he have cause plaintively to ask of England's selection committee, "Whither go ye, O lords?" Perhaps Kingston's great misfortune was John Palmer's propensity, as his partner at flyhalf, for putting his boot to the ball about eight times in ten. Thus, Roger Pallow and Steve Donovan in the centres languished and neither Watkins nor Rafter was adequately brought into the play. When the cold shower drenched the field and the players, some of the better qualities deteriorated. However, from go to whoa the play was perfectly good-tempered and this made up for many facets which might otherwise have been criticised. It even helped to make up, a bit, for the Unicorn's little boxes.

The theme of "Quo vadis" was suitable to any selection of airs about the match with Midlands at Welford Road, the home of the famous Leicester Tigers. It was especially appropriate to the lock-forward, Nigel Horton, who at his own request had been repatriated early from the 1977 Lions' tour of New Zealand after suffering a broken bone in a hand. Horton rather ranked as a boy wonder when he was first capped in 1969. He played in all four internationals of the Five Nations Championship and to all appearance had it made. But in the following season, either the selectors, or Horton or all of them went off the boil. He did not play again for England until 1971, when he won three caps. He was then put to grass until 1974, when he played against Scotland. In 1975, they wanted him against Wales. They then let him be until 1977 when, amazingly, he again played the full programme. But in 1978, he was, so to speak, again on half-pay, being needed only against France and Wales. At Easter of 1978, the famous Scottish prop-forward, Ian McLauchlan, arrived in New Zealand for festival matches. Being a blunt man, his first question was: "How did or could the Lions lose their last test last year when they had so much of the game?" That was easy: "Phil Bennett, the captain." McLauchlan ruminated. Then he rumbled: "Any team which can omit Nigel Horton and Tony Neary (another Englishman of the gone-but-not-forgotten brigade) must be, it *has* to be, a great side." Ian spoke as an expert. He had played against all of the world's great forwards. As to Horton, the appalling mystery was why, in a decade in which England had suffered so many defeats, he had been capped only 15 times. The ready explanation was that he was a man given to offering unpopular opinions because he believed in their rightness. You could go further. He could be, undeniably, cantankerous. At a dinner in Gore during the 1977 Lions' tour, he spoke out against the Press as if they had conducted a campaign of personal vilification against him. On the return journey to Invercargill, he continued the attack. A piece in the *New Zealand Herald* which had described the unsatisfactory play in lineouts of the Lions' tour and which sought to convey that the relevant laws were the principal fault had been, Horton asserted, "planted" at the instance of the New Zealand union, in order to direct referees' attention to nefarious activities of the Lions' forwards. He would not listen to the retort that the *Herald* as a newspaper with a world-wide reputation for probity would never countenance "planted" stories of any sort on any activity. The suspicion was fixed in his mind. This was a cantankerous attitude the more strange because he had for years been a policeman and as such should have had a care for evidence. It seemed not unreasonable to suppose that Horton at times might have spoken with comparable bitterness about English selection methods. Indeed, rightly or wrongly, this was his reputation. If justified, it was a fault. Yet the greater fault, the much, much greater fault, lay with selectors who, guided by whim or personal resentment had so consistently inconsistently treated his undeniable qualities as a tall, strong, fast and gifted forward. Living in a more egalitarian community, Horton, cantankerous or not, would have been a first choice, a man you would not dream of leaving out of a side simply because you didn't care for the cut of his jib. As a partner for, say, Colin Meads, he would have been a fixture until age attacked his joints. In England's rugby society, which is not, regrettably, egalitarian, his moods and opinions were disapproved. So he was left out of the English team to play the All Blacks and, later, was called into the team for a succeeding international. By now, Horton was well established as a restaurateur in Toulouse. Who could blame him if, confronted by the extraordinary comings and goings of the English selectors, he adopted the French posture of lifting his hands, shrugging his shoulders and muttering a good old schoolboy "Non compris"?

Another player of the Midlands' pack who might have tempted other selection committees, Will Dickinson, had been neglected, it was said, because at 5 feet 10 inches he was too short for tighthead prop, not to mention for blocking and other duties in the middle of the lineout. At 29, Will was now in the sere, if not in the yellow as well. At 29, he was also in the prime of life as a front-row forward. As was proved when he packed so low against Johnstone that Peter Wheeler, admittedly aided by the considerable licence as to posture which he was allowed by Alan Hosie, was able to win four heels against the head, an extraordinary superiority. Johnstone was again to bend like a bow when the Barbarians played sere and serene old Will and Wheeler, wearing a smile not entirely seraphic, said quietly, "He should have been there for England against the All Blacks, shouldn't he?" It was hard not to laugh out loud, though not with easy mirth, when, after the tour, Dickinson did win his first cap. His qualities, it had to be asserted, could not possibly have taken 29 years to discover. Yet again rose the cry, directed by laser beam at the selectors, "Whither goest thou?"

It was T. P. McLean of the *New Zealand Herald* who wrote of the All Blacks' display against Midlands that while the forwards thundered, the backs blundered. It was John Reason of the *Daily Telegraph* who offered the opinion, during the play, that the New Zealanders, especially the backs, were displaying "unalloyed mediocrity". No question about it, the game was, for New Zealanders, a writhing sort of experience. Penalties conceded were effortlessly turned into goals by the infallible Hare, who scored all of Midlands' points. Donaldson skewed the ball into the scrum at a cost of at least five free-kicks. As McLean later remarked, the immortal Sid Going, freely identified by John Reason as a champion at crooked put-ins to the scrums of 1972-73, could laze out his days in the quiet, lovely Maromaku Valley where he farms. He was never in the class of Donaldson.

The powerful wind sweeping downfield was undoubtedly a deterrent to the subtler sorts of attack. But strong winds are bread-and-butter stuff to most New Zealanders and this was no sufficient excuse for ineptitude. As a student of Victoria University during the critical days of his post-adolescent development, Mourie had also had ample opportunity to study the wind. It was clever of him, on winning the toss, to decide to play into it. It was also extremely clever of him, just on half-time and after Hosie had penalised Chris Gifford for emulating Donaldson with a crooked put-in, to call up the replacement fullback for Clive Currie, Richard Wilson, to take the kick at goal. Wilson was still heavy with jet-lag after his rapid flight to join up with the team and under ordinary circumstances could not possibly have been considered fit for play so soon after his arrival. But at 11 o'clock on match-morning, McKechnie was medically advised to stand down. It would not have been much of a problem for the All Blacks to substitute Williams, or Taylor, or Jaffray, or Bruce, because an adequate replacement would have been available for each man. But when Wilson, a cheerful lad, said "Why not?" Jack Gleeson chucked him in at the deep end.

Cooper soon tested with a Garryowen. Wilson fumbled, an offside was ruled and "Dusty" within two minutes of kick-off had landed his first. Then Wilson failed a penalty goal from about the quarter-line and a moment or two later sliced, from about the same spot, his attempt to convert Williams' try — a try obtained from a beaut miskick of a drop at goal by Bruce which slewed in the wind across the goalposts but with enough weight to carry into the in-goal area, which was where Williams hungrily planted the ball down. For much of the rest of the half, until Gifford was caught in the act, Wilson's body, lathered in lassitude, was failing to respond precisely to the directions from his brain. When, therefore, Gifford was penalised about 24 metres out and Mourie called up Wilson, the reaction was "Oh, Lor'. What next?" With four goals by Hare, one of them the long drop from the free-kick, to Williams' try, Midlands were leading 12-4. If Wilson missed, the eight points would take some catching in the second half.

It was fine judgment by Mourie. Wilson tapped the ball and with a strong dropkick smashed it through the wind for the goal. At 7-12, with the wind still doing a Johnnie Walker, the All Blacks, you could say, had only to stand up to win.

No one admired Mourie's play of the day more than one of the greatest of all flankers, the one and only Kelvin, or "Bunny", Tremain, who had rightly been installed from his early times as an All Black as a Crown Prince of flank-forward play. "Gee, he can run." said Bunny. "I always had a few doubts whether he was as good as they said. Not now. You tell me how a flank-forward playing open-side can get to the blindside — which takes some doing — and still score a try?" Easy, for the admirable Mourie. Despite an easy Richard Wilson goal from 15 metres three minutes into the second half, reducing the Counties' lead to two points, Mourie was having to crank up his men more than somewhat. Williams, for example, dropping grades below his normal form, twice failed scoring opportunities. McGregor, driving at the line, got there. Alas, the ball had been lifted from his grasp. Midlands were not giving away foolish penalties like the All Blacks in the first half and with Horton, Dickinson, a remarkably effective wing-forward in John Shipsides, a crafty captain in Wheeler, excellent scrumhalf play by Gifford and the menacing "Dusty" at the back, they were doing a fair amount of cranking up themselves.

The critical points of the game were, of all things, a dropout from the quarter-line by Bruce and Mourie's try. Counties had made a strong attack after a well-planted kick-ahead by Paul Knee which Mourie and Fleming covered and at which New Zealand forced. Rapidly advancing to the quarter-line, Bruce let fly, left-footed, with a dropkick. It was an enormous blow of at least 70 metres before it bounced into touch. From the succeeding lineout, Fleming drove strongly to the right on the open flank. He was checked. Donaldson, sprightly as a squirrel, swiftly moved left with the ball, bringing Williams into the act. When Williams was checked, Mourie, who had come from God knows where, took his pass at unstoppable speed to score at the corner.

The All Blacks' lead, 14 to 12, was still narrow; and at one attack by Paul Dodge, Knee, Shipsides and Brian Hall, their defence was very badly shaken. Zestful Taylor ended the anxiety. As a lineout was being formed, Counties threw very long, over the top, in the All Blacks' quarter. Taylor flashed to the spot. Using his strength, he wrestled the ball from the arms of the flanker, Ian Smith, and, on the burst, set off for the open countryside. When Hare came at him, Taylor found Osborne thundering. When Counties' gallants got to Osborne, in their own quarter, Haden, swallowing great gulps of ground, took the pass. When Counties' gallants — by gum, they could run — got to Haden, Taylor was at his side; and Taylor it most deservedly was who scored one of the most exhilarating tries of the tour. It was heartening for young Wilson to top off the try with a goal placed from a fair distance wide of the left upright.

The margin of 20 to 12 (reduced when Hare in the last minute banged over a penalty from about 12 metres) was decisive enough; but there were hair-raising moments after Wheeler with yet another win of a tighthead had given Knee a chance to make a run which all but yielded a try. Wheeler was getting away with murder in his stance in the scrum. It was the old-time style of the 1950s, the sort that was introduced by Danie Craven's Springboks and refined by New Zealand's veteran artist at beating the gun, Has Catley. Backside almost on the ground, both feet stretched toward the mouth of the tunnel — Dalton stood little chance against this sort of activity. On other tours, steps would have been taken to acquaint Wheeler, after appeals to the referee had been ignored, with the more unfortunate features of his approach to the laws. The consequence could have been, you can bet, some deterioration in his blond Nordic looks and a very decent dust-up or two among the opposing factions of the Front-Row Forwards Club. As it was, Mourie's men forbore, battled on and, not without a great deal of blundering around in the backline, did what they had set out to do. Some light early relief was provided when Johnstone and Dickinson argued the merits of each other's stance — Will's, technically, was decisively the better — but that jousting soon settled. Good fun all around, if your stomach was strong enough for blundering or unalloyed mediocrity. At least it did show that Welford Road was devoid of Twickenhamitis. Not a man in the Midlands' team who wasn't proud to be there and more than determined to give a Roland for every All Black Oliver.

"Whither goest thou?" seemed to be a less appropriate salutation than "Farewell, My Lovely" amid the jollification, copious, humorous and memorable, in the hours after no-side of the match against Combined Services. Since the next war, which when it comes will presumably be the War of Total Annihilation, will leave survivors only in the northern fringes of Greenland and amid the eternal ice of the Antarctic, it is unlikely that the British military services will ever be large enough in strength, or command a sufficiency of public sympathy to warrant and field a representative team against a major touring side. The loss will be the touring team's. Once upon a time, the match was always played at Twickers on Boxing Day, usually in the sporting spirit which characterises Services' rugby and enjoyable for that reason alone. But the real event was the following dinner-dance at Grosvenor House, one of the great hotels of Park Lane looking out on to Hyde Park. As the dispensing of fermented and spirituous liquors spread more widely and rapidly through the dining room and ballroom, the formalities began to lose stiffness. Eightsome reels turned into madly amusing gallops and by the end of the evening, if you hadn't made fast friends with two-thirds of the attendance, especially the females, you were, at the very least, a dimwit.

It was not the least of the failings of the Seventh All Blacks of '72-'73 that by their own judgment they barred the dinner and ball. The Eighth All Blacks were not offered the ball but the compensation, the formal dinner in the largest of the British Army's training encampments, more than satisfied even their most critical members. All the way back to London, the players, especially the youngsters, kept telling Russell Thomas how greatly they had enjoyed the evening. Russ had been too young to serve overseas in World War Two but he had had enough of military training to get the feel of the good part of it which does not include square-bashing and sadistic sergeant-majors but which does include the fine comradeship among men-at-arms. Thus he was able to say, with satisfaction, "I told you so, didn't I?" And perhaps he could have added that it is a rare experience for hawks and doves alike to dine in the company of admirals and major-generals and air chief marshals and platoons of not much lesser ranks, most of them wearing the ribbons of service against Chinese bandits, Korean Kung Fus, Wild Men of Borneo and the miraculously skilled and brave (one speaks from a technical point of view) Vietcong.

The All Blacks did a bit of Rolanding for an Oliver here when they paraded their "Colonel" — introduced as such and greeted with grave and courteous applause. As a jape at the start of the tour, Mourie had demanded of Robert Kururangi, while the team's bus was trundling along, instruction in the precise Maori inflections of his name. "Is it 'ang' as in 'hang'?" Mourie asked. "Or is it 'arng' as in 'arng'?" "Say it any way you like," said Kururangi. "It's all the same to me." "No, no," said Mourie patiently. "It's very important. When I introduce you to the Queen, I must be sure I am pronouncing your name properly when I say, 'Ma'am, may I present Colonel Robert Kururangi?'" Kururangi all but bounded out of his seat. "Me a colonel? To the Queen?" He paled. "You jokers are having me on." But he moved uneasily for a time. He *couldn't* be sure Mourie *wasn't* going to do it. After Robert had been introduced to the Mess, a dining-partner, Colonel Peter Crookes, leaned across. "What arm of the Service are you in?" he asked. "I'm an apprentice mechanic at Papakura Camp, near Auckland," Kururangi said. "Ah," said Colonel Crookes. "You must know my old friend, Jim Dearsley. After he resigned his commission with us, he emigrated to New Zealand and joined your army. In fact, I do believe he is a half-colonel in your REME." "He's my boss," said Kururangi. "Then please give him my warmest regards," said Colonel Crookes. "Actually," said Kururangi, "I don't see too much of Colonel Dearsley these days."

For sentimentalists reared with a regard for British military traditions, professional skills and regimental glories based upon the consistent production of countless sailors, soldiers and airmen who, like the Pilgrim, were valiant in heart, it was saddening to feel that a sporting association with representatives of the Services was, by the sound of things, about to be terminated. "Farewell, My Lovely" you could say; and not be ashamed of a moistening in the eye. Militarism may be stupid, killing senseless, duty a joke; but could punk rock and associated modern crazes produce peers of the servicemen who, though outweighted, outpowered, out-scienced, still took on the All Blacks as if they were all blood-brothers of Jack the Giant-Killer? Nor could the whither-goest-thou touch be forgotten. Not because he was a West Indian and Black, not because his experience of rugby was not extensive, not because, amid so much of the top brass, he was only an army corporal, but entirely because he was a flank-forward of extraordinary ability was Garston Williams an outstanding figure of the match — so outstanding that you wondered whether the moguls had ever thought to call him to higher rugby service. He could run — he was almost in the Mourie class — he could handle, he could tackle. When ruck after ruck unpiled and he was one of the last to get to his feet, you could bet that the reason was the tackle he had made of Donaldson, or Dunn, or Jaffray, or any other All Black who was running with the ball. No nonsense tackles they were. Biff, bang, crash. Jack Gleeson, ecstatic about the man's abilities, took care to talk to Williams, discover his playing background and compliment him on his game. It was certainly the finest of the Services' efforts — and of the tour, too — and that was some praise because Gillingham, who captained the team, by personal example and leadership produced a stirring effort from his men. John Orwin, also an RAF type, was a fine partner at lock for Gillingham, Steve Hughes at Number 8 hungered for anything in black and both scrumhalves (Gareth Davies, of the British Army of the Rhine, succeeded Ken Pugh when the latter was injured) drew Dead-Eye Dick beads on Donaldson with considerable effect. Steve Jackson and Geoff Fabian in the centres each did well in persuading Jaffray to kick more than he should have and a slender, swift wing in Colin English, a naval lieutenant who in matter-of-fact statements about his career conveyed that special quality which is pride of service, was not easy to nab.

The one man Garston Williams couldn't catch was Robertson because "Brucey", thankfully, was soaring back to his best standards in anticipation and participation, especially, in the latter respect, in running with the ball. As captain of the day, he was an inspiring leader even though, for a fact, he could not get consistent play from his forwards at the lineout. As a compensation, Rutledge, Barry Ashworth, Black and Loveday were all powerful goers with the loose ball. It did the heart good, too, to see Billy Bush playing the role of General Factotum as if he had invented it. From time to time or, rather, as required, Billy joined the set-pieces. Elsewhere, he played what could be described as the game of a nine-eighths, somewhere between heaven and earth and occasionally colliding with, or jostling, Mahomet's coffin. It might have been an idea to team him with Brian Ford in some special place akin, perhaps, to the quarter-back position in American gridiron football. Poor Ford's physical state was no better than fair. He himself said he could not stretch to more than 60 percent of full speed and he was appalled at the possibility that a replacement might be asked for. (It was a tribute to him that the idea was not seriously canvassed.) He did his best with what he could muster in speed and strength and most willingly, had he been asked, would have played anywhere, even at hooker, to stay with the team.

Ford it was who battled to the first try after a heel had been won against the head and Seear, Donaldson, Dunn and Robertson combined before the last pass to Ford was made. With half-time approaching, Services led by 6 to 4 from a 25-metre penalty by Fabian and a drop-goal from a free kick by the flyhalf, Tony Green. Then McKechnie stepped forward with a fine penalty from 22 metres into the wind and, having assured himself that all was well, this day, with his kicking, he proceeded to knock over five more goals, four of them after tries, with superbly accurate shots. Meanwhile, Seear got a pushover try and Jaffray, Robertson and McKechnie himself followed on as try-scorers. Frailties were found. It wasn't the best of international-standard rugby. But it was encouraging for the All Blacks to know Robertson had about come right, Dunn could as he chose desist from punting and McKechnie was middling the ball at his goalkicks. The next hurdle was England. Would Twickenhamitis attack that team? Or would New Zealand get a caning? If England could field men of the spirit and speed of Garston Williams, the match would be hard to win.

CHAPTER SIX

The Glory Has Departed

DURING much of the tour by Mourie's men, England rumbled over the situation of one of its great institutions, Times Newspapers Ltd. Disputes involving some of the 54 unions associated with the publication of *The Times,* the *Sunday Times,* the *Times Literary Supplement* and the *Times Educational Supplement,* each of them a journal of outstanding reputation, had cost the publishers millions of copies and lost them substantial revenues. One printing union was especially obdurate. Except on its own terms, it would not, its leaders said, tolerate the introduction of publishing techniques which would speed the composition and production of the papers. An effect would be, the union contended, a reduction of staff numbers. Meetings became pointless. Discussions were further statements of old points of view. Confrontation became inevitable. Failing a general agreement, so the publishers said, they had decided that on November 30, which was 16 days before the All Blacks' last match, they would suspend publication of each of the four journals.

As the critical day came nearer, frantic attempts were made, within and without the Establishment, to retain in print at least *The Times.* Famous as "The Thunderer" in days of old when one of its editors offered the ultimate statement that the function of the Press was disclosure, *The Times* by tradition was regarded as the foremost daily newspaper published in English. Its departure was regarded as a national tragedy.

In this crisis, the British — or, perhaps, more precisely, the English — reacted by joking. It was their invincible characteristic in adversity. It had carried them through war, crisis, catastrophe, pestilence.

In the issue of November 30, which indeed proved to be the last of 1978 and might be the last of all time, the paper's correspondence columns represented a distillation of the wit, variety and elegance which had made this feature one of the most remarkable of all newspaper activity. Over many years, readers had competed for the privilege of being the first to tell the editor — and the world — that they had heard the first cuckoo of spring. In the last column of this fateful issue, Mr Hamish McLellan, of Wimbledon, made an offering which was both a thought and a joke. Under the heading, "Brief Silence", Mr McLellan wrote the editor thus: "Sir, The last cuckoo?" The editor's footnote was sublimely British stiff-upper-backbone. "Spring," he said, "always returns."

During the previous few days, readers had wondered what the world would be like without their daily brains test which was the finding of the solution to *The Times'* crossword. They reminisced about famous clues and solutions; and Mary D. Stigant, of Dorchester in Dorset, recalled that her grandfather's favourite had been: Clue: "Land of hope and . . ." Solution: ICHABOD — "The Glory is Departed". (Ichabod is mentioned in 1 Samuel, iv. 21.)

Here, in a word, was the ultimate statement as to the England team which on a sunny, cold day with a stiff breeze sweeping over Twickenham, lost to New Zealand by 6 points to 16 and which, if justice had been done, would have been routed. For England, read Ichabod. The glory had departed from what had been, what always should be, one of the great rugby nations, perhaps *the* great rugby nation. Though the Rugby Football Union at Twickenham listed 1893 clubs and 2600 schools as affiliates, teams chosen from this enormous aggregation had for years past been lacking in skills and true grit. The supposition that England no longer bred players of the quality of Peter Jackson and David Duckham, each a peerless wing threequarter; Michael Davis, a Devon lock who insisted on playing out the test match at Christchurch in 1963 rather than quit the field with a dislocated shoulder; Jeff Butterfield, than whom no centre ever more finely judged a pass; "Badger" Jacobs, a prop who stood no higher than a duck's knee but who was all durability; and Beverley Risman, a superb flyhalf, simply did not stand examination. Fundamentally, the problem was a selection system dependent upon the whim of the man the Rugby Football Union committee, a large body, entrusted with the job of finding associates who would sift the wheat from the chaff. Few selectors seem to have been discovered after they had served a decently testing apprenticeship. At the time of the Mourie tour, this committee numbered seven men of which the man chosen as coach, Peter Colston, was the only non-international. "You have had a considerable experience at club, provincial and international level," Jack Gleeson was asked at the final Press conference of the tour. "Would you say that it is possible to choose a team by a committee of seven men?" Gleeson did not waste words. "No," he answered.

One acknowledges that there were other problems. Clubs hidebound by tradition and fixture-lists dating back to the darker ages had reacted with indifferent enthusiasm to the recommendations of a committee of inquiry headed by Sir George Mallaby, a British High Commissioner to New Zealand. This had suggested championship competitions and/or leagues and the formation of eight regions of English rugby for the building of teams of greater than club strength and less than international. The regions, it was urged, should supplant the county championship which by many reliable accounts aroused no public interest and little better than minimal player-enthusiasm. There had been a good deal of talk about other proposals expertly argued by proponents and deftly dismissed by opponents.

One needed to be an insider with the knowledge of a John Reason, who consistently berated the Establishment for its conservatism, to develop the clearest idea of the shortcomings of England at international level. From the outside looking in, however, it seemed clear as day that the fundamental fault was the clumsiness of the selection system. Not counting replacements for injured players, England used 24 men for its four internationals of the Five Nations Championship of 1977-78. Three men played at fullback, six in the four threequarters, six in the second row of the scrummage. The inference to be drawn from the variety was a want of confidence between players and selectors; and this, surely, has been England's bane. An attempt at one stage of the tour to suggest that the English selectors could profitably study the career of Wilson Whineray was not appreciated; yet there can be no doubt whatever that the remark made to Whineray by the selector-coach, Neil McPhail, when he was first chosen for Canterbury — "Whineray, you have four games to prove yourself" — was profoundly important in encouraging the enthusiastic young player to play his natural game. One somewhat critical review by a New Zealander, who admittedly may well have been talking through his hat, was withheld from the English team on the ground that it might have caused them to throw in the towel in their dressing-room. The same sort of piece, written by an Englishman about New Zealand rugby, would have caused All Blacks to tear chunks out of the concrete walls in rage and to say, through clenched teeth, "Where are these pommy bastards? Let us get at them." Graham Mourie in his reasonable, thoughtful way contended that England were a difficult team to chose and train because of the variety of backgrounds in the contestants: Oxbridge university men (not so many these days); middle-class professional men from in and about London; West Countrymen, farmers and the like; and Midlanders and men of the north who, like as not, were working-class artisans in factories. One needed to be diffident about demurring from a Mourie judgment. He was a great hand at informing himself on all available facts. But in this instance, it could be objected that, for once, he had failed to appreciate the value of variety. The great Lions' teams — 1950, 1959 and 1971 in

New Zealand, 1955 and 1974 in South Africa — succeeded primarily because of the varied backgrounds of their players. To an outsider looking in from afar, England's great need appeared to be covered by one word: Leadership. But to an outsider who had had the chance, over most of a decade, of closely inspecting England's structure, the faults were more extensive. Chris Laidlaw, the All Black halfback whose best-selling book, *Mud In Your Eye,* had rocked the Establishments of New Zealand and South Africa, was now settled in London, after a period at Oxford followed by service with the Department of Foreign Affairs in Suva and Paris. As an alumnus of the school of international rugger, he was still closely interested in the game. "The trouble is," he said, "that English club rugby is so extremely boring. There is no real development of play by the backs. The threequarters are starved. English rugby is so full of jargon and 'scientific' coaching that great back-play has disappeared."

Well, leadership failings or not, scientific coaching or not, England was still England. It had twice beaten New Zealand, in 1935 and 1973. Mourie was cautious. England, he said, would be a big one. He found no takers among the scribes of Fleet Street after Sandy Sanders as chairman had released the team (it was a nice touch by John Reason to beat the world by precisely forecasting the composition of the side). All of the critics climbed in on the choice of Barry Nelmes, a trained loose-head prop, at tighthead and of John Scott, a Number 8 at lock. The natural consequence must be, one and all of them said, an unbalanced scrummage and a marked weakness, in default of a place for Nigel Horton, at Number 5 in the lineout. Chris Laidlaw went further. The choice as scrumhalf of Malcolm Young must, he said, restrict England's attack. Young's ploys were the kick over the top and, if he made a break, the turning back of the ball to the loose-forwards. He had no vision of the worth of spreading the attack far from the forward mass.

Doubts that history is capable of repeating itself could be resolved by consulting the international rugby calendar for 1978. Insanity at the lineout is a sure and certain way of conceding points. Insane Act One at Eden Park in September, when on the All Blacks' goalline Andy Dalton threw over the top to Mark Taylor, who was engulfed, yielded the first of the four tries of the match to the bearded Cornstalk, Cornelson. Insane Act Two occurred at Cardiff, also on the goalline, when Stuart Wilson threw over the top to Jaffray, who was engulfed. From the scrimmage, the West Indian, Carl Smith, charged over for a try. Insane Act Three, also at a lineout on the goalline, knocked England cold.

Act Three occurred in the 35th minute when the English, playing rather better than expected against All Blacks who, largely through

Osborne, had already cast away at least two certain tries, were leading by six points from two fine goals by "Dusty" Hare, the man who never missed, to four points from a try scored by Oliver from a charge — marred by an uncalled knock-on — from a lineout.

Peter Wheeler lobbed the ball in high and slowly. In the inevitable jostle, Scott at 5 in going up for the catch or palm-down was compelled into a dramatic misjudgment. He knocked the ball back toward the touchline at an acute angle of descent; and Johnstone, two places removed, timed perfectly his flop on to the ball as it pitched on the goalline. McKechnie placed the goal for a lead of 10 points to 6; and that, quite decidedly, was that so far as England was concerned.

In the last quarter, England moulded together better. Beaumont stirred his forwards as much by example as by exhortation. Michael Rafter responded finely in the backrow, Roger Uttley, not yet at full stretch because of many difficulties with injuries, made some powerful charges and Wheeler was by his captain's side in gallant efforts. But it was desolating that the finest opposing wing threequarter of the tour, Michael Slemen, received only one pass and that Peter Squires on the right, who was probably the next best wing, got only two — from one of which he made a hair-raising dodge past Williams. In short, England lacked quality. Said John Hopkins in the *Sunday Times,* in the last issue of the newspaper for some time: "Twickenham was not a very exciting place to be... One was left exhausted by England's ineptitude."

In the language of American sport, the All Blacks could be credited with an assist. They did some inepting on their own. When Knight was penalised for a block at a lineout, Hare had goaled, easily and accurately, with a drop-kick. In response, the All Black forwards surged downfield as powerfully and terrifyingly as any pack of the past and from a scramble close to the goalline the ball was speared into the hands of Osborne. Robertson and Williams were running to his left, in terms of manpower New Zealand had a 3 to 2, perhaps even a 3 to 1 advantage. No more was needed than smart passes from Osborne to Robertson and on to Williams. Nothing could then have saved England. In a mournful moment which may stay imprinted on his mind forever, Osborne propped, stepped infield off his left foot and tried to cut back against the tide of covering defenders. That was one assist to England's cause.

Not too long afterwards came the next when with the attack now moving to the right a demand was made of Osborne that he pass immediately out to Wilson. That, too, would have been a try. Billy was blinkered. He could not "see". He was, after all, very young and first time at Twickenham in an international is an emotional experience. So he kicked; and once the ball pitched into touch the chance was gone.

But Osborne was not alone in ineptitude. In the sense that you never could be quite sure whether McKechnie would or would not kick goals, he was an exciting man to watch. Now you had him, now you didn't. Once more he went off at half-cock. His attempt to goal Oliver's try could only be described as shocking. Where Hare, as he was later to show with a shot from about 27 metres, would have dusted the ball over the bar, McKechnie's shot did not even trouble the uprights. Not too long after the try, he was offered a penalty of about 27 metres and all the time in the world to place it. No go. It was gratifying for the All Blacks that he managed the conversion to Johnstone's try and he couldn't be blamed when Williams, trying for a penalty of about 58 metres, made a dreadful hash of the kick. But McKechnie was still inepting before the half-time spell was reached when he tried to drop at goal from about 40 metres.

It was after these misfortunes and intertwined with them that the All Blacks did their best to show that they were not to be blamed for any exhaustion which might be felt by any of the 67,750 spectators. Very considerable efforts were made by the team to establish and sustain control of the play. Osborne with one tackle of Dixon offered a sublime touch. He struck into his man with extraordinary accuracy and courage. Rutledge produced a Grade A specimen, too. Uttley, a great, heavy man, powerful in the hips and thighs, ran hard at him, head-on. They clashed. Uttley went back, knocked all of a heap by a shattering thrust. Great stuff this, more particularly to those who had travelled a bit with All Black teams and lamented their incompetence in the mechanics of one of Rugby's noblest arts. Then there was Johnstone who more than once before had shown himself a zealous and proficient tackler. Indeed, if there were to have been special accolades for the more significant All Blacks, the first choices certainly would have been Johnstone and Dalton. Down the left touch on the West Stand in the second half, they made one charge after another. It was heady stuff, schoolboy dramatics and none the worse for that. Knight's first international of the tour was notable for fine concentration, just doing one job capably and getting on to do the next equally well; and concentration was also the special quality of Oliver and Haden at the lineout, beneficially for New Zealand. Beaumont in his great-hearted way was a fine contributor to England's effort but, man to man, Oliver was the better. As for Haden versus Scott, a diligent and disinterested referee would soon have ruled No Contest. As to the backrow, God knows what Malcolm Young and John Horton thought when they saw either Mourie or Rutledge or both constantly hovering about them, while both of the flankers were also everywhere, always at high speed and superlatively sure about what they were doing. The crowd became short-fused when Seear, kicking at the ball, instead copped Beaumont as the latter went down to make the check. But in a charming, memorable gesture, Young instantly stretched out his hand as if to assure Norman Sanson that the kick was unintentional and that the clash had been the rugby equivalent of golf's rub of the green. As for Sanson, he saw it that way, too; and to New Zealand's advantage, he saw two infringements from which McKechnie placed penalty goals from 28 and 35 metres.

Two tries to two penalty goals was some assurance of New Zealand superiority. But there could have been better, there ought to have been better. Perhaps, as a memory of Munster, Donaldson too often tried either to run the ball himself or turn it back to his forwards. Perhaps Osborne was unlucky not to have someone else capitalise on one or two powerful breaks of the defensive line. Perhaps Robertson was unfortunate that one or two chip-kicks did not reach the intended spot or bounce the right way. All in all, however, for want of full development of their potential the All Blacks, in scoring their third international victory failed to satisfy, entirely, their most vigorous critics.

Who happened to be themselves. That was the measure of the quality of the team. All of the time that they were doing well, they were, every man of them, striving to do better. If honesty in self-appraisal is a superior quality, the All Blacks deserved their march onward and upward.

CHAPTER SEVEN

On Into The Ice Age

OF A SUDDEN, the All Blacks lost their luck with the weather. For ten metres in from touch down the grandstand touchline at Rodney Parade at Newport, where the might of Monmouthshire were met and outmatched by 26 points to 9, the field was frostbound. The slivers of ice were dangerous. At Birkenhead Park, South Liverpool, where Billy Beaumont's North of England men were subdued by 9 points to 6, snowfalls had been so heavy that it was questionable, until mid-morning, whether the game could proceed. Aberdeen introduced the All Blacks to a grace many had never heard — "Some hae meat and canna eat/And some hae none but want it/But we hae meat and we can eat/So let the Lord be thankit" — but also to a cold which might have been close to intolerable if it had not been tempered by that other grace which was the warm-hearted hospitality of men of integrity. That opposition, from North and Midlands of Scotland, was downed, after a good deal of maundering about, by 31 points to 3 — the All Blacks led by 4 to 3 at half-time — and then course was set for Murrayfield and the last obstacle to the Grand Slam.

It was cold here, too; and a great, heavy lump, much colder than mere ice, entered New Zealand hearts as the Scottish captain, Ian McGeechan, toward the end of play manoeuvred to score his second drop goal of the game and tie the score at 12-all. But cold was only a part of the problem. Ere this attempt at goal was being made, the sun had long since set, far out beyond the western highlands, and the murk upon Murrayfield had turned into all but impenetrable gloom. Was it because of Scottish blood and Celtic feyness that Doug Bruce at this critical moment became gifted with Caledonian second sight? His buttocks and body interposed between McGeechan's boot and the neighbouring goalposts. The ball rebounded, slithering. Slithering fast, but not nearly so quickly as Osborne. In a stride or two, Billy booted the ball into the vast, empty space which was threequarters of Murrayfield. Robertson, travelling like an Olympic sprinter, joined the hunt. With a judgment which approached the sublime, at maximum speed from ten metres short of the goalmouth, he toed the ball with just sufficient force to put it a few metres into the ingoal area. Again with exquisite judgment, he dived precisely for the try. McKechnie's goal-kick for the winning score of 18 to 9 topped off this magnificent piece of opportunism which assured Mourie's men of their historic place and appointment as the First of the Grand Slammers.

But it was still cold, all through this critical period which in all sorts of ways was to test the character of the team perhaps more decisively than any other experience even up to, and including, the international against Wales. By now the critics of the tour were reaching toward final judgments. On the one hand, they were berating local teams for their failings. It had become, so you rather tended to gather, a British disgrace that a touring team had played 11 hours and 20 minutes of rugby — 680 minutes, begod — without yielding their tryline to an opposing side. On the other hand, these critics on British hearths were becoming patronising about the touring team. The ultimate judgment, by John Dawes, that the All Blacks were the dullest major touring team of modern times, appeared, unsourced, in the *Daily Telegraph* but actually was delivered by Dawes to the *Daily Mirror's* Chris Lander as they stood shoulder-to-shoulder in the gruesome dive which passed for the men's lavatory at Rodney Parade — perhaps both the place and the ice had entered into "Sid's" heart before he offered judgment.

Critics or no, within or without, it was evident that, coinciding with the cold, the heat had been turned on the All Blacks. In terms of forward potential, Monmouthshire might also have been called yet another fifth test. Charlie Faulkner, the aged sage of Pontypool, shared the front-row with his mates of the club and Wales, Bobby Windsor and Graham Price. Behind them at lock packed two more Pontypoolians, Steve Sutton and John Perkins, each of them a Wales B representative, and each of the backrow of Clive Burgess, Jeff Squire and Paul Ringer, was an international. Squire was of Pontypool, too, so that the pack reeked of a club which within recent years had become identified as a leader of the new British down-to-earth style of forward play. Exponent-in-chief of the attitude was Pontypool's greatest character, the prop-forward Ray Prosser who in five years from 1956 won 21 caps for his country and toured New Zealand and Australia with Ronnie Dawson's Lions of 1959. A simple, gentle, gregarious man of infinite warmth and humour, pragmatic, anything but phlegmatic Ray was profoundly impressed by his New Zealand experience — quite as much, in fact, as was, a few years later, that subtle, hyper-intelligent Irish prop, Ray McLoughlin. New Zealand, so each of these men reasoned, had made an accurate appreciation of the main requirements of rugby: The forwards were to get on with the job of outmatching, subduing and overpowering the opposing pack while the backs contrived to make plays which principally placed the ball ahead of the thundering phalanx. As with the Roman centurions of old, the phalanx would by incessant, intelligent activity tear the vitals out of the opposing team. Ray's philosophy was expressed either by or for him in the famous statement: "When the ball gets as far out as the inside centre, we call that a move." Such was the Prosser charisma that Russell Thomas, on the night before the Monmouthshire match, was driven from Porthcawl to Pontypool, a long hike of 50 miles or so over crowded roads and highways, to take sup with the great man. Ray's whisper is like Stentorius' shout — he comes through very loud and clear — and because Thomas came upon him while he was taking a shower at the end of a club training run, Ray thought that in courtesy he ought to make sure he could be heard. The noise, it was later said, was deafening as the two men conversed amiably, Thomas about Wales and Prosser about New Zealand, with rugby mixed up between; but there were genuine tears from Prosser, hard-bitten old Ray, when Thomas presented him with an All Black jumper.

Such a pleasant piece of background, this visit by Thomas. Such a change the next day when he said to the All Blacks, "I would like you to win this one for me, today." The remark was neither spiteful nor malicious. Thomas was always a man to take care with his words. But it was evidence of the pressures which were building upon the All Blacks as they progressed through the tour and which intensified a hundred, perhaps even a thousandfold, when they crossed the border into Wales. First there had been the emotion of Cardiff and the drama of the fifth test at Swansea, then the clamorous cries of cheating as to the international. By now, the Welsh as a nation expected that every man of Monmouthshire would do his duty and die, if necessary, to bring about the defeat of the All Blacks. John Loveday said later that the All Blacks in their changing-room could hear the Monmouthshire men talking and building up and became affected by the experience. "Just before we went on the field," Loveday said, "we were going about in our room almost punching holes through the concrete walls."

Mourie considered later, long after the tour in fact, that Monmouthshire had been the peak of his team's performance. It would be hard to argue against any statement that it was his own noblest performance. The match might be said to have borne his imprint or, to generalise, the imprint of the particular qualities which distinguished his band of All Blacks. It has already been remarked how Dawes disparaged the qualities. At the end of the play, comments quite as critical were general to the crowd. Moving in the mass from the dreadfully seedy, rundown stadium which looked unaltered in any particular since the 1924 All Blacks so narrowly won over Newport, one heard Welshmen agree, one with the other, that the game had been "dull", "grey", "uninteresting", "rubbish", "a bloody shocker, man". Coming from beaten Welshmen, these were the ultimate tributes. Of the left-handed sort, that is. Of the right-handed sort, who among fervent New Zealanders could ask for more than from the famous English flyhalf Richard Sharp, who now writes for the *Sunday Telegraph* and who in 1962 suffered a broken jaw when he was tackled by the Springbok, Mannetjies Roux. (The manager of the Lions touring in South Africa, Brian Vaughn, had to be dissuaded almost physically from rushing out on to the field to call his team from it.) Trained as a schoolmaster and idolised by his pupils after he had scored one of the great tries of Twickenham's international history, Sharp later turned to business. Perhaps the change heightened his dispassionate approach to rugby. "I can never see enough of Mourie's All Blacks," he said. "They fascinate me. They do so many things so well. They have such spirit." It was put to Sharp that other critics were calling the All Blacks dull and boring. He is a mild man. "Bosh," he said. "They absolutely fascinate me. I will be sad when they end their tour. I enjoy every minute of every game they play."

There were impediments to the satisfaction taken by the All Blacks in their decisive defeat of Monmouthshire. Loveridge was given the devil of a time by the 1977 Lions' scrumhalf, Brynmor Williams, who in turn was as strong as a good-sized bull and as slippery as a medium-sized eel in the breaks he made with the ball. Dunn stood too often flatfooted to take his passes. Taylor too often tried to crash through the defensive line. Robertson a little more than necessary tried that chip over the top or that grub-kick through which too often had marked or marred his play in important matches. Kururangi and Wilson as wings did hair-raising things, Kururangi especially by flinging the ball wildly behind when he thought Richard Wilson had come up from fullback to call for a pass; and Wilson especially by rushing from the wing at the Monmouthshire centre to bring off a tackle. The sum of these disgrace-notes, as a specially stern and musically-minded critic might have been tempted to call them, was considerable and perhaps just a bit above average for an international team at a high point of its tour.

But the inspirations of Mourie yielded many compensations, not the least of which a damaging defeat of a team of high reputation. The very particular satisfaction which for a certainty was Mourie's disciplined leadership as well as a carry-over from Russell Thomas' dressing-room plea was the performance of the "junior" forwards, Loveday, Fleming, Graham and, at his appearance after Billy Bush had had to retire with a twanged hamstring, John Ashworth. On background and performance, Monmouthshire were a hard, well-trained Welsh pack, especially good at Burgess, Squire and Ringer, who chased and harried earnestly and effectively. But the pack as a whole was subdued by a New Zealand-style effort which Ray Prosser and Ray McLoughlin as professors of forward play would have highly esteemed. Loveday, bent double, charged like a bull. Graham was seldom less than sniffing distance from the ball. Fleming went up and brought the ball down. Ashworth snorted into tackles. Black, who was more of an understudy than a junior, served nobly in many a purposeful rush. In very difficult conditions, because the part of the field in frost was slippery and dangerous and the rest was glug-glug, these men hewed unceasingly. It was impossible to call their effort dull. It was, as Sharp would certainly have said if asked, fascinating for vigour, vigilance and variety.

Moreover, if the backs seemed prone at times to unnecessary error, perhaps from excessive enthusiasm, they did a fair share; and Loveridge, while responding in kind to many of Brynmor Williams' powerful tackles and thrusts, brought off a try which was the fine point of the game and one of the most memorable episodes of the tour, if not of all touring experience. A stroke of genius, in fact. Windsor heeled at a scrum on his own goalline. Williams followed the ball back, guarding the gate as it were. Loveridge, following, reacted like a striking cobra at the instant that the ball, emerging from the second row, was on the goalline. He sprang over an intervening Monmouthshire body which was Williams' and, an instant before the latter could get there, dabbed his hands down on the ball. With that catlike leap, the All Blacks went on to steal six more points and further depress the gloomy vales of Gwent.

Not that there wasn't quality in Monmouthshire. Williams' effort was far beyond any standard he reached while touring in New Zealand, David Barry as his partner looked a most capable young man and Ian Goslin at left centre, a mere 19 years, ranked high among the promising centres who opposed the All Blacks throughout their tour — not the warmest of tributes, sad to say, but the youngster was one to remember. As for Peter Lewis at fullback, come the day when J. P. R. Williams entered the Gone-But-Not-Forgotten list this chap would jump rather than move toward the greatest prize in Welsh sport, the international rugby cap.

A nice touch of irony entered into the All Blacks' decisive victory. They got their retaliation in first. The phrase had been used, puzzlingly, by Carwyn James at a seminar which discussed the merits and major achievements of the 1971 Lions he so brilliantly coached. Conveying as it did the implication that one team after another had used chicanery and brutality in efforts against the Lions, the phrase was not warmly received in New Zealand where, in truth, the deliberate cheating of the British forwards at the lineout had marred their otherwise well-deserved triumph.

But here, now, Mourie's men were getting their retaliation in first by persuading Richard Wilson to seize the chances of goals offered by the penalties awarded against Monmouthshire by the Irish referee, John West. When Faulkner collapsed the scrum in the second minute, Wilson cracked a 40-metre goal. When Geoff Davies three minutes later lay on the ball, Wilson scored from 25 metres. In the tenth minute, the All Blacks infringed at a lineout and Lewis used the crossbar to help over his kick of 27 metres. But when Goslin got offside at a ruck, Wilson banged again, from 44 metres. So, in 12 minutes, the All Blacks were 9 points to 3 ahead. Before half-time they scored 13 more points while twice conceding penalties which Lewis accurately goaled. When Taylor stepped through and niftily grub-kicked to the goalline Dunn was first there for the try. Richard Wilson goaled yet again from 35 metres and then with a flick of his foot goaled Loveridge's remarkable try. It was, naturally, a criticism that the All Blacks were restricted to four more points in the second half from a try by Robertson because their half-time lead was large enough to assure them of victory. Perhaps the explanation was ill-luck rather than ineptitude. Taylor before half-time suffered a strange injury to the chest. Hard as he tried to gulp air, he felt choked and breathless. Before the break, he was taken off the field for attention. The doctor in the house proved to be Russell Thomas rather than the qualified medical man who could find no ready explanation for the malady. It was Thomas who persuaded Mark to return to play. Upon the reaching of which, he immediately stated his courage by making a searing thrust for almost half the field and almost to the goalline. It was from the scrum after he had been checked that Loveridge scored. Taylor's troubles did not cease with no-side. Like much else as to the ground, Rodney Parade's showering facilities left much to be desired. The cold had supplanted the hot by the time Taylor was ready for hosing. He was still unwell and as soon as possible was whisked back to Porthcawl, 40 miles distant, for rest and recuperation. But so efficient and enterprising a baggage-master as Graham Short was not going to let one of his boys trudge muddied to his hotel. Up and down the street outside Rodney Parade scurried Graham until he found an answer. Yes, said Mrs Passmore, solicitous and helpful; she would be honoured to allow Mr Taylor, an All Black, to use her bathroom. Which, you could bet, was more comfortable than the Parade's. Taylor was still breathing with difficulty but in his pleasant, genial way, he had breath enough to thank Mrs Passmore for her kindness.

"Hell," a poet once observed, "hath no fury like a Kiwi scorned." To play at Birkenhead Park was, for Mourie's men, just another ho-hum affair. Damned cold. Snow, ice, wind, rain, the lot. Could have been postponed. Cancelled. Forgotten. So what? But to an earlier generation Birkenhead Park vividly recalled a man who had scorned New Zealand rugby, or a significant part of it, and who had been reviled for the rest of his life and well beyond. As manager of the British team which toured New Zealand in 1930, winning the first test at Carisbrook, 6-3, with one of the great test-match tries and losing the series, 1-3, principally because of injuries which removed the scrumhalves, Wilf Sobey and Paul Murray, from the tour, James Baxter chose the dinner to the teams of the second match, Britain versus Taranaki, to make a powerful attack on the wing-forward of the 2-3-2 scrummage formation. His words of May 25, 1930, were to have historical repercussions for, in the upshot, they compelled New Zealand to abandon the formation which had been principally responsible for the brilliance of New Zealand back-play, decade on decade. Baxter of Birkenhead Park and Cheshire had already quarrelled that day with the chairman of the Taranaki Rugby Union, James McLeod, because he wanted the teams to remain on the field at half-time, in accordance with international rules, and was overruled at McLeod's insistence that local usage and practice must be observed. Never again, said Baxter stoutly; and at the dinner he fired 15-inch guns. While from time to time a genius might develop, he said, the ordinary man who tried to play wing-forward was nothing more or less than a cheat. "The New Zealand Rugby Union," Baxter went on, "has pronounced against wing-forward play but has thrown the onus of correcting his malpractices on the referee (shades of things to come in other troublous areas of the game!) With all due deference to the controlling body, it has thrown a tremendous responsibility on the referee. No referee can control a wing-forward who is out to beat him. The referee has too much to do at the pace the game is played at today. The onus of correcting the malpractices of wing-forwards is on the clubs. Every club has a committee which picks its players and if this committee says any player is guilty of malpractice it should be perfectly frank. The wing-forward is deliberately trying to beat the referee by unfair tactics. The club can say it will not play a man who is deliberately outwitting the referee."

It would be impossible to measure, now, the magnitude of the controversy Baxter provoked. Commendation of Baxter's opinions from abroad — "His frank utterances," said the *Sydney Morning Herald,* "will have the unanimous support of every country except New Zealand. New Zealand stands in infamous Imperial isolation in its defiance of the canons of a great game" — served only to stir greater indignation. In later years it was alleged that the New Zealand union in any case was independently moving toward agreement with the principle that the front-row of the scrum should comprise not fewer than three men and that the change in the law which followed a year or two after the British tour and which dictated this requirement was unrelated to the bashing by Baxter. But to the New Zealand rugby public, which in those days meant, quite simply, the *whole* New Zealand public, Baxter's statement was the original sin in the altering of the law. All through the 1930s and 1940s and still quite strenuously in the 1950s, lamentations were raised about the decline and fall of New Zealand rugby which had occurred from the time that the 3-2-3 and, much later, the 3-4-1 was substituted. It is an ancient, far-off thing now, not even of academic interest; but still alive are those who can recall how Auckland's Vincent Meredith chose five centre-threequarters in his extraordinarily brilliant backline of the 1920s and how in the same period the awesome Hawke's Bay team which held the Ranfurly Shield against 24 consecutive challengers ran up, through a backline of Jimmy Mill, Lance Johnson, Bert Cooke, Jackie Blake, Bert Grenside, Louis Paewai or Albert Falwasser and the Emperor himself, George Nepia, scores of 77 to 14 against Wairarapa, 58 to 8 against Wellington, 41 to 11 against Auckland and 36 to 3 against Wanganui. Fourteen of the 17 tries scored against Wairarapa were made by backs. There were many other extraordinary feats, for this was the era in which flourished Ifwersen of Auckland, Nicholls of Wellington, Steel of West Coast, Hart of Canterbury, Lindsay of Otago and Lord knows how many more brilliant backs and in which, too, Hawke's Bay in scoring 761 points in 27 matches notched 87 tries by the backs Grenside, Blake, Nepia, Falwasser, Mill and Cooke and only — only, mark it well — 16 penalty goals. No wonder classicists at the universities came to murmur to each other, as the thrust of the Baxter attack took effect, "Eheu fugaces/Anni labuntur, Postume, Postume!" — "Years glide away and are lost to me, lost to me!"

So here were Mourie's men back where "Bim" Baxter used to be king of the castle. Quite a king he had been: President of Birkenhead Park, 1903-40, president of the Rugby Football Union, 1926-27, three times capped for England in 1900, member of England's selection committee, 1906-31, chairman of it from 1913-31, member of the International Board, 1926-39, president of Cheshire, 1904-40. Were Mourie's men conscious of being in the presence of the shade of "Bim"? Doubtful. But they had cause to be thankful that on their behalf McKechnie twice slotted goals between posts of a certain historic significance. As a tribute to the British after their tour of 1930, the New Zealanders gracefully donated to the Rugby Football Union a set of Kauri goalposts. These were intended for Twickenham and Baxter, as the man the union knew all about, was advised of their coming. They were landed, as things turned out, at Liverpool, just up the road from Birkenhead Park; and never, never did they grace Twickers. "Bim" was smart. The posts took the wrong turning. They arrived at

Birkenhead; and there they still stood, this day, welcoming the McKechnie kicks and disdaining, five minutes short of no-side, a 36-metre attempt by Malcolm Young which assuredly would have drawn this most desperately hard and fairly fought match.

After their three days in the walled and historic city of Chester and incarceration in the hotel, the Blossoms, which appeared to have been built in the year Abel Tasman discovered New Zealand — it felt like it — the All Blacks learned with some apprehension that they might encounter at Birkenhead, 20 miles distant, Englishmen who desired to establish that what had gone on at Twickenham in the games played by London Counties and England was effete stuff compared with what was customary in the heart of English rugby to the north. Their apprehensions sharpened at sight of the snow drifting down from the leaden sky overnight and during the morning. Snow was not a New Zealand experience. Nor was the cold congenial. When, later, rain was borne in by the wind, and the word passed around that there would be mud, mud, mountains of mud, the apprehensions rather tended to turn into tensions. The North, it was evident, resented the thought of English incompetence. They proclaimed this with an instant rush by their forwards and a towering kick by John Horton as their reaction to McKechnie's kick-off into the stiff wind. Horton dropped at goal, short, but at a lineout the All Blacks committed the folly of lifting and from 40 metres Young's kick, borne by the wind, became a goal. The pace of play was brisk enough to set up perspiration and the vigour of North's attack stimulated some degree of anxiety. Here, at last, was a backrow — Peter Dixon, Roger Uttley and Tony Neary, blessed by brains, brawn, skill, speed and strength — and as the battle passed from the break-in to the dogfight stage these men, with Dixon pre-eminent, became nuisances of the most confounded sort to the All Black midfield and cover-defence. Nor had many lineouts been played before a 24-year-old lock, John Butler, 6ft 4in and 15½ stones, displayed maturity, courage and craftmanship and, later, stamina, of the most admirable standard. With Billy Beaumont stirring along these gifted troops by example and exhortation, a very high quality indeed began to emerge — sufficient, in fact, to make one wonder why on earth England, almighty England, had not displayed comparable strength. Had not injury robbed the North of Fran Cotton, their huge prop who had been such a powerhouse for the 1977 Lions in New Zealand, it is possible the pack would have been irresistible. But perhaps the inclination of Young and Horton toward safety and, in Horton's case, dependence upon the Garryowen, limited the full exploitation of the forward strength. In Michael Slemen and Peter Squires, North were magnificently served at wing-threequarter and it was a match-saving relief indeed when Squires, squirming rather than dodging down the right touch, mismanaged the infield pass which would certainly have put his fullback Derek Boyd in for a try. Instead he somehow fired the ball into touch.

Great stuff this all was by North of England. When Dixon in the second half initiated one raid after another, the All Blacks could almost be heard saying to one another, "Oh God, here we go again". Nor could the All Blacks escape problems of their own manufacture — Donaldson with at least four crooked puts-in at the scrummage, Haden (when he could get the better of Butler) with difficulties of delivering the ball to Donaldson, Seear with a fumble which cost a pushover try, Williams in an unhappy moment which also cost a try when he was beaten to the bounce of the ball in-goal. When Young from 18 metres put North 6 points ahead after 29 minutes, the New Zealand outlook turned as grey as the day.

But amid all of the assaults and batterings, none smudged by unfairness, Mourie, though not quite himself, still was able to call out the character of his men. Within two minutes of Young's second goal, he gathered McKechnie's kick-out from halfway, sent Rutledge packing with the ball in hand and watched from a distance as Stuart Wilson, given the pass, sped for the goalline. When Wilson was checked, a yard short, McKechnie snapped up the ball and dived to the try. His converting kick, taken from wide out, soared to the goal; and very glad indeed were the All Blacks to be 6-6 at the break and with the wind now to be behind them. The vernacular best fits the strenuous second half. It was one hell of a struggle. It might have been more than that had not Osborne been most grossly obstructed as he chased a kick which returned an attack by Dixon and Beaumont. Referee Burnett marked the place for the penalty at about 32 metres from the goal. McKechnie came up. The circumstances were not dissimilar from those which attended his winning goal against Wales — a noisy crowd (only 10,000 but to a man, woman and child, entirely on the side of the North), a spot 18 or 20 metres in from the left touch, the result dependent upon his skill. Bafflingly, he placed the goal without the least trouble; bafflingly because, in other circumstances he might have foozled it hopelessly. So the All Blacks, with 23 minutes remaining, were three points to the good. Ardently strove the North. Fiercely answered the All Blacks. Absurdly, with five minutes remaining, Jaffray was involved in circumstances which suggested he had late-tackled Slemen. Young was offered the chance of the draw. Under the strain, for it had been a hard and heavy day for all who worked in or next door to the scrummage, he sliced the kick; and the counties of Cheshire, Cumbria, Durham, Lancashire, Northumberland and Yorkshire who were involved in the North of England representative team were beaten; but with the consolation, not at all inconsiderable, that they had decisively demonstrated English pride and English guts. Apparently they had other consolations, too. "Let me buy you a drink," said Dixon. "I'm sure it should be on me," said the New Zealander. "Not a chance," said Peter. "They've been rather good with our expenses this time."

Toward the end of his tour with the British Lions in 1966, Ray McLoughlin, famous as much for his IQ of 140-plus as for his combination of strength and technique as a prop-forward, offered the opinion that New Zealand rugby at administrative level deserved the appointment of a secretary-manager, at a salary of £25,000, who would become the game's dictator. Thus, thus and not otherwise, McLoughlin argued, would the faults and failings which had distressed his team and, on occasion, New Zealanders as well, be overcome. The man as a true professional would know how to anticipate and look after everything, he would become the equivalent of that brilliant administrator, Sir Stanley Rous, who by expert management raised English soccer to victory in the World Cup of 1966.

The McLoughlin suggestion was laughed to scorn. The New Zealand Rugby Union, so its champions said — no vast army, this — deserved to be warmly commended, this day and every day, for its organisational skill, its attention to detail, its constant thought for the good and welfare of its players.

Ha-bloody-ha. So you could say after considering the tour of Mourie's men — aspects such as the absence of a secretary for the honorary manager, travel arrangements by coach instead of train, neglect by the Four Home Unions of charter air-travel where this was desirable. For a certainty a secretary-manager worth £25,000 in the mid-sixties — the best part of $100,000 in 1978 — would not have dreamed of sanctioning the journey from Chester after the North of England match to Aberdeen for the match against North and Midlands of Scotland. The snows and winds and cold of winter were all about as the All Blacks placed their luggage in the foyer of the Hotel Blossoms — once experienced, never, never forgotten, or gone back to — at 8 o'clock on a Sunday morning, plunged into their bus at 9 and set off for Glasgow Airport, six mortal hours and more of driving broken by lunch. Airports are the same the whole world over; and the stay at this one was gratifying, but only for the Press and only for a short time, because the bar was open; at least at an airport you can be an alcoholic and stay anonymous and none will care. Then it was whoop-de-doo for 45 minutes or thereabouts by BAC aircraft to Aberdeen, where the welcomes were warm and the luggage was late. It was preposterous, this waste of a day, and a secretary-manager-dictator who let such things occur, at home or abroad, would have been for the guillotine without the option. To his credit Russell Thomas had complained and asked for a chartered aircraft from Manchester or Liverpool directly to Aberdeen. No go, said the Four Home Unions. A plane was not available. Bosh, and bosh again. No matter the cost, there should have been a *demand,* from New Zealand, for the charter. In default, the programme should have been changed to let the All Blacks play South of Scotland in a Border town. The British can be tough traders where their own welfare is concerned. Time enough, then, for the New Zealand union to be tough, too. After all, they had done British rugby a service by agreeing to substitute the All Blacks, at getting on for the eleventh hour, when the South African Rugby Board decided that it would be inappropriate to attempt to fulfil their projected full-scale tour of the British Isles by the Springboks during 1978 and 1979.

This messing-about by British authorities was unfortunate because the warmth of Scotland's welcome belied the grey cold of Aberdeen's granite heart. No All Black team touring the British Isles has ever been so diligent as were Mourie's men — largely, it ought to be said, at the instance of Russell Thomas — in visiting schools and the principal celebrant was the Robert Gordon College founded in Aberdeen in the 18th century. At Chester, Thomas had bespoken four All Blacks and various New Zealand Pressmen to attend at the school for luncheon. On the morning before match-day, the word drifted about that the occasion was to be rather important. A dozen more of the team immediately volunteered. At about the same time, Doug Bruce as a schoolmaster began to doubt that the chosen dress, blazer with white skivvy, would be quite suitable to the visit. Mourie agreed. Formal Number Two dress was ordained — blazer, collar and All Black tie. Thus the All Blacks were a trim and anything but grim band as they sauntered through the gates. Never was there such a welcome. Billy Bush appeared to be in danger of going down for the third time under the weight of autograph-seekers. Mourie, Williams, Bruce, Thomas, the best — wherever you looked you saw scads of kids surrounding the men in black. Lunch with wine! Wine, at a secondary school? And salmon, Scotch salmon, half as big as whales and monumentally delicious! Gad, sir, Scotland and Scottish education must be going right to the dogs; and a great pleasure it was to go with them, too. A great pleasure, also, for all New Zealanders to be in any way associated with Robert Gordon College. During the 1930s, the family of Captain Bisset Smith, founded the Otaki Scholarship, the terms of which provide that an outstanding pupil of the school spends several weeks each year touring New Zealand. Captain Bisset Smith was in command of the *Otaki,* of the New Zealand Shipping Company, when it was attacked in the Atlantic in 1917 by a German raider. So gallantly did the merchantman fight before its inevitable disappearance that the German ship itself was almost blown out of the water. Captain Bisset

Smith was awarded a posthumous Victoria Cross.

By the look of some of the Otaki Scholarship winners, including the most recent one, to whom the All Blacks were introduced, Robert Gordon College produced men of outstanding quality. One such was Chris Snape, the lock who captained North and Midlands. By personal example, not least in battles for possession at the lineout, Snape fostered in his team courage of the *Otaki* sort. Referee Roger Quittenton dished out penalties against them by the mile, no fewer than 13 in the first half and six in the second — with 13 awarded to the North, this was one of the big penalty-days of the tour — the massive All Black scrum won at least nine heels against the head and the Scottish cause looked hopeless, at least on paper. But, thanks principally to all-round gallantry, next to an extraordinarily talented backrow of Colin Watt, Ian Paxton and Tony Ingle-Finch, and thirdly to a 37-year-old scrumhalf, Ian McCrae, whose 20 years of first-class rugby had begun before Peter Robertson on the wing had been born, the All Blacks were compelled to rely upon wind and weight to roll out their barrel-load of 27 points in the second half. McCrae's career as Scotland's halfback ended after six caps when he played against Sid Going in the 1972-73 international. Scottish selectors have in their time been no less whimsical than England's and, by the sound of things, McCrae's gift for speaking his mind had settled his hash. Strange experience! On his play at Aberdeen, in quickness of pass, including a snappy reverse, and a spearing left-foot punt of stunning speed and accuracy, he still looked Scotland's finest scrumhalf, certainly far beyond the international, Alan Lawson. But there — once you offend in Scotland, the mark is upon you, never to be expunged. It was McCrae's fast pass which first rocked the All Blacks. The ball reached the outhalf, Colin High, at such speed that he had all the time he wanted, and more, for the drop-goal of 27 metres which opened the scoring. Only two minutes gone and the mighty New Zealanders already humbled. They did manage to scratch to a one-point lead on the call of half-time when a break by Loveridge, Knight and Williams put the ball into the arms of Richard Wilson, who scored in the corner. It was one of those days when poor Richard really had to do something. In 11 shots at goal, three of them in the first 13 minutes, he succeeded only twice. Much therefore depended upon Oliver in securing his defensive lines against the raiding Scots, especially John Adams with one mighty midfield cleavage, and the crisp, cool wind which swept down Linksfield in a setting most remarkably like St Kilda in Dunedin. Then he could safely set his men to the offensive of the second half. This was well done especially by Loveday and Knight (who had his finest game of the tour) among the forwards and by Robertson and Kururangi in the backs. It had been a toss-up whether

Jack Gleeson would play McGregor or Barry Ashworth. It would have been a fine thing for a McGregor to appear far in the north, on the verge of the Highlands; but the vote instead went to Ashworth, who celebrated with two tries to build up the scoring also marked by Richard Wilson (a try and two conversions), Rutledge, Robertson and Kururangi, with a drop-goal by Dunn chucked in. A sad experience for McGregor to sit out once more. A silent man by nature, he kept his thoughts to himself; which, yet again, was a tribute to the character in the team.

It was a victory, as expected; but perhaps the visit to Robert Gordon College was the more memorable. Even so, the effort of the All Blacks on the field and in social contact during the brief visit to Aberdeen will be, it is to be hoped, more warmly remembered than the execrable performance of a large team of New Zealand supporters who invaded the hotel dining-room and lounge toward the end of the formal and charmingly-humoured dinner to the teams and who could not be persuaded to leave. The Scots and the All Blacks found sanctuary in a distant bar of the hotel and there took much pleasure in each other's company, leaving behind a discordant shambles.

CHAPTER EIGHT

The Riddle of the Tour

AS A LEADING honorary life-member, for services over and beyond the call of duty, of the Front-Row Forwards Club, which is an organisation of pragmatic, hard-minded men, Ian ("The Mighty Mouse") McLauchlan was bound to use a style of interrogation rather different from the Biblical. Accordingly when he asked *his* question, which was also a teaser, it was natural that his subsequent actions differed from Pilate's (Pontius, if you remember your Bacon, asked his celebrated "What is truth?" and stayed not for answer). Every so often, in the ante-room of the North British hotel in Edinburgh, amid the pleasant after-dinner talk which characterises the gracious Scots, "The Mouse" gave out. "What," he demanded, "is a great team? I ask you, What is a great team?"

What *was* the answer? He refused to supply it. He had already said Mourie's was the finest New Zealand pack he had played against. No small compliment this. He may even have said that this was the greatest of all of the packs he had played. *That* really would have been something. Yet the difference between the best pack he had played and the best New Zealand pack, if he was differentiating, would not have been material. It followed that Mourie's team was blessed, according to the stern McLauchlan standards, with excellent forward strength. Since it is improbable, these days, that any team can be great unless its forwards are of the finest standard, it seemed reasonable to infer that "The Mouse" considered this was a great All Black team. McLauchlan had played, on this day of the Grand Slam, his 38th international for Scotland, with a number of others chucked in for Lions' teams in New Zealand and South Africa — was it not his follow-up to his charge-down of Alan Sutherland's clearing-kick which set the 1971 Lions to scoring in the first test against the All Blacks? And was not that try, in hindsight, decisive to the Lions' historic achievement of beating the All Blacks in the series? He was thus, by the record, no muggins; and the subtle suggestion, implicit in that demanding question, "What is a great team?" that Mourie's men had forged from their finest players a team of sufficient quality to be called great was as powerful a tribute as could have been paid.

Yet there was a nagging edge to the question, all the same. Would a great team have contained players capable of making blunders as crass as those which were committed by Bruce and Stuart Wilson against a Scottish attack which yielded a try to their left-wing, Bruce Hay? Would Bryan Williams, as a member of a great side, have permitted himself extravagances which looked, potentially, of deadly significance to the hopes of the Grand Slam? Would there have been blunders by Bruce in fielding passes, by Donaldson in having a clearing-kick charged down, by Mourie in conceding a penalty in the last frantic minutes when the All Blacks, 18-9 ahead, could not lose? (One rather thought, as to the Mourie incident and being aware of the man's cool long-headedness, that he might have said to himself, "Ah well, what's three points? They'll take time." But there was a hell of a clamour, all the same, when Andy Irvine's kick at the goal rebounded from upright or crossbar.) Would Haden, as a final thought, have struck down Alastair McHarg with a mighty punch more or less in the full presence of Referee John West, if this had been a truly great All Black team?

No matter. Just as beauty is determined by the eye of the beholder, so, surely, was the answer to "The Mouse's" tantalising question a matter for individual taste and judgment. Faintly might it be wondered whether the New Zealand Rugby Union's council, meeting in Wellington on the morning before the international, had helped the All Blacks in their march upon first the Grand Slam and second the greatness that victory in all four internationals would presumably be vest in the team. Early in the tour, Ron Palenski, head of the New Zealand Press Association's London bureau and the PA's correspondent for the tour, had beaten all comers to a story alleging that the Northern Transvaal Rugby Union wanted to celebrate 1979 by forming a South Pacific Barbarians' team made up of 13 New Zealanders, including 10 or 11 of Mourie's team, Australians, Fijians and perhaps other Islanders for a tour of South Africa. It was a big story which became bigger when the rugby council, having decided that it would be inappropriate to pass on the invitations because of the heavy programme of international and other fixtures already scheduled for 1979, promptly received protesting cables from a number of the All Blacks who said they wanted to tour. This was potentially upsetting to the morale of the All Black party; and as late as 24 hours before kick-off at Murrayfield further grief threatened with the news from Wellington that the council, after reconsidering the whole question, had decided to pass on invitations to six players. The possibilities of disturbance to the tour were evident in some player reactions to the news from Wellington. In the foyer of the North

British, Mourie made a tart retort when asked if he was likely to be one of the six. He was, he said, "not interested" in the project; and though, then and later, he kept his opinions to himself, it was reasonable to suppose that he held strong views against association with South Africa. Haden was known to be a key man in Northern Transvaal's eyes — gifted lineout players are, practically speaking, the Cullinan Diamonds of modern rugby. Oliver, too, was warmly spoken of. But these, and other players, parried questions as to their intentions and gave the impression that they disliked the intrusion, which was also potentially upsetting. Russell Thomas, though he said that, as a councillor, he supported the change of mind, and Jack Gleeson were evidently disturbed at the introduction of the wretched South African question at this fateful hour of their tour. Indeed, the council was less than intelligent in its timing.

In the preliminaries to the build-up to the big test, it was enlightening to hear opinions about British rugby from a Scottish expert, not least because in the 72 hours of build-up to the game, the play in it and the celebrations of victory, much that happened could be said to represent some kind of answer to McLauchlan's persistent and nagging question, "I ask you, What is a great team?" As has been mentioned, British experts in the Fleet Street area bounded by Holborn on one end and the Strand on the other were reaching toward and delivering final judgments upon the All Blacks' abilities. To the sensitive, the thrust of the blow from Dawes at Rodney Parade through Lander to the columns of the *Daily Telegraph,* that the All Blacks were the most boring touring international team of modern rugby, was severe as a criticism of the All Blacks. But there was also severity in the view that British rugby, because of the inability of its players to score tries against and/or beat the All Blacks, had gone to the dogs.

These judgments of the mighty men of the media, few of whom had close connection with the selecting and training of teams at first-class level, including internationals, contrasted significantly with the appreciation of the physical education lecturer at Jordanhill College in Glasgow, Bill Dickinson, who for years until 1977 had been, as the Scottish Rugby Union coyly called its coach, "adviser to the Scottish captain". Dickinson's training methods, amply reliant upon the watch as a means of judging the improvement in the pace-rate and through it the work-rate of players, might seem academic but as to his knowledge of the game and players no questions arose. At Hamilton in New Zealand in 1977, he was introduced to a famous coach of 20 years before, Dick Everest, whose Waikato teams of the 1950s not only won and held the Ranfurly Shield but also brought off one of the great sensations of all time, the defeat of the 1956 Springboks in their first match in New Zealand. Few would cavil at Everest's ranking as a profound judge of the game. He and Dickinson talked agreeably for a moment or two. Then something set Bill going and for several minutes he expounded one technique or another, nicely balancing his judgments and firmly delivering his opinions. He was called elsewhere. "Well," said Dick, wide-eyed and the least bit astonished, "he's decisive — and knowledgeable."

Thus when Dickinson, a day or two before the Grand Slam contest, said of British rugby of the late 1970s that it "is very much more highly organised than it was in 1967" — he was making a comparison between the teams led by Mourie and Brian Lochore — and that British teams were now more difficult to play, his opinions suggested that the tendency to denigrate British teams rather than praise the All Blacks might be rooted in anti-Colonialism. Dickinson himself had some critical opinions of Mourie's team. He thought they were unable to play with the freedom Lochore's men had enjoyed. Their play had been slightly inhibited; they had greater potential than they permitted themselves to believe. But, said Bill — and he spoke as an expert — "Jack Gleeson has done wonders in coaching his team. By comparison with the standards of the All Blacks against the Lions in New Zealand in 1977, by comparison, too, with the play in the early matches of the 1978 tour, Jack has tidied things up remarkably well."

Shrewd judgments, these. Dickinson's crystal ball was awesomely efficient when it told him that "Scotland cannot win this match — but they could steal it".

Mourie, much later, cast his mind over the international. "If we had not let Scotland score their try," he said, "I believe we would have had no difficulty in winning decisively." Precisely. That was where the stealing came in. That was why, too, McLauchlan kept up his patter — "I ask you, What is a great team?" It was a dreadful moment for the All Blacks in the eighth minute of the game when Hay scored wide out on the left and from a mark just inside the touchline Andy Irvine placed the converting goal. The circumstances were a reflection on at least two of the All Blacks. Stuart Wilson tumbled full-length when turning on the soft and skiddy field to deal with a slicing punt artfully placed by McGeechan behind the All Black line of backs. When the ball was fly-kicked ahead, Bruce, coming back as a cover-defender, made a dismal hash of his attempt to nudge the ball two or three yards into touch. Hay had three Scotsmen thundering at his side. One, lying full-length on the ground out of play, deflected the ball back infield with his hand. Another made a pass to Hay. Everything was a terrible scramble, most of all in the All Blacks' defence, as Hay charged over the tryline and, not too long afterwards, Irvine goaled.

To reflect adversely upon the competence of Wilson and Bruce was not to belittle the Scottish effort. It was a masterpiece of opportunism distinguished above all by speed. At the moment of Hay's try, the great Scottish heart burst asunder with pride. At the sign by the touch-judges that Irvine's kick was a goal, the joy was renewed. Now was the time, indeed, for Mourie and his men to wonder whether the blight that had affected New Zealand teams in the British Isles from 1905 onwards was to hit them, too. The preliminaries to kick-off showed how strong, and potentially menacing, was the Scottish pride. On the green, green field on a calm, calm but darkening afternoon, the 31-piece band of the Royal Highland Fusiliers marched up and down, first quickly then at a slow pace, to the "Ode for Joy" of Beethoven's Ninth — whimsy had seized the programme editor who described the composer as "Beat". The 30-piece band of pipes and drums of the Queen Victoria School at Dunblane was no less rewarding, not least because, coming from a school founded for the sons of Scottish servicemen, it was a reminder of the 200,000 names of Scottish dead retained at Edinburgh Castle as a reminder of the nation's vast bloodletting in the two great world wars. Yet here were descendants and kinsfolk of the dead gathered at Murrayfield to display Scottish cleverness — not least in stealing — speed, resource, intelligence and, above all, courage. Nor seemed there to be, just before kick-off, many devolutionists in the audience of 70,000. The taking up of and carrying through with the National Anthem was seemly, yet fervent, an invocation quite as significant as the wild and cheerful yells greeting the Scottish team's appearance and the bands' playing of the magnificent "Scotland the Brave".

What to do, six points down and Bruce and Osborne mishandling passes? When the attack shot past Donaldson, another piece of stealing seemed promised. It might have occurred but for a timely penalty to New Zealand. Williams flicked into prominence and drooped out of it with despair when he mishandled a ball which came to him. Whoops of joy were raised by New Zealand supporters when, at last, a Scottish mistake — McGeechan getting offside — gave McKechnie a chance to goal from 30 metres. The chance was well taken. Scotland now led by 6 to 3 and the All Blacks, encouraged, began to "go". One of them all too soon nearly went. Exasperated by McHarg's continual and blatant obstruction, Haden at last turned executioner with a punch so well timed that the Scot fell flat, arms akimbo, and had to be restored by that old-fashioned but unusual rugby device, smelling-salts under the nose. Referee West, as he was bound, spoke acidly to Haden. It seems that he also spoke to McHarg on the lines of "I saw that and we'll have no more of that sort of business". West also said he was not impressed by McHarg's theatrical descent after the punch. The All Blacks were impressed by his reaction but still, wondered why he had not tidied up the Scot before the punch became necessary. (Of McHarg, Dickinson had said, with some fondness, that "Really, I always think of Alastair as the original serpent in rugby's Garden of Eden".)

If strange misadventures pursued Williams, so, too, was Irvine cursed by unaccustomed mistakes. Twenty-four minutes into the play, he of all people knocked on at, of all places, his own goalmouth a plunging kick by Donaldson. At the scrummage so close to the tryline, the All Blacks heeled. Then they strove, steadily pushing back the Scots. At a finely-judged moment, Seear picked up the ball. No one could stop his try. It was simplicity for McKechnie to place the goal.

So they fought on, both teams dogged and determined, all men, not least the sufferers, committed to the despatch of the opposing side. David Leslie had to retire with an injury and Ian Lambie came on, first cap, in a light which was turning from gleaming to gloom and to join a forward contest so fierce that when the two packs faced each other, waiting to pack down at the scrummage, the cloud of steam rising from their bodies suggested a geyser on the blow, a miniature Pohutu at the least. At a lineout penalty — and Scotland was growing over-excited, it was giving away too many — McKechnie took a shot from 42 metres. Too far, surely too far. Remarkably, the ball sailed over. At 12 to 6, with 20 minutes to play, New Zealand seemed safe.

Safe for just three minutes. At the end of which, McGeechan with the snappiest of shots dropkicked a goal. 12 to 9 to New Zealand; and, from the Castle not too far distant, the ghosts of Scotland's honoured past began to call to McGeechan and his men, commanding them to strive beyond the call of duty. Magnificent were the Scots in these great last minutes in which they rammed at the New Zealand goal, were repulsed, returned to ram again. The daylight was going, going, gone. Sometimes, in the more desperate moments, it looked as if New Zealand was as well. "For some dreadfully tense seconds which seemed to stretch into hours," an account of the time remarked, "the All Blacks, within a couple of minutes of no-side, were required to attend at a lineout within two yards of their own corner-flag, Scotland to throw in. One blunder at the lineout, another at the succeeding scrummage, could cost them the game and all the fame they have now garnered. Instead the blunder, too critical to believe, was McGeechan's attempt at a chip-kick which was charged down by Bruce."

Who could hope ever to expunge from the minds of the millions who watched in person or on television as Bruce's body interposed between the kick and the goalposts, the ball rebounding sharply metres behind McGeechan. Irvine was up in the line. A great space of Murrayfield lay empty. Osborne, with instant timing, chased upon the ball, booting it hard. In the darkness, which was all but Stygian, he chased the ball beyond the halfway, into the Scottish quarter. Perhaps because his fair head stood out like a Davy's lamp, Robertson was to be seen, running so fast that he looked to be streaking up to and past

Alastair Cranston. By now the ball was slithering gently not many metres short of the uprights.

How Roberston managed to toe the ball ahead into the in-goal area without losing the advantage of his colossal speed passed human understanding. But even in the murk, it was possible to see that with his dive he fairly collected the ball in his arms for the try which McKechnie converted and which was the winning trick in the Grand Slam. The Poet's Corner of New Zealand rugby immediately enlarged itself to take care that the efforts of Bruce, of Osborne and, most particularly, of Robertson, would not now, or ever after, be forgotten. "Wonderful, wonderful Copenhagen," says the song. Ah, but they should see Robertson.

Irvine kicked deep, Mourie was penalised, Irvine's attempt at goal rebounded. All of a sudden, the All Black bomb once more exploded. As before, though this time it was even more difficult to see, a great streaming rush developed from the All Blacks' quarter to the Scottish goal. A dim figure established as Rutledge dived at the goalline. The whistle sounded. It was the end of the game. "I scored," said Rutledge. "I am sorry," said John West. "I was unsighted." Who could blame him, in that murk?

In any case, there was no thought of protest. The deed had been done, the slam had been made. Bodies gleamed whitely in the darkness as foeman swopped jerseys and trooped exhausted from the field. For a time, a long, long time, Scotland had looked capable not of winning the match but of stealing it. Its men like McHarg and Alan Tomes had won fine ball at the lineout, its hooker, Colin Deans, had won a heel against the head, its backrow of Mike Biggar, Leslie (and Lambie) and Gordon Dickson had swarmed all over the field. The pace was greater than of any team which had opposed the All Blacks; and every so often, McGeechan, Jim Renwick and the other backs threatened to slit the defence. But now, "Retreat" had been sounded. They all surged through the gloom to their hot tubs, to their drinks, to their companionship at the dinner, to the revelry of the dance. All was glorious, for victor and vanquished. And round and round, stealing about, went "Mighty Mouse" with his baffling question, "I ask you, What is a great team?"

What, indeed? But Mourie's men had to be memorable. How could distinction be denied to the mighty Slammers?

CHAPTER NINE

Hubbub And Hullabaloo

IT LOOKED TO be about the silliest situation in all of All Black history — Mourie as captain summoning three or four forwards to perform a haka with him while Loveridge, his halfback, was footling about at halfway with a tap-kick penalty. It looked even sillier moments later when one of the haka team, Knight, in rushing after the ball conceded a penalty. Though the distance was 55 metres from goal, Andy Irvine, the Scot of palpitating brilliance, struck so monstrous a blow that the ball hit the crossbar. Had it slid over instead of rebounding, that would have been the end of the matter. However, in the ten vigorous minutes which remained of their tour, the All Blacks while hurling themselves all over the field were awarded, as an act of heavenly grace, a scrum-five metres. (It was not one of the most popular awards of Referee Norman Sanson's career.) The New Zealanders won the heel. Loveridge immediately fired out a long pass. Dunn with all the practised care of a man in his 30th international when in fact he had never played in one carefully sighted his right-footed drop at goal. As the ball sailed over the bar, the last fine threads of the tour by Mourie's men were stitched. They had compiled a record of 17 wins in 18 matches. More, they had won a place in Rugby's Destiny as the first Grand Slammers from Down Under.

But a haka? Here, on of all places, Cardiff Arms Park? The sight was more than disturbing, it was desolating. Not at any level does one mock the traditions of a great game.

"Rugby is a fun game," said Mourie, lamely. "It was a fun thing to do." What had disturbed the sense of values in this remarkably sensible and intelligent man? Later, the truth came out. "I knew what was coming," said Russell Thomas. "I did not disagree. We felt we had to do something, *anything,* to lessen the tensions of the Bridgend business."

Fond the hopes, genuine the intention, sad the come-down. In the moment of the fifth minute of play when John Ashworth, who claimed later he was raking for the ball, inflicted a grievously deep wound on the face of J. P. R. Williams, Bridgend ceased to be the name of a Welsh club celebrating its centenary and became the symbol of a bitterness which might not be expunged for a long time. For 16 matches, the All Blacks by command and earnest wish had played rugby of a sporting kind unparalleled in modern international tours. The command and wish, principally enunciated by Jack Gleeson and earnestly supported by Mourie, were not new.

"You mean," said Frank Oliver during the Wallabies' tour in New Zealand, "that we can't have a go at them when they come the rough stuff on us? And we are All Blacks!"

"That's what I mean," said Gleeson. "No rough stuff, today or ever."

The moment of the fifth minute all but destroyed the grace of the tour. "It was the kind of game," said Mourie, "which was bound to produce an incident." True enough. True, too, that Bridgend, fired up by *hwyl* and supreme determination to prove that at least one team in Wales was as good as Munster or, more precisely, better than the All Blacks, fired the first bullets. The knees which were lifted in the front row of the first scrum were menacing. The early tackles were next best to king-hit jobs.

It was also true that Ashworth later said that if rugby required him to kick men on the ground, he would not play the game. He appeared to be appalled by the extent of Williams' injury. Here and there, he said he was sorry. He wished the incident had not occurred.

Necessarily, one chooses words with care. Nevertheless, the criticism must be made. Ashworth moved each foot, or boot, in the time-honoured motions of raking for the ball. The first movement might be forgiven. Williams' head was a long way from the ball; but in these early minutes, the passion in the play was extreme; even a saint might have rushed, as Ashworth did, to win the ball for his team. The second movement was inexcusable. He rucked without due care and attention. Within the Road Code, driving without due care and attention can be a fatal fault. If Ashworth could not see that no possible advantage could accrue to his team from his act, he was displaying an indiscipline out of character with the tour and the tenets of the game. Bridgend was his business. It was a bad business.

At sight of Williams' face as he stood up, irresolute whether to leave the field yet determined to keep his stamp on Bridgend's play while he was absent, the dogs of war were let slip. The sight of the streaming blood was indeed shocking. So began the process of radios screaming, headlines blaring, television dissecting. Fleet Street moved in for the kill. It was not remembered that Mourie and his men for 16 matches had behaved with so scrupulous an attention to fair and sporting play that the reasonable inference was that this was their only approved method. Now, so it was to be understood, the Colonials, having blundered, must be taught by their seniors how they should behave. In the *Guardian,* David Frost, a mild man, said Ashworth's act had cast a blight on the tour. Most of the rest were much more harsh. Hubbub and hullabaloo were all around. The response of a haka during the game against the Barbarians was ill-chosen. It was ingenuous. Even worse was John Ashworth's provocative response to jeering when at the start of the second half of the Baa-Baas' match he took the place of the injured Johnstone. He flung his fists above his head as if to say, in the phrase so well known to students of BBC television, "Get knotted".

Perhaps it was inevitable that with two Bs, Bridgend and Barbarians, involved, this should turn out to be a bastard of a week. The Baa-Baas did their bit. Their game was sensational for movement, variety, pace and excitement. At their dinner, their speakers conveyed profound appreciation of the New Zealand Rugby Union's action in agreeing to supplant, at late notice, the abandoned tour of the Springboks. The club's president, Herbert Waddell, in a sense dismissed Bridgend by recalling how the British team in South Africa in 1924 fielded "three dirty buggers" one of whom, Blakiston, a de-frocked priest who later was made knight baronet, was deliberately set upon and kicked from pillar to post. Each time he went down seemed certain to be the last. Each time, Waddell said to him, "Are you all right, Blackie?" Blakiston staggered back into consciousness and in the second half the Springbok who had done most of the damage to him was carried from the field, knocked cold — by Blakiston. The point of Mr Waddell's story seemed to be that atavistic impulses were sometimes bound to stir in men who were involved in the more passionate events of rugby and that their occasional appearance should not be taken to herald the end either of the world or the game. It was an amusing story. No less diverting was the dinner-table conversation of an eminent Irish rugby man who frankly deplored the manners and attitudes of the Welsh in rugby and who baldly said that the English, the Scots and the Irish would much prefer to confine rugby in Britain to themselves. The man, important enough to be manager of an Irish international team, lamented that it was the Welsh who had marred the "wonderful" tour of Mourie's men. "Unfortunately," he said, "the Welsh are necessary to our rugby."

This was biting stuff from non-Welshmen. But Welshmen themselves could be critical of their kind. Almost as sensational an event of the week as the wounding of Williams was the walk-out of All Blacks and Bridgend players when the father of Williams, Dr Peter Williams, in his capacity as president of the club was making an unscheduled speech at the dinner to the teams. Dr Williams was distressed. He had, he said, encouraged each of his four sons to play the game. He now regretted this. He regretted, too, that at least two All Blacks had used methods which were outside the bounds of sportsmanship. He did not belabour the points. Essentially, no more than half a dozen sentences bore upon the unfortunate events of the afternoon. But the action of a number of players was decisive. Overlooking the right of any man, not least an official, to criticise — even if the speech was unscheduled — overlooking, too, the courtesies which are fundamental to formal dinners, they moved from the dining-room to an ante-room in which was located, conveniently, a bar. It might have been a guess that the Welsh international, Steve Fenwick, was the first to rise and march. A statement that J. P. R. Williams himself took the long walk from the top table was smartly denied by Williams himself; no one troubled to discover where he was when Mourie, turning to make the usual presentation of an All Black tie (of which J. P. R. probably had a fair collection already — unless he had traded them for other ties), found that his man was not present. It was a fact that Russell Thomas was unhappy with the All Blacks. Indeed the march was a condemnation of the players rather than a tribute to their courage. But the point was that a West Wales' man who happened to be president of the Welsh Rugby Union, Mr D. L. James, was profuse in his apologies to Russell Thomas over the remarks of Dr Peter Williams. Moreover, other Welshmen at the dinner assured Thomas that their sentiments did not accord with Dr Peter's. Mr James, always "D.L." and always such a charming, courteous and genial companion that he could be termed, as the highest of compliments, a dear little man, was West Welsh to the backbone. It is in West Wales, of all parts of rugby of the four Home Unions, that pragmatism is most often practised in fearsome local derbies which appear to be warmly appreciated and remembered by players and public. Pragmatism did not excuse John Ashworth's act; but it might be held to explain it.

Pragmatism was certainly in the decision of the Bridgend committee to play at hooker their celebrated striker, Geoffrey Davies. Within the preceding fortnight, Davies and the hooker of the Cardiff club team, Mike Watkins, both of them members of the Wales B squad, had been arrested for being drunk and disorderly. Brought to Court, each had been fined.

The Welsh Rugby Union immediately dropped the two from the B squad. Cardiff also swooped. Watkins was suspended for the rest of the season, a sentence of, in effect, five months. No man, according to law, ought to be punished twice for the same offence. Yet the Welsh at the real heart of the game, the Welsh who so warmly welcomed "Bunny" Tremain's touring supporters party after the Welsh international, take great pride in their rugby. Instinctively, they wish it to be *sans peur et sans reproche*. Bridgend's decision to play Davies appeared not to be warmly appreciated by this portion of the community.

The little chap — comparatively; he stood 5 feet 10 inches — certainly was primed to the eyeballs with *hwyl* at the first scrum. It was rich irony that Davies is by occupation a sweet operative. Ian Stephens and Meredydd James, his props, were quite as wound up. So was the rest of the team. Who could blame them, young and impressionable men that they were? When Mourie went to J. P. R. Williams for the toss a long time before kick-off — some accounts said he did this an hour beforehand — he found all of the Bridgend men already togged for the game. So they were out there to die for both dear old Bridgend and dear old Wales.

The confounded pity of the first scrum, which at Bridgend's instigation was violent and dirty, and of most of the rest of the game was that Bridgend's concentration on illegal and nefarious practices and the inevitable response in kind by the All Blacks detracted pretty substantially from the club's considerable skill. Next to Wales, this was by far the best Welsh team to be fielded against the All Blacks. Roy Evans and Billy Howe (two pounds short of 18 stone, begod) were magnificent locks who gave Haden and Loveday the devil of a time. Stephens, Davies and James were a stern, strong front-row. The backrow-men, Gareth Jones, Steve Ellis and Gareth Williams all got about the field as if they had ants in their pants. Gerald Williams was a dandy scrumhalf, quite undismayed by the masses of mud which were stirred up by the furious forward contest. He not only threw fast and accurate passes but, faithful to his occupation as a heating engineer, gave Loveridge the hottest of times. Through the outer backs, from Ian Williams at flyhalf to the centres Fenwick and Lyndon Thomas, to the tiny, 5 feet 7 inches tall Vivian Jenkins on one wing and the 21-year-old Ian Davies on the other and to the lord and master, J. P. R. himself, all was potential glory. They had speed, courage and a very decent idea of attack. Next to Gerald Williams', the memorable display was J. P. R.'s. Playing for Wales against the All Blacks, he had been doleful and dreadful, uncertain in handling, as slow as a carthorse in movement. Today, J. P. R. was restored in all his glory. He made one catch over his head, his back turned and in the grandest style turned about to set up a strong counter-attack. He did many other things expertly and with that quality of courage which had always been his hallmark.

When it was possible to forget the ancillaries of boot and fist, the central portion of the game, the football itself, was interesting and stimulating. Kururangi in the ninth minute fielded in his own quarter.

Bearing left, he ran at full speed, beyond the quarter-line, up to halfway. Bridgenders reached for him, clutched the air and tore their hair. Robert rushed on. Rather beyond halfway, having evaded uncountable opponents, he passed to Taylor. Taylor, too, ran at speed. He had Bryan Williams in support. Every so often, Taylor changed gear, not so much for a different speed as for a different idea. He fiddled with his hands. A pass was certain. He stopped fiddling. You could not be sure (for one damned good reason; Mark wasn't either) what he would do. He fiddled again. He ran. Finally, he offered a dummy, left, and bore right, plunging to the goalline for the try. Much of the tour will go, inevitably, from the minds of those whose daily duty it was to watch and report it. When most is gone, the long, lovely run of Kururangi and Taylor, so strong, so brave, so daring, so glorious, will be remembered in fine detail.

The All Blacks made other significent contributions, too, to the technical side of the game. "Mourie the Peacemaker", as he had to be during odious moments of conflict, raced all about the field, scored a relatively simple try at the end — a try none the less — and was especially effective in wheedling his men to go with him when he made peels from several mauls. Bridgend mud was not much different from Carisbrook mud and Seear, back on the old home stand, so to speak, reacted joyously, not least in fine work at the back of the lineout. The pack stirred and struggled without failing to conquer its principal fault of saying to Loveridge, in effect, "Over to you", as it shovelled the ball in all sorts of ways at him. Taranaki mud is not much different from Bridgend's, either, and Loveridge was not discommoded. But on this day when he found that Bridgend mud was not much different from Lancaster Park's, "Olly" Bruce reverted completely to the type cast at Lancaster in such conditions years ago. He kicked with the left foot, he kicked with the right, more or less invariably he kicked. It was not a just reward that before the half he was late-tackled by Ian Williams so hard as to be all but knocked out; but it was a criticism, the All Blacks being as generally superior as they were to the liveliest club team in Wales, that the yield of all their effort was an early penalty by Richard Wilson, another fine, long one of more than 40 metres after the Taylor try, a 20-metre goal by the same man early in the second half and finally, three minutes from no-side, the Mourie try from a Bridgend misfield at a lineout on their goalline. Before the break, and after the All Blacks had led 10-0, Fenwick twice goaled, once from 22 metres, the second time from 35 metres. Steve had a chance, when Knight was convicted of holding James' head more or less in chancery while he biffed powerful right rips into the body, to goal from little more than 25 metres six or eight minutes before the end and a score then might have caused Bridgend to step into overdrive. But, as before remarked, Bruce was playing his sterile style; and the All Blacks remained unbeaten by the Welsh in Wales; no insignificant effort, considering that such a feat, only previously performed by the Invincibles of 1924, had been denied the teams of 1905, 1935, 1953, 1963 and 1972.

On the shady side, the match was black. It was surely a misfortune for the authorities to appoint an Englishman, Laurie Prideaux, as the referee of such a match. No doubt Mr Prideaux's qualifications were excellent, no doubt, too, that he deserved to break into the big-time. But he was small in stature, a misfortune for a referee confronted with a match likely to rate high in the Passionate Stakes. Nor did he react with alacrity to the signs of trouble implicit in the first scrum, which was collapsed and in which, at the re-form, those Bridgend knees resembled pistons. Mr Prideaux did not stand a chance of detecting the fault when Ashworth made his second strike and J. P. R.'s head snapped and jerked from the sickening impact. He was on duty, as he should have been, on the other side of the ruck. But Mr Prideaux, perhaps because he was a reasonable man who did not expect footballers to fight, wanted in the composure, the presence, which conveys to the angriest of players that they would be better advised to tread warily. Hence, early on, Geoff Davies fought Knight. Hence, throughout, the elbow jab was a standing order for most of the forwards. Hence the belting by Knight of James. Hence a slugging match between Geoff Davies and Haden staged as a sideshow to a great go up the field by Mourie and Ashworth. The match soon generated a fetid atmosphere. An experienced referee of decisive mien, especially a man of the Alan Welsby (West Wales fixture) kind, would soon have sorted things out.

But that is not to absolve the two teams of responsibility for a dirty, dreadful contest. Incontestably, the first fault was Bridgend's. They were out on the Brewery Field to win at all costs. But the worst fault was John Ashworth's.

Which was an explanation of, but not an excuse for, the extraordinary sight of the haka led by Mourie in the last critical phase of the match against the Barbarians in which the All Blacks, by incompetence in finishing off brilliant attacks and ruinously bad goalkicking by McKechnie, fiddled away what should have been a decisive victory established by the most dynamic rugby of the tour and were in danger until the forwards, and Loveridge and Dunn, all operating at maximum efficiency, produced the winning drop goal.

The selection of the Barbarians is done on the recommendation of a small committee — two from each of the four Home Unions — and various bigwigs of the club and appeared in 1978 to be principally the work of the club's secretary, Geoffrey Windsor-Lewis, who after a distinguished career (at least in rugby) at Cambridge was twice capped for Wales in 1960. Geoffrey came of good stock. His father, for many years a medical man in Cambridge, played for the University and several times for Wales during the 1920s and with the passing of time was becoming one of the survivors of the great band of Barbarians — Emil de Lissa, Jack Haigh Smith, Glyn Hughes, Herbert Waddell, Jock Wemyss, Ernie Crawford, Rowe Harding and so on — who not least through Barbarianism had acquired some measure of immortality within their own lifetime. They set rigorous standards. When Noel Stanley as manager of the 1974 All Blacks sat on Herbert Waddell's right at the club's dinner at the London Hilton, he was startled that Herbert, pointing a menacing finger and growling in his grittiest Glaswegian, exclaimed: "That man will never play for the Barbarians again." That man, Fran Cotton, had lit his cigarette before the loyal toast. Such social faux pas had counted, in Baa-Baa eyes, against many men and had been used, when discovered, for the industry of sneering at the club. Yet the club, rightly or wrongly, adhered to standards which were set when the Right Reverend W. J. Carey, one of the earliest members, composed the celebrated words, "Rugby football is a game for gentlemen of all classes but never for a bad sportsman in any class."

Rightly or wrongly, too, the club preferred that teams it fielded against touring international sides, a fashion started in 1947-48 to relieve the financial stress of the tour of Bill McLean's Australian Wallabies, should not be taken to represent British Isles rugby. This stigma attached, not with complete justification, to the club's team which in the last match beat the hitherto victorious Springbok team of 1960-61, again to the team of 1973 which with some of the most glorious rugby ever seen at the Arms Park defeated Ian Kirkpatrick's All Blacks and yet again to the team of 1974, which had the eight forwards and the great scrumhalf, Gareth Edwards, who among them had been principally responsible for the majestic effort by the 1974 Lions of beating South Africa 3 to 1, with the last drawn. It was the dream of others than the Barbarians that British Isles' teams should be fielded as a matter of course against such visiting teams as All Blacks and Springboks. On a quiet afternoon of their great tour of 1971, the Lions' managers of the time, Dr Douglas Smith and Mr Carwyn James — each, incidentally, a Baa-Baa — mused at a Press conference over the idea. They believed, strongly, that the dice were loaded against national teams which played strong teams touring the British Isles. A Lions' side, well chosen and trained, would, they said, correct the imbalance. The impact upon British sporting affairs of British teams beating the invaders in, say, three of four test matches, one in each country, would be dynamic. Smith and James pursued their idea at the end of the '71 tour, pleading to the Four Home Unions that they should accept the proposal *in toto*. When the Home Unions rejected the plea, the proposers, supported by some influential journalists, urged that the Barbarians at the least should accept a role as banner-bearers of British rugby. Impalpably, pressure was upon Geoffrey Windsor-Lewis to field in the club's colours a team which would appear to all initiates to represent the best of the British game.

Though he himself would not have said it, it was greatly to the credit of Windsor-Lewis that he chose to ignore the pressure and instead field a team capable of expressing the club's time-honoured precept of Up-Guards-and-at-'em. Specially intriguing were the choices of the great French flankers from the Toulouse club, Jean-Claude Skrela and Jean-Pierre Rives, each of them a mighty contributor to French rugby in the past few years and each, too, a Barbarian. It was good to see, too, Will Dickinson, the Midlands' man who ought to have been chosen for England against the All Blacks, Neil Hutchings, an uncapped Aberavon centre who was said to have a little more flair and pace than either Fenwick or Gravell of the Welsh team — it would be difficult to have less of these qualities than these leading members of the Welsh Heavy Brigade — and Elgan Rees, who had played for the Lions in New Zealand but who had yet to win his cap for Wales. It was a coup for the club to have persuaded the brilliant Welsh flyhalf Phil Bennett to return to the big time after his decision of months before to quit international rugby. Perhaps not too much strong-arming was needed. After his miserable tour with the British Lions in 1977, bowed down by captaincy, the weather and an amazing, widespread and utterly unfounded rumour that he had committed a serious social solecisim, Bennett must have been dying for the chance to show the skills which had made him the heaviest points-scorer in international history.

Jack Gleeson reacted warmly to the Barbarians' team. He wanted, he said, a good game, not a test match, to round out the tour. He himself experimented. Fleming had been coming along nicely at Number 8, moving more nimbly and with better physical coordination than Seear. Donaldson was out of the question because of injury but in any case Loveridge deserved preferment. If not so strong as Donaldson as a runner, he had the better blindside break, his clearing pass was a little faster, he looked to be rather nippier in some of the more important activities of halfback play. Dunn deserved preferment, too, if only as a gesture to that future in which he could become, for three or four years, a strong point in New Zealand teams. The great question was Bryan Williams. Gleeson took time over this one. He was convinced Kururangi had developed as Williams had declined and therefore justified encouragement. (He was as puzzled as were all others by Williams' decline.) But it might be a dreadful thing at what might be the end of Williams' career to publish his want of confidence in the great man. So Jack tarried, decided; and was as glad as were all the rest to see Williams cut back inside for the try which carried his scoring aggregate for New Zealand to 401, fifth in the honour roll behind D. B. Clarke, W. F. McCormick, R. A. Jarden and R. W. H. Scott.

Loveridge's selection and the assault upon Russell Thomas after the game were indictments of Bridgend and/or its supporters. Nearing the end of the Bridgend game, Loveridge claimed a fair catch of a ball which had been kicked from deep behind the first line of Bridgend players. As he made the catch, he was set upon by several Bridgend forwards who were manifestly offside. Theirs was a violent assault, as sickening in its own right as the assault upon Thomas in the Arms Park grandstand. Loveridge's right thigh was mercilessly booted. It swelled so much that he had to be sent to bed immediately after the game. Twenty-four hours before kick-off against the Barbarians, the thigh was swollen by an inch and a quarter. Brian McKenzie, the physiotherapist, treated the leg diligently and Loveridge, after a fitness trial on match-morning over one and a half miles, was found to have reduced the swelling by an inch. But the bandaging over his thigh as he took the field was extensive. In a great run he made in the second half, he would, if fit, have undoubtedly scored. Brynmor Williams caught him from behind not because Loveridge lacked the natural pace but because his speed was inhibited by the wound and the plastic banding.

British rugby made great play, from 1973 onwards, of the film of the Barbarians-All Blacks' match of that year. Scores, hundreds of showings at club dinners, coaching schools and the like, inferentially demonstrated that when it came to class rugger, old boy, as against that wretched winning stuff those fellows from New Zealand insisted on playing, no one was in the class of the British. Who could blame the patriots? The match epitomised the greatnesses of well-played rugby.

It might not now be unwarranted for New Zealand clubs and coaching schools to use the Barbarians' match of 1978 for showing at dinners and other entertainments. For sure there would be strong words from perceptive audiences at the chances offered to and not taken by the All Blacks, not least by Bryan Williams in the first half. There would be, too, tongue-clicking at the sight of McKechnie bashing away at goal-kicks, nine times in all, for a reward of only one conversion, a penalty of about 23 metres just before half-time. ("Yeah," he casually said, the next day. "I did miss a few, didn't I?") There might be cries of disgust from the most junior of wing threequarters at sight of Williams being sucked into the centres for a tackle while Slemen, whom he should have been marking, took a pass for the easiest of tries. And even in Southland, powerful criticisms might be made of Oliver for his stupidity in pushing Billy Beaumont before the latter had caught the ball from a drop-out from the All Blacks' quarter-line, conceding the penalty by which Bennett put the Barbarians ahead by 16 to 15 with only seven minutes to play.

But the showings of warts and all would still be justified. This was a match of exhilaration. In the first half, as the All Blacks attacked and attacked and attacked, the basic speed of their movements was unbelievably high. One might best convey a sense of this by filming a succession of waves rolling upon an ocean beach and projecting the picture in treble time. All was breathtaking. Men attacked, supported, backed-up, countered, passed and re-passed the ball. The yield of this amazing 40 minutes, only seven points from a try by Johnstone and the McKechnie goal, admittedly was a criticism of All Black techniques because there should have been several more tries, not least the incontestable one by Mourie before half-time which referee Norman Sanson unaccountably refused to award. Yet it was marvellous stuff. Here was running rugby, thrills, spills and chills; and if clubs and coaching conferences and, most particularly, young players, could be shown the film, over and over, they might feel compelled to emulate the effort. Most seriously may it be doubted whether any All Black team, and this takes into account the staggering first half of the match against England by the Invincibles, has ever played with such speed, such momentum.

From the turn-around, taken with a lead of only 7 to 4 after Hutchings had brilliantly pitched a kick into no-man's land which was soon occupied for a try by Slemen, the match became even more dramatic after Bennett had placed a penalty from a scant few metres. Loveridge, breaking right, was taken, Robertson moved the ball ahead, Fleming twice figured in goes at the goalline. When Fleming was checked the second time, Rutledge, the silent one who was always there or thereabouts, nimbly floored the ball in the right place (and ought to have said harsh words in the Southland dialect when his fellow from Far South, McKechnie, foozled the kick at goal). The Barbarians were all mixed up by a shrewd kick by Osborne but unscrambled in time to save disaster. Which soon came when Loveridge and Dunn, moving the ball to the blindside, foxed the cover-defence as Williams, driving inside Dunn, took his pass to crash over for a try in the tackle of Derek Quinnell.

The lead of 15 to 7 looked sufficient, an encouragement to the team to resume, with greater accuracy, the glorious smash-hit rugby of the first half. But the Barbarians had other ideas. Skrela and Rives were plunging about in offence and defence. Bennett once displayed, startlingly, his acceleration. Not for the first time, Allan Martin was giving Haden a bit of a hiding at the lineout. Brynmor Williams, if clumsy and technically deficient in his passing, threatened danger with the power of his break. Backed once by only six men, Peter Wheeler twice stole heels on Dalton's head and Loveridge and Dalton between them compounded this misfortune by conceding free-kicks for crooked put-ins. Jim Renwick, a lad of dainty feet, lost the ball in going in for a try. Irvine hovered menacingly, Rees raced, the energy in the team improved with each passing part of the hour. Fourteen minutes from no-side, the Barbarians were given a penalty in front of the All Blacks' posts and with commendable cunning Brynmor Williams fiddled about with a tap-kick before darting the ball left, toward Slemen. Who, being utterly neglected by Bryan Williams, scored the simplest of tries which, converted by Bennett, brought the Baa-Baas to 13-15 and going like the clappers.

Ten minutes from the end, Mourie raised the haka and Irvine all but raised the flags. A substantial portion of the audience of 47,500, surely not all of them from Bridgend, who had been disagreeable in their manners toward the All Blacks, now began to give keener support to the Barbarians and cheered most lustily when Bennett converted that penalty so idiotically conceded by Oliver in his assault upon Beaumont. So now it was 16 to 15 to the Barbarians and the hell to pay with all portions of the audience, agreeable and disagreeable. It was in this period of seven minutes that referee Sanson became a name of bitter import to the Welsh. They yelled blue murder when, down by the Baa-Baas' quarter, he penalised Rees; and they accompanied two McKechnie attempts at penalty-goals, one from about 22 metres, the other from 27, with those groans and jeers which sometimes make the Arms Park a distressing memory for New Zealanders. Referee Sanson was jeered again when an attempt by Osborne at a drop goal descended into Irvine's arms just as Robertson, travelling at terminal velocity, made contact with a thunderous charge, one Scot to another. The criticism, especially loud from those furthest from the scene, was that Irvine was in his own ingoal when knocked to the ground with the ball in his arms, thereby being entitled to a drop-out at the quarter-line. Television replays established beyond all doubt that Handy Andy was, in fact, a step infield and thus had conceded the scrum-five metres ordered by Sanson.

It was here and now, with all the world yelling the bluest of blue murder, that Dalton heeled, Loveridge passed and Dunn goaled.

The score of the match was 18 to 16. The score of the tour was 17 to 1.

Bad things were to come: The assault upon Thomas; vilification because of Bridgend; crazy statements by J. P. R. that he could have died; indictments of the All Blacks.

Yet the scores stood, especially the score of the tour.

Mourie's men might not be the greatest team of all time. But they were the first Grand Slammers. They were the component parts of the team that found itself. In the finding, they established themselves as a gracious part of the legend of international touring teams.

APPENDICES

PREVIOUS ALL BLACK TOURS

1905-06 (First All Blacks)
Played 32; Won 31; Lost 1. Points for 830, Against 39
New Zealand 12; Scotland 7
New Zealand 15; Ireland 0
New Zealand 15; England 0
New Zealand 0; Wales 3
Captain: D. Gallaher (Auckland)

1924-25 (Second All Blacks)
Played 28; Won 28. Points for 654, Against 98
New Zealand 6; Ireland 0
New Zealand 19; Wales 0
New Zealand 17; England 11
Captain: C. G. Porter (Wellington)

1935-36 (Third All Blacks)
Played 28; Won 24; Drew 1; Lost 3. Points for 431, Against 180
New Zealand 18; Scotland 8
New Zealand 17; Ireland 9
New Zealand 12; Wales 13
New Zealand 0; England 13
Captain: J. E. Manchester (Canterbury)

1953-54 (Fourth All Blacks)
Played 29; Won 25; Drew 2; Lost 2. Points for 438, Against 115
New Zealand 8; Wales 13
New Zealand 14; Ireland 3
New Zealand 5; England 0
New Zealand 3; Scotland 0
Captain: R. C. Stuart (Canterbury)

1963-64 (Fifth All Blacks)

Played 30; Won 28; Drew 1; Lost 1. Points for 508, Against 137
New Zealand 6; Ireland 5
New Zealand 6; Wales 0
New Zealand 14; England 0
New Zealand 0; Scotland 0
Captain: W. J. Whineray (Auckland)

1967 (Sixth All Blacks)

Played 11; Won 10; Drew 1. Points for 207, Against 78
New Zealand 23; England 11
New Zealand 13; Wales 6
New Zealand 14; Scotland 3
Captain: B. J. Lochore (Wairarapa)

1972-73 (Seventh All Blacks)

Played 26; Won 20; Drew 2; Lost 4. Points for 521, Against 227.
New Zealand 19; Wales 16
New Zealand 14; Scotland 9
New Zealand 9; England 0
New Zealand 10; Ireland 10
Captain: I. A. Kirkpatrick (Poverty Bay)

1974

Played 8; Won 7; Drew 1. Points for 127, Against 50
New Zealand 15; Ireland 6
Captain: A. R. Leslie (Wellington)

STATISTICAL RECORDS

The 1978 All Blacks in the British Isles

Fullbacks	*Age*	*Height*	*Weight*	*Occupation*	*Caps*
B. J. McKechnie (Southland)	24	5. 8	12. 4	Accountant	4
C. J. Currie (Canterbury)	22	6. 0	13. 7	Student teacher	—
*R. G. Wilson (Canterbury)	25	5.11	11.13	Sports-store asst.	—
Threequarters					
B. G. Williams (Auckland)	27	5.10	14. 4	Lawyer	34
S. S. Wilson (Wellington)	23	6. 0	13. 7	Sales clerk	5
B. R. Ford (Marlborough)	26	6. 0	14. 2	Driver	2
R. R. Kururangi (Counties)	21	5.10	13	Soldier	—
B. J. Robertson (Counties)	26	6. 1	13. 7	Sales rep.	23
W. M. Osborne (Wanganui)	23	5.10	13. 4	Stock agent	9
Five-eighths					
J. L. Jaffray (Otago)	28	5.10	13	Stock agent	6
N. M. Taylor (Bay of Plenty)	28	5.10	13. 4	Insurance agent	7
O. D. Bruce (Canterbury)	30	5.10	11.10	Schoolmaster	10
E. Dunn (North Auckland)	23	5. 7	11. 5	Schoolmaster	—
Halfbacks					
M. W. Donaldson (Manawatu)	22	5. 9	11.10	Sports-store manager	5
D. S. Loveridge (Taranaki)	26	5. 9	11. 8	Pig farmer	—
Number 8s					
G. A. Seear (Otago)	26	6. 5	16	Draughtsman	5
A. A. McGregor (Southland)	25	6. 1	14.12	Farmer	—
Flankers					
G. N. K. Mourie (Taranaki)	26	6. 0	13. 5	Farmer	2
L. W. Rutledge (Southland)	26	6. 1	14. 7	Freezing worker	3
W. G. Graham (Otago)	21	6. 2	15	Stock agent	—
B. G. Ashworth (Auckland)	28	6. 2	14. 8	Sheet-metal operator	2
Locks					
F. J. Oliver (Southland)	29	6. 3	16.11	Forestry contractor	10
A. M. Haden (Auckland)	27	6. 6	17. 2	Property officer	9
J. K. Loveday (Manawatu)	29	6. 3	16.12	Chiropractor	—
J. K. Fleming (Wellington)	25	6. 4	15. 7	Driver	—

Props

G. A. Knight (Manawatu)	26	6. 2	17. 2	Salesman	5
J. C. Ashworth (Canterbury)	27	6. 2	16. 7	Farmer	3
W. K. Bush (Canterbury)	29	6. 0	16	Freezing-worker	9
B. R. Johnstone (Auckland)	27	6. 1	16. 2	Contractor	5

Hookers

A. G. Dalton (Counties)	26	5.10	14. 8	Farm advisory officer	4
J. K. Black (Canterbury)	27	6. 0	14. 8	Management trainee	1

*R. Wilson was called in as replacement after Currie, injured in the game with Wales, was invalided from the tour.

RECORD OF APPEARANCES

	Cambridge	Cardiff	W. Wales	London C.	Munster	IRELAND	Ulster	WALES	S. Counties	Midlands	C. Service	ENGLAND	Monmouth	N. England	N. Scotland	SCOTLAND	Bridgend	Barbarians
McKechnie	FB	—	FB	—	FB	—	FB	+FB	—	—	FB	FB	—	FB	—	FB	—	FB
Currie	—	FB	—	FB	—	FB	—	FB	—	—	—	—	—	—	—	—	—	—
R. G. Wilson	—	—	—	—	—	—	—	—	—	FB	—	—	FB	—	FB	—	FB	—
S. S. Wilson	—	W	W	—	W	W	—	W	+W	W	—	W	W	W	—	W	—	W
Williams	—	W	W	—	W	+W	W	W	W	W	—	W	—	W	—	W	W	W
Ford	W	—	—	W	—	W	—	—	—	—	W	—	—	—	W	—	—	—
Kururangi	W	—	—	W	—	—	W	—	W	—	W	—	W	—	W	—	W	—
Robertson	C	—	—	C	C	—	C	C	C	—	C	C	C	—	C	C	—	C
Osborne	—	C	C	—	+C	C	—	⅝	—	C	—	⅝	—	C	—	⅝	C	⅝
Jaffray	—	⅝	—	—	⅝	—	⅝	—	⅝	—	⅝	—	—	⅝	—	—	—	—
Taylor	⅝	—	⅝	⅝	—	⅝	—	—	FB	⅝	—	—	⅝	—	⅝	—	⅝	—
Bruce	⅝	—	⅝	—	—	⅝	—	⅝	—	—	—	⅝	—	⅝	—	⅝	⅝	—
Dunn	—	⅝	—	⅝	⅝	—	⅝	—	⅝	⅝	⅝	—	⅝	—	⅝	—	—	⅝
Donaldson	½	—	½	—	½	½	—	—	—	½	½	½	—	½	—	½	—	—
Loveridge	—	½	—	½	—	—	½	½	½	—	—	—	½	—	½	—	½	½
Seear	—	8	8	—	—	8	—	8	8	—	8	8	—	8	—	8	8	—
McGregor	8	—	—	—	8	—	—	—	—	F	—	—	—	—	—	—	—	—
Graham	—	—	F	—	F	—	8	—	F	—	—	—	F	—	—	—	F	—
Mourie	F	F	F	—	F	F	—	F	F	F	—	F	F	F	—	F	F	F
Rutledge	—	F	—	F	—	F	F	F	—	—	F	F	—	F	F	F	—	F
B. G. Ashworth	F	—	—	F	—	—	F	—	—	—	F	—	—	—	F	—	—	—
Fleming	L	—	L	8	—	—	L	—	L	8	L	—	8	—	8	—	—	8
Oliver	—	L	—	L	L	L	—	L	—	L	—	L	—	L	L	L	—	L
Haden	—	L	L	L	L	L	—	L	—	L	—	L	L	L	—	L	L	L
Loveday	L	—	—	—	—	—	L	—	L	—	L	—	L	—	L	—	L	—
J. C. Ashworth	P	—	—	P	—	—	P	—	P	—	P	—	+P	P	—	—	P	+P
Johnstone	—	P	P	—	P	P	—	P	—	P	—	P	P	—	P	P	—	P
Bush	P	—	—	P	—	P	P	P	—	—	P	—	P	—	—	—	—	—
Knight	—	P	P	—	P	—	—	—	P	P	—	P	—	P	P	P	P	P
Dalton	—	H	—	H	—	H	—	H	—	H	—	H	—	H	—	H	—	H
Black	H	—	H	—	H	—	H	—	H	—	H	—	H	—	H	—	H	—

+ Denotes replacement

INDIVIDUAL SCORING

(Internationals are indicated by (1), (2), (3), (4)).

	Matches	Tries	Conv.	Pen.	DG	Total
McKechnie (+2, 3, 4)	10	2	12	19	—	89
R. Wilson	4	1	4	8	1	39
Williams (+1, 2, 3, 4)	13	4	1	4	—	30
S. Wilson (1, 2, 3, 4)	12	5	—	—	—	20
Robertson (2, 3, 4)	12	5	—	—	—	20
Currie (1, 2)	4	—	6	2	—	18
Dunn	9	3	—	—	2	18
Kururangi	8	4	—	—	—	16
Mourie (1, 2, 3, 4)	14	3	—	—	—	12
Taylor (1)	9	3	—	—	—	12
Donaldson (1, 3, 4)	9	2	—	—	—	8
Oliver (1, 2, 3, 4)	11	2	—	—	—	8
B. G. Ashworth	5	2	—	—	—	8
Ford (1)	5	2	—	—	—	8
Rutledge (1, 2, 3, 4)	11	2	—	—	—	8
Johnstone (1, 2, 3, 4)	11	2	—	—	—	8
Seear (1, 2, 3, 4)	10	2	—	—	—	8
Bruce (1, 2, 3, 4)	9	—	—	—	2	6
Black	9	1	—	—	—	4
Knight (3, 4)	11	1	—	—	—	4
Osborne (1, 2, 3, 4)	11	1	—	—	—	4
Dalton (1, 2, 3, 4)	9	1	—	—	—	4
Loveridge (2)	9	1	—	—	—	4
Jaffray	6	1	—	—	—	4
		50	23	33	5	360

The All Blacks were awarded one penalty try. Seear was in possession at the time.

Other match appearances were: McGregor, 3; Graham, 6; Haden (1, 2, 3, 4), 13; Loveday, 7; Fleming, 10; J. C. Ashworth, 9; Bush, (1, 2), 7.

Opposing teams scored 7 tries, 4 conversions, 30 penalties and 7 dropped goals.

RECORD OF THE TOUR

FIRST MATCH

Cambridge University 12, All Blacks 32.

Grange Road, Cambridge, October 18. Fine, overcast, well-grassed, perfect pitch. Attendance of 8,500 a ground record, with hundreds denied admission. Half-time, 21-0.

Cambridge University:
Ian Metcalfe (King Edward's, Birmingham, and St Catharine's); Paul Frackleton (Royal School, Dungannon, and Pembroke); Matthew Fosh (Harrow and Magdalene); Andy Laycock (St Michael's, Leeds, and Emmanuel), Richard Tyler (Cheltenham Grammar School and Fitzwilliam); James Thornton (Dulwich and Magdalene), John Robbie (The High School, Dublin, and Christs), captain; Eddie Butler (Monmouth and Fitzwilliam); Steve Glanvill (Exeter and Pembroke), Nigel Heath (Solihull and Downing), Justin Ford (Millfield and Emmanuel), Chris O'Callaghan (St Joseph's, Port Talbot, and St John's); Richard Broonan (Merchant Taylor's and Trinity), Jerry Grant (Haileybury and St Catharine's), Steve Killick (Dulwich and Queens).

All Blacks:
McKechnie; Kururangi, Robertson, Ford; Taylor, Bruce; Donaldson; McGregor; Mourie, Fleming, Loveday, Barry Ashworth; John Ashworth, Black, Bush.

Referee:
Ken Rowlands (Welsh Rugby Union).

2 minutes: Penalty goal, McKechnie, 23 metres, 3-0.
8: Penalty McKechnie, 31 metres, 6-0.
13: Penalty McKechnie, 21 metres, 9-0.
18: Try Taylor, after 40 metres break, conversion McKechnie, 15-0.
22: Try Donaldson, after 18-metre sprint, conversion McKechnie from sideline, 21-0.
48: Try Tyler, after cut-through by Thornton, conversion Robbie, 21-6.
53: Penalty Robbie, 45 metres, lineout infringement, 21-9.
65: Penalty McKechnie, 22 metres, offside at lineout, 24-9.
67: Penalty Robbie, 44 metres (Robbie's kick-off after McKechnie's goal crossed the bar), 24-12.
68: Try Donaldson after Fleming break on blind, 28-12.
75: Try Ford after Donaldson reverse pass and kick-ahead, 32-12.

Bruce and Taylor each failed with a dropkick at goal. Robbie missed one attempt at a penalty from 30 metres and another awarded at halfway after the All Blacks had been penalised for misconduct while the ball was out of play after Tyler's try. Cambridge were awarded 12 penalties (9 in the first half, 3 in the second) and the All Blacks 10 (7-3).

SECOND MATCH

Cardiff 7, All Blacks 17.

The Arms Park, Cardiff, October 21. A perfect day for a perfect rugby place. Before play began, Bryan Williams was presented with a silver salver to mark his 100th game for New Zealand. He headed the All Blacks onto the field and then led the team in its haka. Crowd 43,000. Half-time 9-3.

Cardiff:
Paul Rees; Dave Thomas, Mike Murphy, Pat Daniels, Chris Camilleri; Gareth Davies, Terry Holmes; John Scott; Carl Smith, Hans de Goede, Robert Norster, Richard Dudley-Jones; Barry Nelmes, captain; Mike Watkins, Mike Knill.

All Blacks:
Currie; Williams, Osborne, Stuart Wilson; Jaffray, Dunn; Loveridge; Seear; Mourie. Oliver, Haden, Rutledge; Johnstone, Dalton, Knight.

Referee:
Roger Quittenton (Rugby Football Union).

13 minutes: Penalty goal Currie, 24 metres, after he had caught his own Garryowen and Cardiff conceded a penalty, 3-0.

19: Drop-goal Davies after a free kick called against Donaldson for an illegal put-in at the scrummage, 3-3.

28: Try Wilson, from 65-metres gallop after an interception, conversion Currie, 9-3.

42: Try Osborne from Dunn lob-kick caught on full by Jaffray, pass to Osborne for 35-metre run, 13-3.

67: Try Wilson on right wing from set-piece play joined by Williams from left wing, 20-metre run to corner, 17-3.

73: Try Smith after long throw-in on goalline to Jaffray, caught in possession, 17-7.

Cardiff were awarded 15 penalties (6-9), the All Blacks 14 (8-6). Davies missed his one penalty attempt. Currie goaled one of five penalty attempts, Williams failed his only one.

THIRD MATCH

West Wales 7, All Blacks 23.

St Helens Swansea, October 25. Grey cool day, fresh breeze from west. "Now Is the Hour" sung by a band of youths and girls before kick-off. Half-time 7-0.

West Wales:
Roger Blyth (Swansea); Elgan Rees (Neath), Ray Gravell (Llanelli), Ray Bergiers (Llanelli), *J. J. Williams (Llanelli); Dai Richards (Swansea), Clive Shell (Aberavon); Derek Quinnell (Llanelli), captain; *Trevor Evans (Swansea), Geoff Wheel (Swansea), Allan Martin (Aberavon), Gareth Roberts (Swansea); John Richardson (Aberavon), Jeff Herdman (Swansea), Paul Llewellyn (Swansea).

*J. J. Williams suffered a deep gash on the leg in the movement which yielded Knight's try. He was replaced by David Nicholls.

Evans retired hurt at half-time and was replaced by Richard Moriarty.

All Blacks:
McKechnie; Williams, Osborne, Wilson; Taylor, Bruce; Donaldson; Seear; Graham, Haden, Fleming, Mourie; Johnstone, Black, Knight.

Referee:
Alan Welsby (Rugby Football Union).

25 minutes: Try Knight, after dazzling 50-metre running attack by Donaldson, Wilson, Donaldson, Seear and goalline plunge by Knight, 4-0.

40 (including eight minutes of injury-time): Penalty Williams, 54 metres, lineout infringement, 7-0.

43: Try Bergiers from wild mis-kick by McKechnie, 7-4.

48: Penalty McKechnie, 35 metres, 10-4.

50: Penalty Blyth, 31 metres, after failure by Bruce to find touch, 10-7.

55: Try Wilson, from 35-metre blindside break by Donaldson and Seear, conversion McKechnie from touchline, 16-7.

77: Penalty McKechnie, 22 metres, after strong attack initiated by Donaldson to Rutledge to Mourie, 19-7.

79: Try Wilson, from blindside intervention by Williams into midfield, drawing Nichols, 23-7.

West Wales were awarded 12 penalties (9-3) and the All Blacks 16 (5-11). Blyth goaled his only attempt. In eight shots at goal, the All Blacks scored only with Williams and McKechnie. With injury-time, the first half lasted 48 minutes, the second 47. Moriarty as replacement was concussed in his first play and was off the field for nine minutes.

FOURTH MATCH

London Counties 12, All Blacks 37.

Twickenham, London, October 28. Fine, clear, grey, calm. Twickenham lawn at least two inches long. Recorded music instead of band. Crowd 23,000. Half-time, 18-6.

London Counties:
*Keith Bushell (Harlequins and Kent); Bob Demming (Bedford and Eastern Counties), Keith Hughes (London Welsh and Surrey), Peter Warfield (Rosslyn Park and Surrey), Derek Wyatt (Bath and Eastern Counties); Ronald Wilson (London Scottish and Middlesex), Alan Lawson (London Scottish and Middlesex); Adrian Alexander (Harlequins and Middlesex); Robert Mordell (Rosslyn Park and Middlesex), Chris Ralston (Richmond and Middlesex), Maurice Colclough (Angouleme and Sussex), Sandy Pratt (London Scottish and Surrey); Terry Claxton (Harlequins and Middlesex), Philip d'A Keith-Roach (Rosslyn Park and Eastern Counties), captain, Andrew Cutter (Harlequins and Surrey).

†Bushell was concussed in the 54th minute and replaced by Ian Williamson.

All Blacks:
Currie; Kururangi, Robertson, Ford; Taylor, Dunn; Loveridge; Fleming; Barry Ashworth, Oliver, captain, Haden, Rutledge; John Ashworth, Dalton, Bush.

Referee:
Clive Norling (Welsh Rugby Union).

5 minutes: Try Kururangi after Wyatt mulled fielding a hook-kick by Dunn, conversion Currie, 6-0.

17: Try Kururangi after break by Taylor and sidestep past Bushell, conversion Currie, 12-0.

20: Penalty goal, Bushell, 22 metres, 12-3.

27: Try Robertson after charge-down of Warfield's clearing kick, conversion Currie, 18-3.

30: Penalty Bushell, 18 metres, scrummage penalty, 18-6.

42: Try Dunn, blindside break and dummy, 22-6.

44: Penalty Bushell, 36 metres, infringement at ruck, 22-9.

50: Try Oliver, capitalising break by Loveridge, Rutledge, conversion Currie, 28-9.

62: Try Ford, from slice kick-through by Dunn, Ford toed on, conversion Currie, 34-9.

67: Penalty Williamson, 34-12.

75: Penalty Currie, 32 metres, 37-12.

London Counties were awarded 12 penalties (5-7) and goaled four of five attempts. The All Blacks were awarded 10 penalties (5-5) and goaled one in six attempts.

FIFTH MATCH

Munster 12, All Blacks 0.

Thomond Park, Limerick, October 31. Bright sunshine after rain through the night. Pitch well grassed and firm. Forty-piece youth band from time to time obliged with "The Floral Dance", "Po Kare Kare" and "Now Is the Hour". Having lost the toss, the All Blacks played into the sun and light wind. Half-time 0-9.

Munster:
Larry Moloney (Garryowen); Moss Finn (University College, Cork), Seamus Dennison (Garryowen), Greg Barrett (Cork Constitution), Jimmy Bowen (Cork Constitution); Tony Ward (St Mary's College), Donal Canniffe (Lansdowne), captain; Donal Spring (Dublin University); Colm Tucker (Shannon), Moss Keane (Lansdowne), Brendan Foley (Shannon), Christy Cantillon (Cork Constitution); Gerry McLoughlin (Shannon), Pat Whelan (Garryowen), Les White (London Irish).

All Blacks:
McKechnie; Williams, *Robertson, Wilson; Jaffray, Dunn; Donaldson; McGregor; Mourie, Haden, Oliver, Graham; Johnstone, Black, Knight.
* Robertson retired hurt in the ninth minute and was replaced by Osborne.

Referee:
Corrie Thomas (Welsh Rugby Union).

9 minutes: Try Cantillon, from cross-kick by Ward, pick-up and 50-metre sprint and dodge by Bowen, back-up by Cantillon, conversion Ward, 6-0.

16: Drop goal Ward, 15 metres, from knock-on 8 metres in front of posts by McKechnie, 9-0.

68: Drop goal Ward, 18 metres, from scrum 5-metres after Wilson had touched down while falling on ball bouncing in the in-goal, 12-0.

Munster were awarded six penalties (3-3) and the All Blacks 5 (4-1). Neither side took a penalty kick at goal.

SIXTH MATCH

IRELAND 6, NEW ZEALAND 10.

Landsdowne Road, Dublin, November 4. Fine, firm pitch, with troubling wind blowing across the field. Crowd 50,000. Half-time 3-3.

Ireland:
Larry Moloney (Garryowen); Terry Kennedy (St Mary's College), Michael Gibson (Northern Ireland Football Club), Adrian McKibbin (London Irish), Alfred McLennan (Wanderers); Tony Ward (St Mary's College), Colin Patterson (Instonians); Willie Duggan (Blackrock College); Seamus Deering (St Mary's College), captain, Moss Keane (Lansdowne), Donal Spring (Dublin University), Fergus Slattery (Blackrock College); Philip Orr (Old Wesley), Patrick Whelan (Garryowen), Edward Byrne (Blackrock College).

New Zealand:
Colin Currie (Canterbury); Stuart Wilson (Wellington), Bill Osborne (Wanganui), *Brian Ford (Marlborough); Mark Taylor (Bay of Plenty), Doug Bruce (Canterbury); Mark Donaldson (Manawatu); Gary Seear (Otago); Graham Mourie (Taranaki), Frank Oliver (Southland), Andy Haden (Auckland), Leicester Rutledge (Southland); Brad Johnstone (Auckland), Andy Dalton (Counties), Bill Bush (Canterbury).
*Ford suffered a knee injury in the 47th minute and was replaced by Bryan Williams.

Referee:
Clive Norling (Welsh Rugby Union).

13 minutes: Drop goal, Bruce, 18 metres, after heel from scrummage, 3-0.
15: Penalty, Ward, 39 metres, against Seear for picking the ball out of the scrum, 3-3.
43: Drop goal Bruce, 18 metres, from Donaldson pass from ruck, 6-3.
50: Penalty Ward, 25 metres, late-charge of Ward after kick-ahead, 6-6.
78: Try Dalton, from blindside break around front of lineout by Donaldson, 10-6.

Ireland were awarded 15 penalties (7-8) and New Zealand 9 (5-4). Ward goaled two of four attempts. Currie failed with three attempts and Williams with one.

SEVENTH MATCH

Ulster 3, All Blacks 23.

Ravenhill, Belfast, November 7. Grey, gloomy day with strong south wind blowing over a firm pitch. Recorded music included a selection of Maori songs sung by the St Joseph's Maori Girls' College in Napier. The commentator on the ground broadcasting system remarked to the crowd of 23,000: "If you meet a New Zealand supporter, I suggest you shake him by the hand and make him welcome." As a prelude to the match, Russell Thomas in the presence of both teams laid a wreath on the Memorial Gates at the entrance to the ground.

Ulster:
Ronnie Elliott (Bangor); Joey Miles (Malone), Alan Irwin (Queens University, Belfast), Michael Gibson (Northern Ireland Football Club), Chris Gardiner (Northern Ireland Football Club); Adrian Goodrich (Ballymena), *Colin Patterson (Instonians); Harry Steele (Ballymena); Alan McLean (Ballymena), Dermot Dalton (Malone), Willie Anderson (Dungannon), Stewart McKinney (Dungannon), captain; Alan Henry (Malone), Guy Beringer (London Irish), Barney O'Kane (Ballymena).
*Patterson retired hurt in the 76th minute and was replaced by Ricky Stewart.

All Blacks:
McKechnie; Kururangi, Robertson, captain, Williams; Jaffray, Dunn; Loveridge; Graham; Barry Ashworth, Fleming, Loveday, Rutledge; John Ashworth , Black, Bush.

Referee:
Peter Hughes (Rugby Football Union).

25 minutes: Penalty Williams, 35 metres, 3-0.
31: Try Williams from Robertson break past Gibson, 7-0.
41: Penalty McKechnie, 44 metres, 10-0.
44: Penalty Goodrich, 27 metres, breach of 10-metre lineout gap, 10-3.
67: Try Black, from drive by Fleming, conversion McKechnie, 16-3.
72: Try Kururangi from break by Graham carried on Robertson, 20-3.
81: Penalty McKechnie, 36 metres, amidst strong booing — the crowd wanted action, not goals, 23-3.

Ulster were awarded 11 penalties and two free-kicks (1-10), and the All Blacks 12 (7-5). Goodrich placed one out of four, McKechnie two out of four.

EIGHTH MATCH

WALES 12, NEW ZEALAND 13.

The National stadium (Arms Park), Cardiff. Grey day, perfect pitch, fresh breeze blowing diagonally down the field from the west. Maximum crowd of 47,500. A Maori among the spectators rushed onto the field to join the All Blacks as they performed their haka. Half-time, 12-7.

Wales:
J. P. R. Williams (Bridgend), captain; J. J. Williams (Llanelli), Ray Gravell (Llanelli), Steve Fenwick (Bridgend), Clive Rees (London Welsh); Gareth Davies (Cardiff), Terry Holmes (Cardiff); Derek Quinnell (Llanelli); Jeff Squire (Pontypool), Geoff Wheel (Swansea), Allan Martin (Aberavon), Paul Ringer (Ebbw Vale); Charlie Faulkner (Pontypool), Bobby Windsor (Pontypool), Graham Price (Pontypool).

New Zealand:
*Clive Currie (Canterbury); Bryan Williams (Auckland), Bruce Robertson (Counties), Stuart Wilson (Wellington); Bill Osborne (Wanganui), Doug Bruce (Canterbury); David Loveridge (Taranaki); Gary Seear (Otago); Graham Mourie (Taranaki), Frank Oliver (Southland), Andy Haden (Auckland), Leicester Rutledge (Southland); Brad Johnstone (Auckland), Andy Dalton (Counties), Billy Bush (Canterbury).
*Currie was injured in the seventh minute and replaced by McKechnie.

Referee:
Roger Quittenton (Rugby Football Union).

4 minutes: Penalty goal Davies, 22 metres, after a late tackle of J. P. R. Williams, 0-3.

7: Penalty Davies, 24 metres, after Currie's claim for a fair catch had been disallowed, 0-6.

22: Penalty Fenwick, 40 metres, after a late-tackle call against B. G. Williams for a tackle of J. J. Williams, 0-9.

24: Try Wilson, after a slanting kick to the in-goal area by Osborne, 4-9.

26: Penalty Davies, 10 metres, after a call of late tackle against Osborne on Gravell (who had not, in fact, had the ball — Fenwick's was the kick-ahead to the goalmouth), 4-12.

38: Penalty McKechnie, 22 metres, Holmes offside, 7-12.

56: Penalty McKechnie, 31 metres, after Wales had breached the 10-metre lineout gap, 10-12.

79: Penalty McKechnie, 35 metres, after a call against Wheel for using Oliver's shoulder to climb for the ball, 13-12.

Wales were awarded 10 penalties and two free-kicks (7-3) and goaled four of six attempts. New Zealand received 18 penalties (8-10) and goaled three of five attempts.

NINTH MATCH

South and South-West Counties 0, All Blacks 20.

Memorial Ground, Bristol, November 15. Dry, cold, blustering wind blowing over pitch bare in many places. Winning the toss, the All Blacks played into the wind. Half-time, 4-0.

South and South-West Counties:
Peter Butler (Gloucester and Gloucestershire); Alan Morley (Bristol and Gloucestershire), Steve Donovan (Torquay and Devon), Roger Pallow (Falmouth), Richard Mogg (Gloucester and Gloucestershire); John Palmer (Bath and Somerset), Peter Kingston (Gloucester and Gloucestershire); John Scott (Cardiff and Devon); Mike Rafter (Bristol and Gloucestershire), captain, Paul Ackford (Rosslyn Park and Devon), Roger Corin (St Ives and Cornwall), John Watkins (Gloucester and Gloucestershire); Barry Nelmes (Cardiff and Gloucestershire), Steve Mills (Gloucester and Gloucestershire), John Doubleday (Bristol and Gloucestershire).

All Blacks:
Taylor; Williams, Robertson, *Kururangi; Jaffray, Dunn; Loveridge; Seear; Mourie, Loveday, Fleming, Graham; John Ashworth, Black, Knight.
*Kururangi retired hurt and was replaced by S. Wilson.

Referee:
Norman Sanson (Scotland).

36 minutes: Try Williams, from long pass by Dunn beyond Taylor to Robertson, Williams sprint for corner, 4-0.

45: Penalty Williams, 31 metres, against Scott for holding Seear, 7-0.

50: Try Dunn after a kick-up by Jaffray, a tackle of Mogg, and a dribble and dive for the score, 11-0.

64: Penalty try Seear when Counties collapsed the scrum as Seear strove to go on the blind, conversion Williams, 17-0.

78: Penalty Williams, ruck, 20-0.

Counties were awarded eight penalties (3-5) and the All Blacks 15 (10-5). One of Butler's two attempts at penalty goals passed under the bar from 51 metres. Williams missed three shots at goal.

TENTH MATCH

Midland Counties 15, All Blacks 20.

Welford Road, Leicester, November 18. Grey, cold, windy day. Crowd 16,000. Before kick-off, the public address system asked for the All Blacks' coach-driver (Richard Smith) to "go to the players' entrance, please". "The All Blacks," said the voice, "have had enough of it already." The All Blacks won the toss and played into the wind. Half-time, 10-12.

Midland Counties:
"Dusty" Hare (Leicester and Notts, Lincs and Derbyshire); John Duggan (Leicester and Leicestershire), Paul Dodge (Leicester and Leicestershire), Brian Hall (Leicester

and Notts, Lincs and Derbyshire), Paul Knee (Coventry and Warwickshire); Martin Cooper (Moseley and Staffordshire), Chris Gifford (Moseley and Warwickshire); Garry Adey (Leicester and Leicestershire); Ian Smith (Leicester and Leicestershire), Nigel Horton (Toulouse and North Midlands), Barry Ninnes (Coventry and Warwickshire), John Shipsides (Coventry and Warwickshire); Robin Cowling (Leicester and Leicestershire), Peter Wheeler (Leicester and Leicestershire), captain, Will Dickinson (Richmond and Notts, Lincs and Derbyshire).

All Blacks:
Richard Wilson; Williams, Osborne, Stuart Wilson; Taylor, Bruce; Donaldson; Fleming; Mourie, Haden, Oliver, McGregor; Johnstone, Dalton, Knight.

Referee:
Alan Hosie (Scottish Rugby Union).

2 minutes: Penalty goal, Hare, 25 metres, offside, 0-3.

7: Drop goal after free kick, Hare, 40 metres, Donaldson crooked feed into scrum, 0-6.

9: Try Williams, dropkick by Bruce sliced into Counties' in-goal, Williams first to ball, 4-6.

28: Penalty Hare, 54 metres, Bruce penalised in maul, 4-9.

37: Penalty Hare, Johnstone in error at lineout drive, 4-12.

39: Drop goal after free-kick, Richard Wilson 25 metres, 7-12.

43: Penalty Richard Wilson, 15 metres, Smith penalised at drive in scrum, 10-12.

57: Try Mourie, drive by Fleming, Donaldson blindside to Williams, Mourie up for inside pass, 14-12.

70: Try Taylor, 70 metres rush begun by Taylor at quick throw-in by Counties, support play by Osborne, Haden back to Taylor, conversion Richard Wilson, 20-12.

80: Penalty Hare, 12 metres, 20-15.

Midlands were awarded five penalties (3-2) and four free-kicks for illegal put-ins by Donaldson. Hare missed nothing. The All Blacks were given eight penalties (6-2) and two free-kicks. Richard Wilson, drafted to the tour to replace the injured Currie, was called into service at 11 a.m. after an adverse medical report on McKechnie. Wilson's drop goal from a free-kick just before half-time was crucial to the victory.

ELEVENTH MATCH

Combined Services 6, All Blacks 34.

Military Stadium, Aldershot, November 21. Grey day, slight wind, glorious pitch. Crowd 7,000. Half-time, 7-6.

Combined Services:
Lieutenant Paul Lea (Camborne and Royal Navy); Lieutenant Colin English (Devonport Services and Royal Navy), Corporal Steve Jackson (Blackheath and Army), Lieutenant Geoff Fabian (Devonport Services and Royal Navy), J-Technician Steve Rogers (Lincoln and Royal Air Force); Corporal Anthony Green (Wasps and Royal Air Force), J-Technician Ken Pugh (United Services Portsmouth and Royal Navy); Lieutenant Steve Hughes (Devonport Services and Royal Marines); SAC Graham Still (Ebbw Vale and Royal Air Force), SAC John Orwin (Gloucester and Royal Air Force), Flying Officer Nigel Gillingham (Leicester and Royal Air Force), captain, Corporal Garston Williams (Headingley and Army); Corporal Norman Gray (Rosslyn Park and Army), Corporal Bob Matthews (Aldershot Services and Army), Lieutenant Jock Ackerman (United Services Portsmouth and Royal Navy).

(Rosslyn Park and Army), Corporal Bob Matthews (Aldershot Services and Army), Lieutenant Jock Ackerman (United Services Portsmouth and Royal Navy).

All Blacks:
McKechnie; Ford, Robertson, captain, Kururangi; Jaffray, Dunn; Donaldson; Seear; Barry Ashworth, Fleming, Loveday, Rutledge; John Ashworth, Black, Bush.

Referee:
Ken Parfitt (Welsh Rugby Union).

8 minutes: Penalty goal Fabian, 25 metres, lineout infringement, 0-3.

13: Try Ford, break by Seear from tight-head, to Donaldson, Dunn, Robertson, Ford, 4-3.

17: Drop goal after free-kick, Green 20 metres, Donaldson penalised for put-in, 4-6.

32: Penalty McKechnie, 22 metres, Fleming barged at lineout, 7-6.

44: Penalty McKechnie, 22 metres, scrummage infringement, 10-6.

51: Try Seear, pushover at scrummage, conversion McKechnie, 16-6.

56: Try Jaffray, fast follow-up when Robertson tackled, conversion McKechnie, 22-6.

60: Try Robertson, Kururangi and Robertson in fast break, support by Ford, infield to Robertson, superb move, conversion McKechnie, 28-6.

67: Try McKechnie, swift attack on right, Kururangi nearly through, kick-up, McKechnie support, conversion McKechnie, 34-6.

Combined Services were awarded 9 penalties (4-5) and two free-kicks and scored from two of three attempts. The All Blacks were awarded eight penalties (4-4).

TWELFTH MATCH

ENGLAND 6, NEW ZEALAND 16.

Twickenham, London, November 25. Cold, stiff north-west wind, gleaming sunlight. Lawn reduced in height but still troublesome for McKechnie's goalkicks. Fine singing from 67,750 crowd of "Land of Hope and Glory" and National Anthem. Half-time, 10-6.

England:
"Dusty" Hare (Leicester and Notts, Lincs and Derbyshire); Peter Squires (Harrogate and Yorkshire), Anthony Bond (Sale and Lancashire), Paul Dodge (Leicester and Leicestershire), Michael Slemen (Liverpool and Lancashire); John Horton (Bath and Lancashire), Malcolm Young (Gosforth and Northumberland); Roger Uttley (Gosforth and Northumberland); Mike Rafter (Bristol and Gloucestershire), John Scott (Cardiff and Devon), Bill Beaumont (Fylde and Lancashire), captain, Peter Dixon (Gosforth and Cumbria); Robin Cowling (Leicester and Leicestershire), Peter Wheeler (Leicester and Leicestershire), Barry Nelmes (Cardiff and Gloucestershire).

New Zealand:
Brian McKechnie (Southland); Bryan Williams (Auckland), Bruce Robertson (Counties), Stuart Wilson (Wellington); Bill Osborne (Wanganui), Doug Bruce (Canterbury); Mark Donaldson (Manawatu); Gary Seear (Otago); Graham Mourie (Taranaki), Frank Oliver (Southland), Andy Haden (Auckland), Leicester Rutledge (Southland); Brad Johnstone (Auckland), Andy Dalton (Counties), Gary Knight (Manawatu).

Referee:
Norman Sanson (Scottish Rugby Union).

5 minutes: Penalty (drop goal) Hare, 35 metres, Knight penalised for block at lineout, 0-3.

16: Try Oliver, drive from end of lineout by Mourie, 4-3.

25: Penalty Hare, 27 metres, drive by Uttley and Rafter, ruck infringement, 4-6.

35: Try Johnstone, tap-down by Scott at lineout on England's line, Wheeler's throw-in, conversion McKechnie, 10-6.

53: Penalty McKechnie, 29 metres, ruck penalty after attack by Osborne and Donaldson, ball crossed bar after striking upright, 13-6.

73: Penalty McKechnie, 36 metres, scrummage infringement, 16-6.

England were awarded 14 penalties (8-6) and two free-kicks. New Zealand were awarded 17 penalties (8-9) and one free-kick. Hare's attempt from 47 metres rebounded from the bar. McKechnie and Williams missed two each, Williams' kicks being taken at halfway or thereabouts.

THIRTEENTH MATCH

Monmouthshire 9, All Blacks 26.

Rodney Parade, Newport, November 29. Fine, clear but freezing cold. Pitch ice-bound for ten metres down grandstand touchline. Wheezing sound-system for "Land of My Fathers" largely ignored by capacity crowd. Half-time, 22-9.

Monmouthshire:
Peter Lewis (Pontypool); Tony Browning (Newbridge), David Burcher (Newport), Ian Goslin (Ebbw Vale), Geoff Davies (Pontypool); David Barry (Newport), Brynmor Williams (Newport); Jeff Squire (Pontypool); Paul Ringer (Ebbw Vale), John Perkins (Pontypool), Steve Sutton (Pontypool), Clive Burgess (Ebbw Vale); Charlie Faulkner (Pontypool), captain, Bobby Windsor (Pontypool), Graham Price (Pontypool).

All Blacks:
Richard Wilson; Stuart Wilson, Robertson, Kururangi; Taylor, Dunn; Loveridge; Fleming; Mourie, Loveday, Haden, Graham; Johnstone, Black, *Bush.
*Bush retired in the second half with a hamstring and was replaced by John Ashworth.

Referee:
John West (Irish Rugby Union).

2 minutes: Penalty Richard Wilson, 40 metres, collapse of scrum by Faulkner, 3-0.

5: Penalty Richard Wilson, 25 metres, Davies penalised for lying on ball, 6-0.

10: Penalty Lewis, 26 metres, lineout infringement, 6-3.

12: Penalty Richard Wilson, 44 metres, Goslin offside at ruck, 9-3.

20: Try Dunn, Taylor breakthrough, grub-kick to goalline, Dunn first to ball, 13-3.

25: Penalty Lewis, 18 metres, Taylor offside after Richard Wilson fumbled and Stuart Wilson failed to find touch, 13-6.

27: Penalty Lewis, 26 metres, lineout penalty after wild pass to no one by Kururangi with Richard Wilson up on the attack, 13-9.

30: Penalty Richard Wilson, 35 metres, offside at ruck, 16-9.

40: Try Loveridge, dive over Monmouthshire backrow at their heel on goalline, fractionally first to ball ahead of Brynmor Williams, conversion Richard Wilson, 22-9.

67: Try Robertson, kick ahead by Taylor, fast heel, 26-9.

Monmouthshire were awarded 12 penalties (4-8) and the All Blacks seven (6-1). Lewis missed one penalty and Browning two.

FOURTEENTH MATCH

North of England 6, All Blacks 9.

Birkenhead Park, North Birkenhead, December 2. Bitter cold, strong east wind, remarkable recovery of ground after overnight and morning snowfalls. Crowd 10,000 housed in primitive conditions. All Blacks play into wind. Half-time, 6-6.

North of England:
Derek Boyd (West Hartlepool and Durham); Peter Squires (Harrogate and Yorkshire), Richard Cardus (Roundhay and Yorkshire), Tony Bond (Sale and Lancashire), Michael Slemen (Liverpool and Lancashire); John Horton (Bath and Lancashire), Malcolm Young (Gosforth and Northumberland); Roger Uttley (Gosforth and Northumberland); Tony Neary (Broughton Park and Lancashire), John Butler (Gosforth and Cumbria), Bill Beaumont (Fylde and Lancashire), captain, Peter Dixon (Gosforth and Cumbria); Frank Blackhurst (Waterloo and Lancashire), Roy Tabern (Fylde and Lancashire), John Bell (Gosforth and Yorkshire).

All Blacks:
McKechnie; Stuart Wilson, Osborne, Williams; Jaffray, Bruce; Donaldson; Seear; Mourie, Oliver, Haden, Rutledge; John Ashworth, Dalton, Knight.

Referee:
David Burnett (Irish Rugby Union).

4: Penalty Young, 40 metres, lifting in lineout, 0-3.
29: Penalty Young, 18 metres, lineout infringement, 0-6.
31: Try McKechnie, great rolling run by forwards, out to backs, Wilson to McKechnie, conversion McKechnie, 6-6.
57: Penalty McKechnie, 35 metres, Osborne obstructed while hurtling toward loose ball, 9-6.

North of England were awarded 14 penalties (7-7) and five free-kicks. The All Blacks were awarded 15 penalties (10-5). Young missed two kicks at goal, including one from 36 metres five minutes before no-side — he sliced his kick. Seear and Williams each missed attempts from about halfway and McKechnie missed two.

FIFTEENTH MATCH

North and Midlands of Scotland 3, All Blacks 31.

Linksfield Stadium, Aberdeen, December 5. Clear, cold day, bumpy field, crisp downfield breeze into which the All Blacks, by choice, played first. Half-time, 4-3.

North and Midlands of Scotland:
Alan Croll (Gordonians); Steve Mackenzie (Kirkcaldy), John Adams (Glenrothes), Stewart Irvine (Glenrothes), Peter Robertson (Gordonians); Colin High (Highland), Ian McCrae (Gordonians); Ian Paxton (Glenrothes); Tony Ingle-Finch (Highland), Chris Snape (Gordonians), captain, Andy Dunlop (Highland), Colin Watt (Gordonians); Gregor Mackenzie (Highland), Alan Hardie (Gordonians), Gordon Brown (Dunfermline).

All Blacks:
Richard Wilson; Kururangi, Robertson, Ford; Taylor, Dunn; Loveridge; Fleming; Barry Ashworth, Loveday, Oliver, captain, Rutledge; Johnstone, Black, Knight.

Referee:
Roger Quittenton (R.F.U.).

2 minutes: Drop goal High, 27 metres, after heel from scrum, 0-3.
40: Try Richard Wilson, support play for Loveridge and Knight in drive to goalline, 4-3.
43: Try Rutledge after Steve Mackenzie fumble of long kick by Dunn, long throw-in from touch to Rutledge, 8-3.
53: Try Robertson, fast move from tighthead heel, Williams breakthrough, Robertson back-up, conversion Richard Wilson, 14-3.
58: Drop goal Dunn, tighthead heel after strong scrum drive, 17-3.
65: Try Barry Ashworth, pushover after strong scrummage thrust, conversion Richard Wilson, 23-3.
68: Try Kururangi on left wing after supporting Loveridge and Dunn in long run, 27-3.
75: Try Barry Ashworth, supporting Dunn in swift blindside break, 31-3.

SIXTEENTH MATCH

SCOTLAND 9, NEW ZEALAND 18.

Murrayfield, Edinburgh, December 9. Damp, calm, well-grassed but skiddy pitch. Music by Royal Highland Fusiliers, 31 pieces, including "Ode to Joy" from Beethoven's Ninth (composer named in programme as "Beat"), and pipe and drums of Dunblane Queen Victoria School for sons of Scottish Servicemen (30 pieces). Fine singing of National Anthem from 70,000 crowd. Half-time, 9-6.

Scotland:
Andy Irvine (Heriot's F.P.); Keith Robertson (Melrose), Jim Renwick (Hawick), Alastair Cranston (Hawick), Bruce Hay (Boroughmuir); Ian McGeechan (Headingley), captain, Alan Lawson (London Scottish); *David Leslie (Galashiels); Gordon Dickson (Galashiels), Alastair McHarg (London Scottish), Alan Tomes (Hawick), Michael Biggar (London Scottish); Ian McLauchlan (Jordanhill), Colin Deans (Hawick), Bobby Cunningham (Galashiels).
*Leslie retired hurt in 44th minute and was replaced by John Lambie (Watsonians).

New Zealand:
Brian McKechnie (Southland); Bryan Williams (Auckland), Bruce Robertson (Counties), Stuart Wilson (Wellington); Bill Osborne (Wanganui), Doug Bruce (Canterbury); Mark Donaldson (Manawatu); Gary Seear (Otago); Graham Mourie (Taranaki), Frank Oliver (Southland), Andy Haden (Auckland), Leicester Rutledge (Southland); Brad Johnstone (Auckland), Andy Dalton (Counties), Gary Knight (Manawatu).

Referee:
John West (Irish Rugby Union).

8 minutes: Hay try started by kick-through by McGeechan misfielded by Stuart Wilson, an error grossly compounded when Bruce tried to flykick the ball into touch, Leslie and Biggar carrying it on and allowing Hay to score wide out, Irvine converting with a magnificent kick, 0-6.

15: Penalty McKechnie when McGeechan called offside at 30 metres, 3-6.

24: Try Seear from scrum by Scottish goalposts yielded when Irvine knocked on and Seear drove from the heel, conversion McKechnie, 9-6.

60: Penalty McKechnie, 42 metres, lineout penalty, 12-6.

63: Drop goal McGeechan initiated when Bruce failed to find touch and Seear backed off the scrum as Scotland were heeling, 12-9.

76: Robertson try when McGeechan drop at goal charged down by Bruce, Osborne following to kick ahead, Robertson supporting and with remarkable judgment toeing the ball into in-goal from in front of the posts for the score, conversion McKechnie, 18-9.

Scotland were awarded seven penalties (3-4) and New Zealand 11 (4-7). McKechnie missed one shot at goal.

SEVENTEENTH MATCH

Bridgend 6, All Blacks 17.

Brewery Field, Bridgend, December 13. Rain, mud, cold and slush. Band and pipe band of the RAF Station of St Athan's play "God Defend New Zealand" (and, says a Welshman, sotto voice, "Bridgend, too, I hope"). Crowd 15,000. Half-time, 10-6.

Bridgend:
J. P. R. Williams, captain; Ian Davies, Steve Fenwick, Lyndon Thomas, Vivian Jenkins; Ian Williams, Gerald Williams; Steve Ellis; Gareth Williams, Billy Howe, Roy Evans, Gareth Jones; Ian Stephens, Geoff Davies, Meredydd James.

All Blacks:
Richard Wilson; Williams, Osborne, Kururangi; Taylor, Bruce; Loveridge; Seear; Mourie, Haden, Loveday, Graham; Knight, Black, John Ashworth.

Referee:
Laurie Prideaux (Rugby Football Union).

7 minutes: Richard Wilson penalty, after punch of Haden by Gerald Williams, 3-0.

9: Try Taylor from break from own quarter by Kururangi, pass to Taylor beyond halfway, try in corner from 80-metre movement, 7-0.

26: Penalty Richard Wilson, 42 metres, Bruce kayoed by late tackle by Ian Williams, 10-0.

33: Penalty Fenwick, 22 metres, obstruction of Jenkins by Kururangi, 10-3.

39: Penalty Fenwick, 35 metres, lineout infringement (which touch-judge was it who leaped in the air in signalling the ball's clearance of the bar?), 10-6.

47: Penalty Richard Wilson, 22 metres, ruck, 13-6.

79: Try Mourie, lineout fumble, instant reaction, 17-6.

Bridgend were awarded 11 penalties (6-5) and three free-kicks, the All Blacks 13 penalties (6-7) and one free-kick. Fenwick missed three shots at goal and Ian Williams one. Richard Wilson failed with three shots at goal.

EIGHTEENTH MATCH

Barbarians 16, All Blacks 18.

The Arms Park, Cardiff, December 16. Fine, clear, cold north-east wind, patches of soft ground down touchline and under bar. All of the All Blacks' party on to field for the singing of the national anthems. All Blacks played into bright sun. Crowd 47,500. Half-time, 7-4.

Barbarians:
Andy Irvine (Heriot's F.P., Scotland and 1974-77 Lions); Elgan Rees (Neath and 1977 Lions); Neil Hutchings (Aberavon), Jim Renwick (Hawick and Scotland), Michael Slemen, (Liverpool and England); Phil Bennett (Llanelli, Wales and 1974-77 Lions), Brynmor Williams (Newport, Wales and 1977 Lions); Derek Quinnell (Llanelli, Wales and 1971-77 Lions), captain; Jean-Claude Skrela (Toulouse and France), Allan Martin (Aberavon, Wales and 1977 Lions), Bill Beaumont (Fylde, England and 1977 Lions), Jean-Pierre Rives (Toulouse and France); *Phil Orr (Old Wesley, Ireland and 1977 Lions), Peter Wheeler (Leicester, England and 1977 Lions), Will Dickinson (Richmond).
*Orr suffered a severe gash of the hand in the fifth minute and was replaced by Barry Nelmes (Cardiff and England).

All Blacks:
McKechnie; Stuart Wilson, Robertson, Williams; Osborne, Dunn; Loveridge; Fleming; Mourie, Oliver, Haden, Rutledge; *Johnstone, Dalton, Knight.
*John Ashworth replaced the injured Johnstone at half time.

Referee:
Norman Sanson (Scottish Rugby Union).

24 minutes: Try Johnstone after wonderful movement to the right carried on with a dummy by Dunn and a great forward drive, 4-0.

38: Try Slemen, following break to right turned back by Quinnell and kick-ahead by Hutchings, Slemen toeing ahead and winning race to ball in in-goal, 4-4.

39: Penalty McKechnie, 23 metres, lineout infringement, 7-4.

43: Penalty Bennett, 10 metres, ruck from lineout after an Irvine dropkick at goal had fallen wide, 7-7.

47: Try Rutledge, break on right by Loveridge, charge by Fleming, Rutledge hurled over line with ball, 11-7.

53: Try Williams (his 401st point for New Zealand), blindside break by Loveridge, Dunn, Williams inside pass and over in Quinnell's tackle, 15-7.

66: Try Slemen from tap-kick penalty moved left by Brynmor Williams from 10 metres short of All Black line, Williams sucked in to check Renwick, Slemen in clear for try, conversion from touchline Bennett, 15-13.

73: Penalty Bennett, 24 metres, Oliver early-charged Beaumont at drop-out, 15-16.

79: Drop-goal Dunn from scrum 5-metres awarded when Irvine touched down in Robertson's tackle after fielding a miscued drop at goal by Osborne, 18-16.

The Barbarians were awarded 12 penalties (6-6) and four free-kicks. Bennett and Irvine each missed a shot from a penalty, Irvine's monstrous kick from 58 metres rebounding from the bar. McKechnie in an incredible display goaled only once from no fewer than nine attempts.